Human–Computer Interaction Series

The Human–Computer Interaction Series, launched in 2004, publishes books that advance the science and technology of developing systems which are effective and satisfying for people in a wide variety of contexts. Titles focus on theoretical perspectives (such as formal approaches drawn from a variety of behavioural sciences), practical approaches (such as techniques for effectively integrating user needs in system development), and social issues (such as the determinants of utility, usability and acceptability).

HCI is a multidisciplinary field and focuses on the human aspects in the development of computer technology. As technology becomes increasingly more pervasive the need to take a human-centred approach in the design and development of computer-based systems becomes ever more important.

Titles published within the Human–Computer Interaction Series are included in Thomson Reuters' Book Citation Index, The DBLP Computer Science Bibliography and The HCI Bibliography.

Adalberto Simeone · Benjamin Weyers ·
Svetlana Bialkova · Robert W. Lindeman
Editors

Everyday Virtual and Augmented Reality

 Springer

Editors
Adalberto Simeone
KU Leuven
Leuven, Belgium

Svetlana Bialkova
Liverpool Business School
Liverpool John Moores University
Liverpool, UK

Benjamin Weyers 🄳
Human-Computer Interaction
University of Trier
Trier, Germany

Robert W. Lindeman
HIT Lab NZ
University of Canterbury
Christchurch, New Zealand

ISSN 1571-5035   ISSN 2524-4477 (electronic)
Human–Computer Interaction Series
ISBN 978-3-031-05806-6   ISBN 978-3-031-05804-2 (eBook)
https://doi.org/10.1007/978-3-031-05804-2

This Springer imprint is published by the registered company Springer Nature Switzerland AG
The registered company address is: Gewerbestrasse 11, 6330 Cham, Switzerland

Preface

"Everyday virtual reality" refers to those contexts where virtual reality (VR) or augmented reality (AR) could be used outside of research laboratories or highly specialized professional environments. The interest in VR/AR technologies and applications has increased in the last decade with the availability of consumer-level hard- and software. This increase in relevance has made virtual and augmented reality technology also interesting for everyday scenarios and applications, thus for environments that are far from well-controlled and equipped laboratory setups as often used in research. Therefore, there is a growing need to understand the user's demands, marketing needs, and tech pitfalls in such contexts, in order to create appropriate everyday applications that successfully manage challenges such as heterogeneous user groups, complex and non-standardized physical environments and processes, as well as the use of simple and easy-to-use hardware setups. In an attempt to provide solutions for these challenges, this book encompasses the work of several research groups. It continues successful themes from a series of "Workshops on Everyday Virtual Reality" (**WEVR**), which took place in conjunction with the IEEE Conference on Virtual Reality and 3D User Interfaces from 2015 to 2022, and offers an overview on VR/AR applications in everyday context from education to shopping, as well as describing new trends related to everyday VR.

Although affordable, consumer-level devices are enabling deployment of VR/AR applications in everyday environments such as homes, classrooms, and businesses, there are some challenges, such as low-quality tracking or restricted rendering and projection capabilities. Therefore, the areas of interest of this book focus on the challenges of designing and implementing VR/AR applications for ordinary environments that were not built with the explicit intention of supporting VR systems. These environments are often social environments in which users might be present without access to immersive technologies (cross-reality interaction). It might not be trivial or practical to install the technology required to obtain reliable and robust tracking capabilities, obstacles might be commonplace, and/or space might be restricted. In addition, users might not have access to the full range of 3D input devices that are found in VR/AR laboratories or might start to introduce immersive technologies into existing working processes, which can produce difficulties in coping with and adopting them.

As previously mentioned, the book emerged from a series of impactful and interesting WEVR workshops. Each year, the workshop was attended by more than 20 participants from the main conference. In the last two years, online editions were launched, thus increasing the number of attendees, given the opportunity to access them from anywhere across the globe. The growing interest in WEVR encouraged us to propose the current book, providing a selection of chapters from different labs worldwide, covering various contexts from education, to training, to shopping, gaming, and entertainment.

Additionally, the increase in interest has fostered similar events, such as the **VARECO** workshop[1] conducted in conjunction with the German conference in Human Computer Interaction (Mensch und Computer 2018[2]) or the International Workshop on Cross-Reality Interaction at the ACM Conference on Interactive Surfaces and Spaces.[3]

WEVR core topics cover, but are not limited to:

- Gameplay design and player interaction in consumer VR/AR
- Overcoming constraints of ordinary environments (e.g., locomotion techniques, object avoidance)
- Tangible and haptics support to interaction with the environment
- Interactivity and input modalities
- Co-located and remote social and collaborative VR/AR and related challenges
- 3D user interfaces for desktop or semi-immersive VR
- VR/AR for home, healthcare, and education
- Effects of prolonged VR use in domestic settings
- Cross-reality interaction (e.g., between immersed and non-immersed users)
- New tracking systems (head, hands, body, etc.)
- VR/AR development for non-technical creators
- New trends in VR applications.

The current book encompasses nine chapters. After giving an introduction to the field of everyday VR, which outlines major challenges and their relation to previous publications presented at the WEVR workshops, two chapters will present general scenarios for everyday VR (knowledge work and collaboration/teaming). This is followed by a chapter on work on basic interaction research handing over to a block of three chapters focusing on different application domains (training, teaching, and marketing). We conclude the book with a chapter on evaluation approaches for everyday VR applications, as well as a look into future creation of virtual environments with a neuro-inspired method. Below, we will give a more detailed overview of the various chapters of the book.

---

[1] https://sites.google.com/view/vareco/home.

[2] http://muc2018.mensch-und-computer.de/en/.

[3] ACM ISS 2020, https://xr.famnit.upr.si/.

The first editorial chapter "Introduction to Everyday Virtual and Augmented Reality" introduces readers to the WEVR context, giving a broad overview on previous research and reflecting on earlier editions and key contributions to the WEVR workshop. We further discuss challenges and offer avenues on how to turn these challenges into opportunities when it comes to the application of VR/AR technology for everyday environments.

The second chapter, "Extended Reality for Knowledge Work in Everyday Environments," summarizes the state of the art in the field of extended reality for knowledge work in everyday environments and proposes steps to address the open challenges. While a stream of better, cheaper, and lighter HMDs have been introduced for consumers in recent years, there are still many challenges to be addressed to allow this vision to become reality. In particular, the ability to modify the workers' senses can transform everyday environments into a productive office. This could be achieved by using portable head-mounted displays (HMDs) combined with conventional interaction devices, such as keyboards and tablets.

The third chapter, "The Use of Augmented Reality for Temporal Coordination in Everyday Work Context," gives an introduction to collaborative work, teams, teamwork, and taskwork followed by a broad overview of existing AR-based team supportive methods. On this base, a taxonomy for the development and implementation of AR-based support systems is outlined. Example on its usage in the context of a user-centered design followed by a review of the current research conducted by the authors, as well as a discussion of future work is presented.

The fourth chapter, "Rotational and Positional Jitter in Virtual Reality Interaction in Everyday VR," extends the previous literature by conducting a user study on angular jitter with controllers held with two different grip styles and targets at two different depth distances. The results revealed that user performance decreases (already) with additional jitter. Thus, the authors suggest that practitioners/developers who design 3D user interfaces, controllers, and interaction techniques for daily 3D VR usage should focus on reducing jitter. Decreasing jitter not only improves user performance but also decreases frustration, which improves the user experience.

The fifth chapter, "Development and Validation of a Mixed Reality Exergaming Platform for Fitness Training of Older Adults," presents the conception and field validation of the *Portable Exergame Platform for Elderly* (PEPE). PEPE is a gaming platform with mixed reality (MR) components whose purpose is to fight a sedentary lifestyle by promoting active aging in elderly care centers. The chapter shows that PEPE's custom-made exergames can be successfully used by trainers for delivering sustained long-term training, with benefits in terms of efficiency, elicited physical activity, and perceived effort. Also, PEPE improved the overall perception of the quality of life and social relations in institutionalized older adults.

The sixth chapter, "Networked Virtual Reality and Enhanced Sensing for Remote Classes and Presentations," summarizes the authors' ongoing work to develop and assess VR techniques for remote education. First, two case studies of remote teaching in VR are discussed: a classroom embedded virtual field trip of an energy center guided by a remote teacher, and a remote university class conducted for several weeks in a social VR tool. Then, ongoing research to improve remote educational VR interfaces using enhanced sensing, for example, to visualize or detect student attention based on eye-tracked gaze, is presented. As a result, several practical considerations are identified that will need to be addressed for the long-term success of educational deployments of VR. This can help educators, researchers, and VR developers make informed decisions on how best to use VR technology for designing and deploying educational VR in everyday contexts such as schools and homes.

The seventh chapter, "Enhancing Multisensory Experience and Brand Value: Key Determinants for Extended, Augmented, and Virtual Reality Marketing Applications," offers a survey of literature from the perspective of consumer needs and market demands. Combining theoretical insights with different VR/AR technologies and their real market applications, a framework on how to augment experiences, encompassing processing from attention to action, is suggested. The conceptual framework could be implemented in development of appropriate high-tech VR/AR environments, providing appealing multisensory experiences, and thus, enriching the brand portfolio with innovation going beyond traditional marketing practices.

The eighth chapter, "Using Think-Aloud Protocol in Immersive VR Evaluations," examines whether conventional usability evaluation methods can be directly applied to VR evaluations, and whether they will lead to similar insights when compared to the results of conventional real-world usability lab studies. Therefore, the authors conducted a user study where they compared the results obtained by using the think-aloud protocol to inspect an everyday product, a real microwave oven, and its virtual twin. Results show that 61% of the reported usability problems were shared by both versions, highlighting the potential of immersive virtual reality evaluations (IVREs) as a method to evaluate early design concepts before committing to physical prototypes, which can reduce the need to build expensive physical mock-ups. The implications are discussed, and guidelines are provided for deploying IVREs.

The ninth chapter, "Adaptive Virtual Neuroarchitecture," presents the idea of adaptive virtual neuroarchitecture (AVN), where virtual environments respond to the user and the user's real-world context while simultaneously influencing them both in real time. To show how AVN has been explored in current research, a sampling of recent work that demonstrates reciprocal relationships using physical affordances (space, objects), the user's state (physiological, cognitive, emotional), and the virtual world used in the design of novel virtual reality experiences is included. AVN is hoped to have the potential to help us learn how to design spaces and environments that can enhance the wellbeing of their inhabitants.

The current book could be seen as a manifesto for researchers from computer science to consumer experts, to design appropriate VR/AR applications going beyond traditional lab environments, to be implemented to be user-friendly in the context of daily life.

Leuven, Belgium   Adalberto Simeone
                                             adalberto.simeone@kuleuven.be

Trier, Germany   Benjamin Weyers
                                                   weyers@uni-trier.de

Liverpool, UK   Svetlana Bialkova
                                                 S.Bialkova@ljmu.ac.uk

Christchurch, New Zealand   Robert W. Lindeman
                                          rob.lindeman@canterbury.ac.nz

Contents

Introduction to Everyday Virtual and Augmented Reality

Adalberto Simeone, Benjamin Weyers, Svetlana Bialkova, and Robert W. Lindeman

Abstract Due to emerging consumer hardware solutions, virtual and augmented reality technologies are gaining increasing relevance in everyday contexts, such as living rooms or office spaces. This raises various challenges such as getting immersed in small and cluttered spaces, integrating immersive tools into existing processes and workflows, as well as the involvement of highly heterogeneous user groups in VR and AR applications. The current chapter aims to introduce and characterise this emerging research field by identifying various challenges in terms of the development and investigation of everyday VR and AR systems. Therefore, we give an overview of everyday VR and AR, discuss challenges for the field that we deem central to the continued adoption and integration of VR and AR into the wider public, as well as provide an overview of current everyday VR and AR in various application contexts and discuss some things from a users' perspective. We then review works from previous WEVR workshops, which were established as a platform for the exchange of everyday VR and AR research, to face the main challenges and provide possible solutions. Finally, we discuss the WEVR impact and point out future research avenues.

A. Simeone (✉)
KU Leuven, 3000 Leuven, Belgium
e-mail: adalberto.simeone@kuleuven.be

B. Weyers
Human-Computer Interaction, University of Trier, 54296 Trier, Germany
e-mail: weyers@uni-trier.de

S. Bialkova
Liverpool Business School, Liverpool L3 5UG, UK
e-mail: S.Bialkova@ljmu.ac.uk

R. W. Lindeman
HIT Lab NZ, University of Canterbury, Christchurch 8140, New Zealand
e-mail: rob.lindeman@canterbury.ac.nz

1   Introduction

Virtual reality (VR), together with augmented reality (AR) and mixed reality (MR), is referred to as extended reality (XR). These technologies have been recognised as promising technical innovations and are therefore being widely adopted in various everyday contexts, from automotive to fashion and from banking to entertainment. The rise in adoption of remote working in recent years has also led to a growing interest in these technologies, setting the stage for new enterprises, with an estimate of about 50% increase in use by 2025 (Statista 2022).

The release of commercial VR headsets in recent years marked a significant change in the use and adoption of VR technologies. During the so-called VR Winter times of the early 2000s (Jerald 2015), the use of these technologies remained mostly limited to specialists from universities and industry. Barriers in terms of affordability, usability, and comfort kept widespread access to VR out of reach from all but the most enthusiastic of early adopters. When they became affordable, and commercial VR headsets were released in the second half of the 2010s, the existing VR literature had scarcely confronted itself with the challenges and scenarios that we consider related to everyday VR and AR contexts.

Indeed, typical VR laboratories at academic institutions continue to have large, empty rooms, free from obstacles, that are built for the explicit purpose of supporting VR infrastructure. This contrasts with *everyday* environments, consisting mainly of domestic living rooms, bedrooms, as well as office and production spaces. In such environments, space is limited and obstacles are commonplace (Simeone et al. 2015, 2017). Further, it is not always possible or desirable to install the necessary instrumentation, such as tracking hardware or complex projection systems. Additionally, other aspects, such as obstacles, only become apparent when integrating VR/AR technologies not only into existing physical *spaces*, but also into existing *processes*, such as in the case of production or office work. VR/AR technology and its application needs to outperform existing working tools or add significantly more and new features not available before.

These above-mentioned challenges inspired us to launch the *Workshop on Everyday Virtual Reality* (**WEVR**), which was first held in Arles, France, in 2015 and has been running ever since. We aimed to bring these issues to the attention of the VR community, with the goal of focusing on the specific problems related to the use of VR in everyday contexts. Since then, the "realities" that everyday users can experience have grown to encompass other forms of immersive technologies that became accessible, such as with the release of "prosumer" AR headsets like the Microsoft HoloLens. Although the costs of such devices remain high compared to VR headsets, the issues and challenges affecting everyday contexts are not exclusive to VR and ultimately constitute barriers that hinder more widespread adoption in the public at large.

To overcome these challenges, this book highlights key aspects emerging from WEVR in an attempt to provide possible solutions. In Sect. 2 of this first chapter, we give an overview of everyday VR and AR, discuss challenges for the field that we deem central to the continued adoption and integration of VR and AR into the wider public, as well as provide an overview of current everyday XR in various application contexts and discuss the users' perspectives. In Sect. 3, we then review works from previous WEVR workshops that face these challenges and provide possible solutions. Finally, in Sect. 4, we discuss the role of WEVR research and point out future research avenues in Sect. 5.

2 Everyday Immersive Realities

Experiencing VR/AR in everyday contexts presents a distinct set of characteristics and challenges that differentiates it from other use-cases. For the majority of its history, VR and AR research efforts were directed at specialist settings, such as academic or professional use. The availability of special-purpose infrastructure mitigated some of the problematic aspects of these technologies, such as the disparity between virtual and physical spaces, the naturalness of the interaction, the believability of the immersion.

In such specialised settings, using large walkable spaces in conjunction with redirection techniques helps minimise the number of resets likely to happen when exploring a virtual environment via natural walking. Similarly, accurate tracking of a user's hands, the use of special-purpose controllers and the presence of haptic devices, can drastically improve the range of interaction possibilities available to users. Another significant difference between specialist and everyday settings consists of the often controlled nature of the former. When XR applications or experiences are deployed for use in a laboratory or professional setting, outside influences (e.g. bad or non-uniform lighting or obstacles) are typically carefully minimised. Conversely, everyday settings cannot typically count on these same "ideal" conditions. In everyday settings, life goes on around the immersed users. Such experiences must account for the possibility of interruptions from outside sources. Furthermore, the amount of VR experience of users may differ between professional and everyday contexts. Concerning professional contexts, VR/AR developers can assume that such systems will be used by either VR/AR experts or those who are willing to invest more time to learn working with them. This is not the case for everyday setups, as the user group as well as the use-cases and environments will be more diverse and heterogeneous in various characteristics.

However, everyday VR and AR experiences are not only characterised by limitations, but also opportunities. Consumer VR/AR represents the most common type of immersive technology non-specialists users are likely to experience. Beyond VR or AR entertainment, a range of application classes have surfaced that provide real-world examples of the transformative potential that VR and AR have in fields such as education, design, socialisation, remote work (see Sect. 2.3).

What *are* everyday VR and AR experiences and what is their *relevance* in the wider VR/AR domain? Since everyday VR and AR grew organically around the need to support the requirements of an emerging range of end-user scenarios, there is no strict definition. Rather, we propose a *set of characteristics* that indicate elements that are representative of their "everyday" nature. Framing these experiences, systems and techniques as representative of everyday VR and AR can help readers better understand the reasoning behind design choices, more easily find other related work, and reflect on their effectiveness at supporting end-users.

Successively, we describe these characteristics, in the form of challenges for the field, provide an overview of the main application areas of everyday XR, and discuss the users' perspectives.

2.1 Challenges

Everyday VR and AR face certain challenges that are typically more prevalent in a domestic setting than for specialist stakeholders. Here, we describe the most common.

Physical Space: When VR/AR is used in academic or professional contexts, users can often benefit from the availability of specially built laboratories or environments to use for immersion. These typically consist of large, empty rooms. This is in stark contrast with the everyday settings in which most consumers of VR/AR will immerse themselves, where furniture and other obstacles abound. Everyday VR and AR experiences are either referred to as "Room Scale", if users can walk around their room, or as "Desktop VR" if the user is assumed to be seated while immersed. The latter term has seen an "evolution" in its meaning. In earlier decades, Desktop VR identified semi-immersive VR applications making use of desktop displays (Ware et al. 1993). More recently, the term has been used in conjunction with seated VR experiences (Zielasko et al. 2017), due to the use of semi-immersive displays becoming less common.

Standard Input Devices and Interaction Patterns: To appeal to as broad an audience as possible, everyday VR and AR experiences will make use of retail versions of headsets and the controllers they come with. While on one hand this limits interaction possibilities to some extent, on the other, it promotes standardisation by ensuring that applications are developed around a range of features that are common across different HMD manufacturers. However, significant differences remain. For instance, while VR controllers have largely coalesced around a type of hand-held device offering both buttons and triggers as well as a thumbstick, AR headsets such as the HoloLens do not come with controllers and rely on hand-tracked gestural input. Some areas of VR gaming constitute an exception, especially where special-purpose accessories (e.g. extensions for standard controller, such as for VR golf games) or devices (e.g. Joysticks for flight simulators) demonstrate compelling advantages in terms of immersion or performance over playing with standard controllers.

In contrast to more established paradigms, such as on desktops with WIMP interfaces, or on mobiles via gesture-based input, in VR/AR applications, common interaction patterns have not yet been consistently implemented. For many, VR applications might be the first time they experience 3D user interfaces and 3D interaction techniques. As a result, newcomers to VR or AR need to re-learn the basics, such as distinguishing between what is meant by a button or "trigger" on a controller, or how to perform basic manipulations.

Ease of Use: The current state of VR and AR headsets available in the early 2020s still poses some limitations in terms of how easy it is for a user to immerse themselves. Due to the limited duration of their batteries (2–3 h for an Oculus Quest 2 or a HoloLens 2) and other factors (the controllers' own batteries, barriers to the use of custom content, heat generation for prolonged usage, etc.), an immersive session must typically be planned in advance. This does not favour their spontaneous use, as would be the case for other everyday devices, such as mobile phones, tablets, desktop computers, and laptops. A further challenge is related to the ease with which users can manipulate specific VR applications. For example, they might experience difficulties in using the VR headset and/or the additional devices used for tracking user behaviour (e.g. joysticks, controllers, locomotion devices).

Embedding: In most cases in everyday VR and AR contexts, not only are existing environments enriched by VR or AR technology and applications, but existing processes either in work or private (leisure) contexts are as well. Thus, embedding such technologies into existing processes creates certain challenges, such as keeping boundaries as small as possible, reducing the need to continually put on or raise a headset during a working session, or to better consider existing regulations such as in the case of use in aviation or transportation. Additionally, use of VR and AR in everyday contexts puts special emphasis not only on usability and user experience (considering also inexperienced and novel users), but also on very basic ergonomic aspects. For instance, when using headsets in longer or physically stress-inducing situations, users may sweat, which makes the use of the same hardware by co-workers burdensome.

Dissemination of Results: Common to other disciplines, the dissemination of VR and AR research results is not always immediate. The difficulties for laypersons in accessing academic manuscripts still remain relevant today. This is further exacerbated by the perceived diminished relevance of results obtained decades ago with hardware that is no longer available, where the source code is no longer easily usable (e.g. due to obsolescence or lack of support for the development tools used) or may never have actually been released to the public. These obstacles cast doubts on their adaptability to today's hardware and application scenarios. This has led the community of VR and AR developers to sometimes re-invent the wheel (Steed et al. 2021).

2.2 The User's Perspective

After discussing the actual challenges for everyday VR/AR, we will briefly characterise the user's perspective on everyday VR/AR. Of course, everything we know from other areas in VR/AR research or general HCI also applies here. Still, we would like to highlight certain specific characteristics (type of use, accessibility, teams, and collaborations) as well as known concepts (usability and user experience) with the focus on everyday VR/AR research and applications.

Usability: Experience and knowledge is key in terms of the use of digital systems. This is a well-known aspect and has been manifested in the ISO 9241 Standard[1] in terms of *learnability*, which is significantly influenced by experience and knowledge. Users with previous knowledge of the usage of VR/AR will more likely be faster at learning to use such systems compared to users who are inexperienced. An aspect specifically relevant for everyday usage of immersive technology is that it is necessary to consider a quite high level of heterogeneity in terms of user experience and knowledge. This might be less relevant in professional areas such as office work, but in the context of leisure applications or sports, this problem will need to be specifically addressed by the system's design. This makes the everyday VR and AR scenario quite different to applications tested in laboratory environments with well-controlled samples and environments. Finally, newly introduced systems are confronted with a huge body of prior knowledge which might not only be supportive, but could also be destructive, such that the wrong expectations are built up, or highly automated and trained procedures are disturbed when new systems are integrated in such processes (e.g. in production processes, see also the embedding challenge above).

User Experience: Overarching topics in VR/AR research, but also for interactive systems in general, are usability and user experience. While *usability* reflects the extent to which a system can be used by particular users to achieve specific goals with effectiveness and satisfaction, *user experience* takes a broader view, looking at the individual's entire interaction with the system. In this respect, it is crucial to understand the user's thoughts, feelings, and perceptions resulting from particular interactions. For everyday VR and AR, this is of major importance, specifically considering the previous described challenges, due to heterogeneous user groups, teams, and collaboration, as well as aspects such as embedding new technologies into existing processes and environments. The key parameters emerging from various studies, including those presented at WEVR workshops, are: presence, naturalness, immersion, interaction, and engagement. *Presence* is the subjective experience of being in one place or environment (Witmer and Singer 1998) even when one is physically situated in another environment (McMahan 2003). It reflects the user's sense of "being there" in a scene depicted by a medium (Freeman and Lessiter 2001). Presence involves feeling physically surrounded by a mediated, but seemingly natural and believable, space to the exclusion of "real-world" sensations (Freeman and Lessiter 2001). There are various Likert scales used to measure presence (Lessiter et al. 2001; Usoh et al. 2000; Witmer and Singer 1998). Presence closely relates to immersion, which could be considered an objective property of a VR system's profile (Bowman and McMahan 2007).

---

[1] https://www.iso.org/standard/77520.html.

Development Resources: An advantage that everyday VR and AR applications might have over research experiments is that games and other commercial applications can leverage higher budgets and resources. VR games will typically make use of professional-quality assets and teams of multiple developers, whereas XR research is more often performed by small teams or even single researchers that take on multiple developer roles. Thus, aspects such as graphical realism, sound, virtual characters, general UX factors of the interfaces designed can become overlooked due to the limited amount of time that can be dedicated to them, as they are not seen as the main focus of the research. While there are examples of graphical realism influencing user behaviour (Simeone et al. 2017), there is still limited research into how these background aspects contribute to the overall believability and sense of presence in the experience (Rogers et al. 2022).

Type of Use: Similar to experience, the type of use of VR/AR in everyday situations will differ. This creates the challenge that interaction techniques, environments, and applications not only need to be easy to use but should also consider different types of users and different types of usage of such systems. In this respect, the perspective of cross-reality (which refers to techniques and concepts to let users with different levels of immersion interact with each other; please refer to a more detailed discussion in Sect. 3.2) may be of high relevance such that the users are ultimately able to choose the level of immersion suitable for their task and needs. This is even more relevant if it comes to people with special needs as outlined next.

Accessibility: Each digital interactive system may consider and implement interaction techniques suitable for everyone, specifically including people with special needs. Of course there might be examples of systems that do not apply here, for instance highly specialised system that needs special abilities and training (e.g. fighter jets). However, these are systems that would not be considered as "everyday". Thus, aspects of accessible computing are highly relevant in terms of making VR/AR systems usable by everyone.

Teams and Collaboration: Working together or sharing time and experiences is a key element of everyday life. Thus, supporting teams and collaboration is another element relevant to everyday VR and AR systems. This may not apply to all systems, but still we argue that individual work or interaction with a VR/AR system might be less common in case of everyday working situations, as is the case with highly specialised systems. A recent trend in VR research referred to as "Social VR" (Liu and Steed 2021) is a clear indicator that this research and application domain is of high relevance, not only for everyday VR and AR, but for VR research in general.

2.3 Application Areas

Fundamental academic research in everyday VR and AR typically focuses on abstract scenarios, with the aim of generalising the results and insights to a variety of different use-cases that share some common characteristics. However, when commercial applications are concerned, there is a stronger focus on a specific use-case. Indeed, a variety of VR/AR applications have surfaced for in various domains such as: automotive, architecture and design, banking and finance, food and beverage, entertainment, marketing and commerce, sport and leisure, tourism, etc.

Social Experiences: Online social spaces such as VRChat,[2] AltSpace VR,[3] and Meta Horizon Worlds,[4] represent perhaps the most known and direct point of contact between immersive technologies and everyday users. There, users can interact with other users in shared immersive environments. In contrast, fundamental academic research seldom focuses on multi-user immersive experiences outside of these platforms, due to the high development costs necessary.

Education: VR/AR has found a fruitful application area in the domain of immersive educative materials, available on platforms such as Steam or the Oculus store, or in the form of 360° videos. These experiences can be described as "virtual" tours, where the user takes an observer role along a pre-defined sequence of events with limited interaction possibilities (Simeone et al. 2019).

VR Gaming: Since the release of commercial VR headsets, VR games have become a mainstay of popular online storefronts. The 2022 Steam statistics report that about 1.87% of its active users have SteamVR-enabled headsets from a total of 132 million active users (Statista 2022). However, an equivalent market for see-through AR headsets has not yet become as popular, due to the high cost of such devices.

In summary, for much of its existence, it seems VR and AR have been "solutions looking for problems". However, the greater accessibility of VR and AR to more mainstream users has led to the emergence of the application areas introduced above. Indeed, we have witnessed this emergence in the papers presented over the lifetime of the WEVR workshops, some of which we introduce next.

3 Previous Work Published at WEVR Workshops

To support the previously introduced characteristics and provide examples, we will give an overview of the work published and presented in WEVR workshops from 2015 to 2022. Therefore, we examined the titles and abstracts of all publications from years 2015 to 2022. In a first step, we identified which papers specifically considered the previously described challenges. Therefore, we rated each paper for each challenge in how far the presented work addressed a given challenge on a three-point scale (between *no, some and full*). In the second step, we identified certain sub-categories of these paper topics, which have been addressed in terms of the challenges (such as locomotion or cross-reality interaction). For this, we only considered papers which fully addressed a certain challenge (thus have been rated

---

[2] https://hello.vrchat.com/.

[3] https://altvr.com/.

[4] https://www.oculus.com/horizon-worlds/.

with *full* in the first step). In total, we analysed 66 papers published over the last eight years. Where necessary, we also added further related work to support the presented aspects and widen the scope of the various subsections.

3.1 *Locomotion*—Physical Space

Locomotion is one of the main research directions in the VR field (Nilsson et al. 2018) and is especially representative of the everyday context, as a substantial part of the research output focuses on "Room Scale" settings. Introduced by retail VR headsets, the term **room scale** has come to represent a design paradigm for VR experiences that take place in users' homes. Here, the eponymous room typically refers to a space of 4 m × 4 m, as originally indicated by the SteamVR setup.

These dimensions have guided the development of novel locomotion techniques allowing users to explore VEs much larger than their physical space would permit. Techniques such as *Redirected Walking* are known for their large space requirements, necessary so that users do not notice the effects of rotational and positional gains (Steinicke et al. 2009). Since the release of the HTC Vive headset in 2016, a plethora of such Room Scale techniques have been presented. Here, we review some of the works in this area with a focus on those related to our workshop.

Within domestic settings, this challenging issue is further exacerbated by the presence of furniture and other items that further reduce the space available. To overcome this situation, in 2015, Simeone (2015) proposed the concept of Substitutional Reality, the idea of "substituting" physical objects with virtual counterparts. When these match the location and shape of the original real-world objects, obstacle avoidance is implicit, as users will know that everything they see represents a tangible object delimiting the interactive or walkable space. Later works explored the impact that substituting surface areas had on user behaviour, finding that the choice of material can influence user trajectories (Simeone et al. 2017). Limitations of this approach are that it is ideally suited for 1:1 experiences that can take place within the physically available space. Further, the "Substitutional Environment" needed to be designed in advance. At WEVR, Simeone presented ideas for how 3D reconstruction techniques could detect the physical layout and perform automatic substitutions. These ideas were later followed up by the community and implemented by systems that generate procedural environments by automatically substituting the layout of the physical space with virtual counterparts (Cheng et al. 2019; Shapira and Freedman 2016; Sra et al. 2016).

When it is not necessary to move or it is preferable to remain seated, Zielasko et al. explored the concept of DeskVR in a 2018 WEVR paper (Zielasko et al. 2017), to distinguish the term from *Desktop VR*, which was used in the past to refer to semi-immersive setups (Ware et al. 1993). The authors focused on the use-case of analysts exploring datasets within an immersive setup in their office. This form of stationary (seated or standing) immersion represents a scenario that is one of the likeliest to be experienced by everyday users. This scenario has also been discussed from other perspectives, such as considering the reduction of cybersickness when interacting with such immersive analytic applications while being seated (Zielasko et al. 2018), as well as in the context of using menus, including passive haptics to enhance mid-air menu interaction for such seated use of VR (Zielasko et al. 2019).

3.2   *Cross-Reality Interaction*—User Perspectives and Transitions

Cross-reality is an emerging XR area that shares many themes with everyday XR (Simeone et al. 2020). Given the proliferation of devices enabling immersion at different points of the reality-VR continuum (Milgram and Kishino 1994), users might want to collaborate and interact together. However, the bulk of these applications exist within their own "reality" and do not allow users at other points on the continuum to interact with each other. To this end, Pazhayedath et al. investigated several techniques enabling external users to pinpoint objects they wish the immersed user to focus on, to foster collaboration between the two realities (Pazhayedath et al. 2021). Woodworth and Borst presented a system allowing teachers to use a regular TV as a mirror to enable their reflections to point towards objects or other points of interest in the immersive environment (Woodworth and Borst 2017).

Another focus is supporting the awareness or interaction with external non-immersed users, who might find themselves in the vicinity of the immersed user—a likely occurrence in domestic settings. In 2016, Simeone explored the design of an in-VR "motion tracker" widget based on the device used in the *Aliens* film (Simeone 2016). The widget used a Microsoft Kinect to detect and display the approximate location of other physical users. Langbehn et al. proposed the concept of "Shadow Avatars" (Langbehn et al. 2018), i.e. avatars representing external users in the VE that become increasingly more opaque depending on their distance. Alaee et al. compared two techniques to enable immersed users to interact with their real-world smartphone while in VR (Alaee et al. 2018).

Further work focuses on the transition between different levels of immersion, thus enabling user to adapt their personal level of immersion between partial (AR/AV) and full immersion (VR). This might be used as a technique to engage with non-immersed users, but could also play a central role in the actual task fulfilment. In this regard, Botto et al. (2020) present a prototype of a virtual city tour in which the guide, acting as the primary user, switches between an AR-based perspective of the scene, enabling them to plan a tour, and the actual virtual environment, in which the visitors are immersed. If switched into VR, the primary user can now guide the visitors through the virtual city model. This switch between different levels of immersion might be relevant in other scenarios too, such as those proposed by Piumsomboon et al. (2018).

3.3 *Interaction Techniques and Hardware*—Interaction Devices and Patterns

Selecting or developing the right interaction technique for a given application or problem is a challenge on its own (Bowman et al. 2005). In this context, a body of work has been presented in terms of interaction techniques, such as in the context of locomotion as previously outlined above. Considering that, in everyday VR and AR, simple and versatile display systems, such as Google Cardboard, will be used, and specific interaction techniques for locomotion are necessary as presented by Powell et al. (2016). They present three techniques for navigation when using Google Cardboard without additional controllers or other input devices. Additionally, works have been presented in terms of avoiding collisions with virtual walls (Burgh and Johnsen 2018), as well as how sounds can be used to guide immersed users (Dong and Guo 2016).

In the case of integrating immersive technologies into everyday contexts, it is of specific interest to include physical objects in the near surrounding, such that these can be used for interaction with the virtual environment. In this context, a large body of work exists in terms of passive haptics. Lindeman defines passive haptics as "*...physical objects which provide feedback to the user simply by their shape, texture, or other inherent properties*" (Lindeman et al. 1999) to enhance interaction with the virtual environment. In terms of everyday VR and AR, this technique has been investigated in various contexts. For instance, Zielasko et al. present work on using passive haptics in terms of enhancing mid-air interaction with menus (Zielasko et al. 2019). They compare different types of tapping-based menu interaction techniques, including using an office desk as a surface for a passive-haptic feedback during interaction. Further work addressed issues arising in the case of deploying passive haptics in the field, specifically in the case of lacking hardware for implementing the needed tracking of physical objects. For instance, work by Taylor et al. (2020) focuses on the use of neural networks applied to a video feed to identify the position of a physical object. Work by Hirao et al. (2020) uses standard VR controllers for tracking instead.

Besides these two major aspects related to interaction techniques and hardware, other works have been presented with specific focus on everyday VR and AR. For instance, interaction without additional hardware or hands-free is an issue that works like that by Broussard et al. (2021) and Sidorakis et al. (2015) address using interaction via gaze or consider attention guiding of the user as a major contribution. The audio channel has been also addressed. Works that investigated the effects of music in the perception of the virtual environment by the user (Bialkova and Van Gisbergen 2017) or consider vocal commands as an input modality (Morotti et al. 2020) have reported that audio modality, interplaying with visual modality, is crucial for the VR/AR settings.

3.4   Ease of Use

As discussed above, there are still various factors decreasing the level of ease of use of current VR/AR hardware and applications. However, aspects related to the use of special hardware for reducing boundaries (e.g. problems in physically handling the hardware, such as putting up and down a headset correctly) for immersive technologies have been presented during WEVR workshops. For instance, simple-to-setup projection systems have been proposed. Eubanks et al. (2015) presented a portable VR system using inertial tracking, as is now used by various systems such as the Meta Quest, HTC Focus, and Microsoft HoloLens. In the case of room-mounted displays, the work by Stuerzlinger et al. (2015) presented an easy to setup and portable CAVE system. Furthermore, Hachiuma and Saito (2016) presented an algorithmic approach to track objects for mapping virtual content using in situ projection, work that has also been investigated in production as an AR-based support system (Funk et al. 2015). Another work in this regard has been presented by Botto et al. (2020) looking into the support actually provided by AR for manual assembly tasks.

Challenges associated with specific application areas have also been explored. For instance, in terms of medical applications, users with very specific needs have to be considered, such as in the case of the work by Bozgeyikli et al. (2016). The authors present work on a rehabilitation system in VR for users with Autism Spectrum Syndrome (ASD). Other examples can be found, such as the use of low-cost hardware for content creation (Wallgrün et al. 2019) or the application of small 3D games in a children's museum (Ball et al. 2019). Shopping and retail experiences represent another area where everyday users might come in direct contact with immersive technologies. Authors at the workshop have explored the design of applications leveraging VR and AR to provide retail shopping experiences. Morotti et al. investigated the use of a voice-based assistant in a VR fashion store, finding positive feedback from a sample of fashion students (Morotti et al. 2020). Bialkova and Barr further explored the ease of use and in depth the experience evaluation with AR shopping applications (Bialkova and Barr 2022), as described in detail in Sect. 3.7.

3.5   Environments and Context—Embedding

The challenge of embedding VR/AR technology and applications into everyday scenarios has also been discussed in the workshops, while the integration of such technology into (working) processes received less attention. A strong focus lies on the use and integration of immersive technologies in the office space, for instance in terms of immersive analytics (Lai and Majumder 2015; Su et al. 2015; Zielasko et al. 2018; Lisle et al. 2020). Bellgardt et al. (2017) present a thorough design-space analysis looking, at potential scenarios in the office in the case of seated, standing, and walking, which depends on the spatial situation in which the user is embedded. Additionally, the work by Lai and Majumder (2015) focuses on questions of how to project the virtual environment into the office environment using projection-based systems.

In terms of user experience in office spaces, a 2021 paper addressed employer evaluation (i.e. familiarity, image, reputation, perspectives, attractiveness) of varying office environments in VR (Bialkova and Ros 2021). The work represents a long-term project exploring how VR technologies could be best used to enhance employer branding and to shape human resource management in future (Bialkova and Ros 2018, 2019).

For non-working-related scenarios, sports, training, leisure, and medical therapy applications have also been discussed. Examples for applications in sports and training have been presented either from a hardware perspective regarding tracking by Grani and Bruun-Pedersen (2017) or from an application perspective for creating sports tactics as presented by Cannavò et al. (2018). Other papers dedicated to the potential of VR for architecture and design. For example, Bialkova et al. (2022) invited people for a bicycle ride in VR. In a series of studies, the streetscape of real cities was manipulated to provide a better understating of how to best design infrastructure for safe and attractive cycling (Bialkova and Ettema 2019; Bialkova et al. 2018, 2022). Another application presented the opportunities to enhance virtual museum visits. Studies from different laboratories manipulated various environmental factors, highlighting the potential of VR for creating immersive experiences (Ball et al. 2019; Bialkova and Van Gisbergen 2017; Botto et al. 2020). There has also been some important coverage of the potential of VR for therapy and rehabilitation (Bialkova and Dickhoff 2019; Powell and Powell 2015).

3.6 User Accessibility

In the previous subsections, various user-related aspects and research questions have been addressed in contexts like cross-reality interaction, interaction methods, or ease of use. Still, accessibility is also very relevant in the context of everyday scenarios, as they are clearly aimed at general users, including those with challenges. However, only a few papers have been published in the workshop on accessibility, despite the existing work in the community, such as in case of virtual heritage (Selmanović et al. 2020) or in marketing and tourism (Ozdemir 2021), to name only two examples. One focus lies in the use of audio for people with visual impairments as presented by Dong and Guo (2016). Further work focuses on supporting older adults in communicating with friends and family using social VR systems, for instance to support shared meals (Korsgaard et al. 2020) or therapy and rehabilitation (Lisle et al. 2020; Rings et al. 2020).

3.7 *Commercial Consumer Applications*

With XR technology maturing, the number of commercial applications has increased. This growth of applications is related to several challenges that have been addressed in the WEVR workshops by various papers across the years. One of the earliest works by Bialkova and Van Gisbergen (2017) explored the interplay between sound and vision as a key determinant of human perception. In particular, this work addressed the need to better understand how audio-visual signals manipulated in virtual environments influence perception and human behaviour. The results showed that music altered the way people are engaged in, perceive and experience a VR application. In order to foster systematic investigation and approaches to evaluate the system design of HMDs (e.g. how to care for the user's physical security and their feeling of being secure) and HMD experiences, Mai and Hußmann (2018) drew on work from the research on public displays. The paper aimed to understand how to attract people's attention, how to motivate people to use HMDs and overcome barriers that prevent people from using HMDs presented in public. Additionally, the brand-consumer dynamics was addressed in an attempt to provide the needed understanding on the key drivers of AR experiences and how these might enhance the consumer purchasing experience (Bialkova and Barr 2022). Results showed that interactivity, realism, ease of use, and immersion modulate AR experience evaluation and, thus, user satisfaction. Purchase experience correlated positively with utilitarian and hedonic values, predetermined by aesthetic and information quality. The outcomes of Bialkova and Barr (2022) can be directly applied in practice for designing AR environments to augment the consumer journey and satisfaction.

A 2022 paper by Bialkova (2022) further addressed the consumer demands and brand-consumer dynamics in creating immersive and engaging experiences. The study aimed at providing better understanding of how to augment VR experiences for everyday consumer applications. Based on a literature review, and outcomes from laboratory studies conducted by the authors, a framework is provided which encompasses key determinants from attention to action, hypothesised to augment experiences. The conceptual framework offers ways for brands to reach, attract, and retain customers via multisensory experiences enhancing the brand portfolio beyond conventional shopping environments.

The above WEVR examples, from various applications and contexts, suggest that the technological developments are not just fostering evolution in commerce, but could help brands to implement new strategies. The lessons learned from the WEVR papers demonstrate that the advancement of VR and AR, which are approaching the consumer sphere, could turn challenges into commercial opportunity by making VR- and AR-based shopping experiences easy-to-use, enjoyable, and thus appropriately meeting the demands of various consumers.

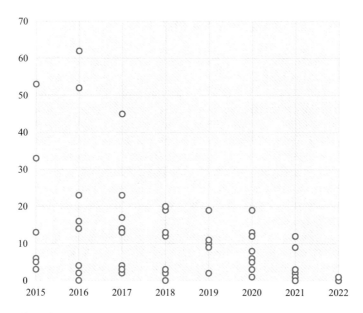

Fig. 1 Citations of everyday VR and AR research papers published in WEVR workshop from 2015 to 2022. Each publication is indicated as circle

4 Impact and Relevance of Everyday VR and AR Research

The major take-away message for the previous section is that the identified challenges are also reflected in the research published in the WEVR workshops over the last eight years. Sixty-six papers have been published over the years and are analysed above. We would argue that this number of publications (more than eight papers each year) highlights the relevance of the topic in the VR and AR research communities. Still, the presented analysis mainly focuses on papers published at the workshops and thus neglects a large body of work published in conferences such as IEEE VR, ISMAR, or ACM CHI, which would further highlight the relevance of the topic.

Additionally, work published in WEVR workshops has had reasonable impact. By reviewing the citations reported for the WEVR papers in Google Scholar, we can observe that papers gained a quite high impact score, as shown in Fig. 1. Some papers from the earlier WEVR versions (three papers in total) were cited more than 50 times. From 2015 to 2020, there are papers cited nearly 20 times each year. When calculating a two-year impact factor (sum of all citations of the last two years 2021 and 2022 divided by the number of papers), WEVR has an impact factor of 2.21. In summary, we argue that the research area of Everyday Virtual and Augmented Reality is an established field and has gained the interest of various scientists working on VR and AR. However, various research questions are still open, inviting further investigation.

5   The Future of Everyday VR and AR

The original goal of WEVR was to raise awareness within the VR/AR community about the challenges related to the use of immersive technologies in such settings. After seven years of organising the WEVR workshop, VR and AR have made significant strides into everyday settings, driven by both commercial and academic interests. We hope that our workshop has contributed to bringing these issues to the foreground, and that together with this book, it will foster further advancements.

However, VR and AR technologies and access to them are still far from the ubiquity that other computing devices enjoy today. While VR devices have entered the mainstream in some domains, particularly in the entertainment and social worlds, see-through AR devices remain in the domain of specialist users, due to the high costs, as well as usability issues.

To continue the work towards increasing the acceptance and uptake of VR/AR technologies, we think there are two future research approaches that are possible. Firstly, researchers should carefully consider the real limitations that everyday users face in terms of access to devices and the likely environments in which the applications will be deployed. Secondly, researchers should use VR to study those everyday situations that are not yet possible with today's technology, but whose derived insights might positively inspire the development of real technologies that are needed, as explored by recent works, e.g. Grandi et al. (2021) and Simeone et al. (2022).

We hope that the WEVR papers, and thus, this book, provide a solid base to conduct controlled laboratory studies to explore VR and AR experiences and, thus, to help (1) understand the factors that affect the acceptance and use of new technology, applications, and VR/AR environments; (2) facilitate end-users to easily derive decisions; and (3) enabling the VR/AR integration into the everyday context. We hope that readers will be inspired to pursue new research paths for the everyday VR/AR of the future.

References

Alaee G, Deasi AP, Pena-Castillo L, Brown E, Meruvia-Pastor O (2018) A user study on augmented virtuality using depth sensing cameras for near-range awareness in immersive VR. In: IEEE VR's 4th workshop on everyday virtual reality (WEVR 2018), vol 10, p 3

Ball C, Ahn SJ, Johnsen K (2019) Design and field study of motion-based informal learning games for a children's museum. In: IEEE 5th workshop on everyday virtual reality (WEVR), WEVR. IEEE

Bellgardt M, Pick S, Zielasko D, Vierjahn T, Weyers B, Kuhlen TW (2017) Utilizing immersive virtual reality in everyday work. In: 2017 IEEE 3rd workshop on everyday virtual reality (WEVR), pp 1–4. IEEE

Bialkova S (2022) From attention to action: key drivers to augment VR experience for everyday consumer applications. In: 2022 IEEE conference on virtual reality and 3D user interfaces abstracts and workshops (VRW), pp 247–252

Bialkova S, Barr C (2022) Virtual try-on: how to enhance consumer experience? In: 2022 IEEE conference on virtual reality and 3D user interfaces abstracts and workshops (VRW), pp 01–08

Bialkova S, Dickhoff B (2019) Encouraging rehabilitation trials: the potential of 360° immersive instruction videos. In: 2019 IEEE conference on virtual reality and 3D user interfaces (VR), pp 1443–1447. IEEE

Bialkova S, Ettema D (2019) Cycling renaissance: the VR potential in exploring static and moving environment elements. In: 2019 IEEE 5th workshop on everyday virtual reality (WEVR), pp 1–6

Bialkova S, Ros E (2018) Augmenting employer brand experiences and evaluation: the role of innovative VR and digital platforms. EMAC2018

Bialkova S, Ros E (2019) Talent management: the potential of VR and digital innovations. EURAM2019

Bialkova S, Ros E (2021) Enhancing employer branding via high-tech platforms: VR and digital, what works better and how? Manag Revue 32(2):128

Bialkova S, Van Gisbergen MS (2017) When sound modulates vision: VR applications for art and entertainment. In: 2017 IEEE 3rd workshop on everyday virtual reality (WEVR), pp 1–6

Bialkova S, Ettema D, Dijst M (2018) Urban future: unlocking cycling with VR applications. In: 2018 IEEE workshop on augmented and virtual realities for good (VAR4Good), pp 1–5

Bialkova S, Ettema D, Dijst M (2022) How do design aspects influence the attractiveness of cycling streetscapes: results of virtual reality experiments in the netherlands. Transp Res Part A Policy Pract 162:315–331

Botto C, Cannavò A, Cappuccio D, Morat G, Sarvestani AN, Ricci P, Demarchi V, Saturnino A (2020) Augmented reality for the manufacturing industry: the case of an assembly assistant. In: IEEE 6th workshop on everyday virtual reality (WEVR), WEVR. IEEE

Bowman DA, McMahan RP (2007) Virtual reality: how much immersion is enough? 40(7):36–43

Bowman DA, Kruijff E, LaViola JJ Jr, Poupyrev I (2005) 3D user interfaces: theory and practice. Addison-Wesley

Bozgeyikli L, Bozgeyikli E, Raij A, Alqasemi R, Katkoori S, Dubey R (2016) Vocational training with immersive virtual reality for individuals with autism: towards better design practices. In: 2016 IEEE 2nd workshop on everyday virtual reality (WEVR). IEEE, pp 21–25

Broussard DM, Rahman Y, Kulshreshth AK, Borst CW (2021) An interface for enhanced teacher awareness of student actions and attention in a VR classroom. In: 2021 IEEE conference on virtual reality and 3D user interfaces abstracts and workshops (VRW). IEEE, pp 284–290

Burgh B, Johnsen K (2018) Camera-geometry interpenetration in virtual reality. In: 2018 IEEE 4th workshop on everyday virtual reality (WEVR), WEVR. IEEE

Cannavò A, Musto M, Prattico FG, Raho F, Lamberti F (2018) A participative system for tactics analysis in sport training based on immersive virtual reality. In: 2018 IEEE 4th workshop on everyday virtual reality (WEVR), WEVR. IEEE

Cheng L-P, Ofek E, Holz C, Wilson AD (2019) VRoamer: generating on-the-fly vr experiences while walking inside large, unknown real-world building environments. In: 2019 IEEE conference on virtual reality and 3D user interfaces (VR). IEEE, pp 359–366

Dong M, Guo R (2016) Towards understanding the capability of spatial audio feedback in virtual environments for people with visual impairments. In: 2016 IEEE 2nd workshop on everyday virtual reality (WEVR). IEEE, pp 15–20

Eubanks JC, Lai C, Mcmahan RP (2015) Portable virtual reality: inertial measurements and biomechanics. In: Proceedings of the 1st workshop on everyday virtual reality, pp 1–4

Freeman J, Lessiter J (2001) Here, there and everywhere: the effect of multichannel audio on presence. In: Proceedings of ICAD2001, Espoo, Finland, 29 July–1 Aug 2001

Funk M, Mayer S, Schmidt A (2015) Using in-situ projection to support cognitively impaired workers at the workplace. In: Proceedings of the 17th international ACM SIGACCESS conference on computers & accessibility, pp 185–192

Grandi JG, Cao Z, Ogren M, Kopper R (2021) Design and simulation of next-generation augmented reality user interfaces in virtual reality. In: 2021 IEEE conference on virtual reality and 3D user interfaces abstracts and workshops (VRW). IEEE, pp 23–29

Grani F, Bruun-Pedersen JR (2017) Giro: better biking in virtual reality. In: 2017 IEEE 3rd workshop on everyday virtual reality (WEVR). IEEE, pp 1–5

Hachiuma R, Saito H (2016) Recognition and pose estimation of primitive shapes from depth images for spatial augmented reality. In: 2016 IEEE 2nd workshop on everyday virtual reality (WEVR). IEEE, pp 32–35

Hirao Y, Takala TM, Lecuyer A (2020) Comparing motion-based versus controller-based pseudo-haptic weight sensations in VR. In: IEEE 6th workshop on everyday virtual reality (WEVR), WEVR. IEEE

Jerald J (2015) The VR book: human-centered design for virtual reality. Morgan & Claypool

Korsgaard D, Bjørner T, Bruun-Pedersen JR, Sørensen PK, Perez-Cueto FA (2020) Eating together while being apart: a pilot study on the effects of mixed-reality conversations and virtual environments on older eaters' solitary meal experience and food intake. In: IEEE 6th workshop on everyday virtual reality (WEVR), WEVR. IEEE

Lai DQ, Majumder A (2015) Interactive display conglomeration on the wall. In: Proceedings of the 1st workshop on everyday virtual reality, pp 5–9

Langbehn E, Harting E, Steinicke F (2018) Shadow-avatars: a visualization method to avoid collisions of physically co-located users in room-scale VR. In: IEEE workshop on everyday virtual reality

Lessiter J, Freeman J, Keogh E, Davidoff J (2001) A cross-media presence questionnaire: the ITC-sense of presence inventory. Presence 10(3):282–297

Lindeman RW, Sibert JL, Hahn JK (1999) Hand-held windows: towards effective 2d interaction in immersive virtual environments. In: Proceedings IEEE virtual reality (Cat. No. 99CB36316), pp 205–212

Lisle L, Chen X, Gitre EJK, North C, Bowman DA (2020) Evaluating the benefits of the immersive space to think. In: IEEE 6th workshop on everyday virtual reality (WEVR), WEVR. IEEE

Liu Q, Steed A (2021) Social virtual reality platform comparison and evaluation using a guided group walkthrough method. Front Virtual Reality 2:668181

Mai C, Heinrich H (2018) The audience funnel for head-mounted displays in public environments. In: 2018 IEEE 4th workshop on everyday virtual reality (WEVR), WEVR. IEEE

McMahan A (2003) Immersion, engagement, and presence: a method for analyzing 3-d video games. In: The medium of the video game, chap 3, pp 135–158

Milgram P, Kishino F (1994) A taxonomy of mixed reality visual displays. IEICE Trans Inf Syst 77(12):1321–1329

Morotti E, Donatiello L, Marfia G (2020) Fostering fashion retail experiences through virtual reality and voice assistants. In: IEEE 6th workshop on everyday virtual reality (WEVR), WEVR. IEEE

Nilsson NC, Peck T, Bruder G, Hodgson E, Serafin S, Whitton M, Steinicke F, Rosenberg ES (2018) 15 years of research on redirected walking in immersive virtual environments. IEEE Comput Graph Appl 38(2):44–56

Ozdemir MA (2021) Virtual reality (VR) and augmented reality (AR) technologies for accessibility and marketing in the tourism industry. In: ICT tools and applications for accessible tourism. IGI Global, pp 277–301

Pazhayedath P, Belchior P, Prates R, Silveira F, Lopes DS, Cools R, Esteves A, Simeone AL (2021) Exploring bi-directional pinpointing techniques for cross-reality collaboration. In: 2021 IEEE conference on virtual reality and 3D user interfaces abstracts and workshops (VRW). IEEE, pp 264–270

Piumsomboon T, Lee GA, Hart JD, Ens B, Lindeman RW, Thomas BH, Billinghurst M (2018) Mini-me: an adaptive avatar for mixed reality remote collaboration. In: Proceedings of the 2018 CHI conference on human factors in computing systems, pp 1–13

Powell V, Powell W (2015) Therapy-led design of home-based virtual rehabilitation. In: Proceedings of the 1st workshop on everyday virtual reality, pp 11–14

Powell W, Powell V, Brown P, Cook W, Uddin J (2016) Getting around in google cardboard—exploring navigation preferences with low-cost mobile VR. In: 2016 IEEE 2nd workshop on everyday virtual reality (WEVR), pp 5–8. IEEE

Rings S, Steinicke F, Picker T, Prasuhn C (2020) Enabling patients with neurological diseases to perform motor-cognitive exergames under clinical supervision for everyday usage. In: IEEE 6th workshop on everyday virtual reality (WEVR), WEVR. IEEE

Rogers K, Karaosmanoglu S, Altmeyer M, Suarez A, Nacke LE (2022) Much realistic, such wow! A systematic literature review of realism in digital games. In: CHI conference on human factors in computing systems, pp 1–21

Selmanović E, Rizvic S, Harvey C, Boskovic D, Hulusic V, Chahin M, Sljivo S (2020) Improving accessibility to intangible cultural heritage preservation using virtual reality. J Comput Cult Heritage (JOCCH) 13(2):1–19

Shapira L, Freedman D (2016) Reality skins: creating immersive and tactile virtual environments. In: 2016 IEEE international symposium on mixed and augmented reality (ISMAR). IEEE, pp 115–124

Sidorakis N, Koulieris GA, Mania K (2015) Binocular eye-tracking for the control of a 3d immersive multimedia user interface. In: Proceedings of the 1st workshop on everyday virtual reality, pp 15–18

Simeone AL (2015) Substitutional reality: towards a research agenda. In: Proceedings of the 1st workshop on everyday virtual reality, pp 19–22

Simeone AL (2016) The VR motion tracker: visualising movement of non-participants in desktop virtual reality experiences. In: 2016 IEEE 2nd workshop on everyday virtual reality (WEVR). IEEE, pp 1–4

Simeone AL, Velloso E, Gellersen H (2015) Substitutional reality: using the physical environment to design virtual reality experiences. In: Proceedings of the 33rd annual ACM conference on human factors in computing systems. ACM, pp 3307–3316

Simeone AL, Mavridou I, Powell W (2017) Altering user movement behaviour in virtual environments. IEEE Trans Visual Comput Graph 23(4):1312–1321

Simeone AL, Speicher M, Molnar A, Wilde A, Daiber F (2019) Live: the human role in learning in immersive virtual environments. In: Symposium on spatial user interaction, pp 1–11

Simeone AL, Khamis M, Esteves A, Daiber F, Kljun M, Pucihar KČ, Isokoski P, Gugenheimer J (2020) International workshop on cross-reality (XR) interaction. In: Companion proceedings of the 2020 conference on interactive surfaces and spaces, pp 111–114

Simeone AL, Cools R, Depuydt S, Gomes JM, Goris P, Grocott J, Esteves A, Gerling K (2022) Immersive speculative enactments: bringing future scenarios and technology to life using virtual reality. In: CHI conference on human factors in computing systems, pp 1–20

Sra M, Garrido-Jurado S, Schmandt C, Maes P (2016) Procedurally generated virtual reality from 3d reconstructed physical space. In: Proceedings of the 22nd ACM conference on virtual reality software and technology, pp 191–200

Statista (2022) Number of monthly active users on gaming platform steam worldwide from 2017 to 2021. https://www.statista.com/statistics/733277/number-stream-dau-mau/

Statista (2022) Virtual reality (VR)—statistics & facts. https://www.statista.com/topics/2532/virtual-reality-vr/

Steed A, Takala TM, Archer D, Lages W, Lindeman RW (2021) Directions for 3d user interface research from consumer VR games. IEEE Trans Vis Comput Graph 27(11):4171–4182

Steinicke F, Bruder G, Jerald J, Frenz H, Lappe M (2009) Estimation of detection thresholds for redirected walking techniques. IEEE Trans Vis Comput Graph 16(1):17–27

Stuerzlinger W, Pavlovych A, Nywton D (2015) TIVS: temporary immersive virtual environment at simon fraser university: a non-permanent cave. In: Proceedings of the 1st workshop on everyday virtual reality, pp 23–28

Su S, Chaudhary A, O'Leary P, Geveci B, Sherman W, Nieto H, Francisco-Revilla L (2015) Virtual reality enabled scientific visualization workflow. In: Proceedings of the 1st workshop on everyday virtual reality, pp 29–32

Taylor C, McNicholas R, Cosker D (2020) Towards an egocentric framework for rigid and articulated object tracking in virtual reality. In: IEEE 6th workshop on everyday virtual reality (WEVR), WEVR. IEEE

Usoh M, Catena E, Arman S, Slater M (2000) Using presence questionnaires in reality. Presence 9:497–503

Wallgrün JO, Masrur A, Zhao J, Taylor A, Knapp E, Chang JS-K, Kippel A (2019) Low-cost VR applications to experience real word places anytime, anywhere, and with anyone. In: IEEE 5th workshop on everyday virtual reality (WEVR), WEVR. IEEE

Ware C, Arthur K, Booth KS (1993) Fish tank virtual reality. In: Proceedings of the INTERACT'93 and CHI'93 conference on human factors in computing systems, pp 37–42

Witmer BG, Singer MJ (1998) Measuring presence in virtual environments: a presence questionnaire. Presence 7(3):225–240

Woodworth JW, Borst CW (2017) Design of a practical TV interface for teacher-guided VR field trips. In: 2017 IEEE 3rd workshop on everyday virtual reality (WEVR). IEEE, pp 1–6

Zielasko D, Weyers B, Bellgardt M, Pick S, Meibner A, Vierjahn T, Kuhlen TW (2017) Remain seated: towards fully-immersive desktop VR. In: 2017 IEEE 3rd workshop on everyday virtual reality (WEVR). IEEE, pp 1–6

Zielasko D, Meißner A, Freitag S, Weyers B, Kuhlen TW (2018) Dynamic field of view reduction related to subjective sickness measures in an HMD-based data analysis task. In: 2017 IEEE 4th workshop on everyday virtual reality (WEVR). IEEE

Zielasko D, Krüger M, Weyers B, Kuhlen TW (2019) Passive haptic menus for desk-based and HMD-projected virtual reality. In: 2018 IEEE 5th workshop on everyday virtual reality (WEVR). IEEE

Extended Reality for Knowledge Work in Everyday Environments

Verena Biener, Eyal Ofek, Michel Pahud, Per Ola Kristensson, and Jens Grubert

Abstract Virtual and augmented reality (*VR* and *AR*) have the potential to change information work. The ability to modify the workers senses can transform everyday environments into a productive office, using portable head-mounted displays (*HMDs*) combined with conventional interaction devices, such as keyboards and tablets. While a stream of better, cheaper, and lighter HMDs has been introduced for consumers in recent years, there are still many challenges to be addressed to allow this vision to become reality. This chapter gives an overview of the state of the art in the field of extended reality for knowledge work in everyday environments, identifies challenges and proposes steps to address the open challenges.

1 Introduction

Extended reality (XR) covers a spectrum of diverse technologies ranging from augmented physical (*AR*) environments to fully virtual (*VR*) environments. While XR technologies have been studied for decades in laboratory settings, the shift toward affordable consumer-oriented products allows exploring the positive and negative qualities of such technologies in everyday environments. Among diverse application

V. Biener (✉) · J. Grubert
Coburg University of Applied Sciences and Arts, Coburg, Germany
e-mail: verena.biener@hs-coburg.de

J. Grubert
e-mail: jens.grubert@hs-coburg.de

E. Ofek · M. Pahud
Microsoft Research Redmond, Redmond, USA
e-mail: eyalofek@microsoft.com

M. Pahud
e-mail: mpahud@microsoft.com

P. O. Kristensson
University of Cambridge, Cambridge, UK
e-mail: pok21@cam.ac.uk

domains, spanning entertainment, medical and industrial use (Slater and Sanchez-Vives 2016; Billinghurst et al. 2015), supporting knowledge work has attracted increasing interest in recent years.

The notation '*Knowledge Work*' follows the definition initially coined by Drucker (1966) where information workers (or *IWs*) apply theoretical and analytical knowledge to develop products and services. Much of the work might be detached from physical documents, artifacts, or specific work locations and is mediated through digital devices such as laptops, tablets, or mobile phones, connected through the Internet. This unique nature of knowledge work enables better mobility—the ability to work far from the physical office—and raises new possibilities to both overcome difficulties and enable services that are natural for physical offices, such as streamlined communication and collaboration and environments designed for creativity, privacy, and other factors.

In this chapter, we intend to explain our vision that moving the worker further into a digital immersive environment opens up options not limited by the physicality of the worker's devices and environments. We hypothesize that a virtual work environment enables workers to do more than they could before, with less effort, and may also eventually level the playing field between workers regardless of their physical locations, physical limitations, or the quality of their physical work environment. Doing knowledge work in XR is still an emerging field and current devices entail quite a few drawbacks compared to current physical work environments. Therefore, we summarize both existing research on supporting knowledge work through XR technologies and challenges that should be addressed to move the field forward.

The focus of this work is to explore research in the area of extended reality that takes place in a knowledge work context.

Our search includes diverse papers from journals and conferences and is not limited to certain venues or years. Most papers were found through ACM Digital Library, IEEE Explore, and Google Scholar. We did not conduct a strictly formal and complete literature review, as the topic is an emerging field and terminology is not yet consistent enough to find all relevant papers with a predefined set of keywords. The following search terms were used in different combinations: virtual reality, augmented reality, knowledge work, text entry, collaboration, office environment, and long-term use. These were used in the advanced search engines of aforementioned databases. Additionally, we considered papers that referenced, or were referenced, by relevant papers, that would not have been included through the keyword search alone. We primarily examined the title and abstract to decide, based on our own expertise in the field, whether a paper was relevant. We used the following criteria: (1) the paper included an XR technology which means systems or devices that enhance or replace the physical surrounding, and (2) the paper had a connection to the field of knowledge work.

This chapter is divided into several sections, each investigating a different aspects of knowledge work in XR. As this is an overview of literature in an emerging field the literature does not provide an agreed upon set of sub-categories. We identified our subsections during the literature review process, by clustering the papers according to their main contents. Section 2, *Interaction Techniques*, reviews research on interaction techniques that can facilitate knowledge work in XR, including techniques for text entry (Sect. 2.3)—a crucial task in knowledge work. Section 3, *Collaboration*, explores the collaborative aspects of information work, which are crucial to allow the worker to maintain group working from remote and new environments. Section 4, *Environment*, considers the influence of the environment on the knowledge worker and how XR can help optimize it, as well as the social implications arising from the use of XR. Section 6, *Application*, presents practical applications of XR in the area of knowledge work. Finally, we envision the worker to use the XR environment as an alternative to the limiting physical environment, resulting in the use of XR for extended time periods. Therefore, Sect. 5, *Long-term Immersion*, provides insights into the current research status in this area. Toward the end of this chapter, we provide a summary, discuss future challenges, and synthesize our main conclusions.

2   Interaction Techniques

Envisioning work in XR spaces, we look at ways that information workers are doing their task today, and how they can be done in XR space. The transition to XR space, where the user's senses are being modified by devices such as head-mounted displays (HMDs) and different interfaces for the hands are challenging and require new interaction concepts (Bowman et al. 2004). Some tasks such as typing that are crucial in today's work are dependent on good combination of senses (such as vision, proprioception, and haptics).

Another aspect of interest is embedding the, mostly 2D, information work in three-dimensional space. The use of a 3D immersive space enables several capabilities that were not available to workers using standard 2D monitors and input devices, such as a very wide display space around the user, a depth display that is not limited to one plane as most monitors, and storing data in the same space as the user's body, enabling new and direct methods to interact with data using natural gestures (Fig. 1). Different works look at how to efficiently map user's 3D motions in space to the 2D space of the task (Andujar and Argelaguet 2007; Brasier et al. 2020) or documents (e.g., spreadsheets or letters), while other looked at how to use the additional dimension of display given by XR to expose more meta-data about the task that can help the worker (Biener et al. 2020; Gesslein et al. 2020).

2.1   *Working with 2D Content in 3D*

Toady's most common knowledge worker tasks, such as document editing or spreadsheet applications, are done in 2D on 2D displays. Therefore, in order to leverage on the existing data, tools, and user's familiarity, many approaches that combine knowledge work with XR three-dimensional environments keep the 2D nature of such tasks and develop techniques for interacting with 2D content in a 3D environment.

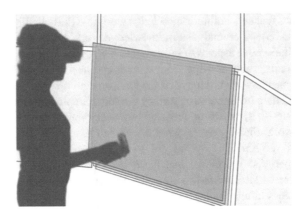

Fig. 1 Using a head-mounted display adds several capabilities over conventional 2D displays. First, the effective display field of view engulfs the user; second, the HMD's stereo display enables the position of data at different distances from the user, and is not limited to a planar display. Finally, positioning the user and the data in the same space enables new and direct ways for the user to interact with the data using natural gestures

Immersive 3D environments offer a large space around the user that can be used to display more information. However, directly interacting with the content, for example, through gestures, can be fatiguing, especially for large displays. This problem can be tackled by indirect interaction. Simple interactions on 2D data in a 3D virtual environment could be done by simply using existing devices like mice or touchpads. This is for example supported by Oculus Infinite Office (Oculus 2021) where a bluetooth keyboard including a touchpad can be connected to the Oculus Quest 2, is visualized in VR and can be used to interact with different applications. However, such devices might not scale well from use on standard displays to the large interaction space XR. Also, their interaction space is limited to the 2D plane on which they operate, limiting the possibilities provided by XR, like depth visualization. Huang et al. (2017) compared mouse input with gesture input for manipulating graphs in VR and results from their user study indicate that gestures can be more efficient for complicated graphs. To interact with data visualized in 3D, one could also employ 3D mice such as presented by Perelman et al. (2015) , which allows interaction on a two 2D plane as well as in 3D space.

For example, Andujar and Argelaguet (2007) proposed to interact with 2D windows inside virtual reality by decoupling motor space from visual space. To this end, users interacted with a controller pointing on a virtual pad, which mapped movements to the respective 2D window (see Fig. 2). They compared the technique with direct manipulation raycasting and the performance results indicated that there is a small overhead. However, authors argue that it is a good trade-off for more flexibility and comfort. Later, this idea was also studied within AR (Brasier et al. 2020) where results suggested that indirect input can perform equally to direct hand raycast and produces less fatigue. Also, Hoppe et al. (2020), proposed a set of tools to further

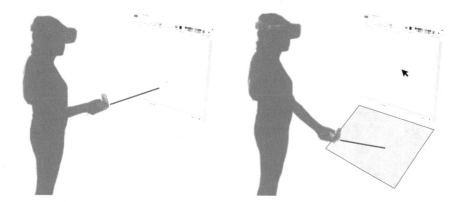

Fig. 2 Sketch of the virtual pad as proposed by Andujar and Argelaguet (2007). On the left, the user directly interacts with the 2D content through raycasting. On the right, the user casts the ray onto a virtual pad which redirects the movement to the 2D content and allows a more comfortable position. Image courtesy by Ferran Argelaguet

interact with 2D Window content, such as a workbench tool for copying and pasting 2D content within 3D or a macro tool, inside 3D virtual environments.

Normand and McGuffin (2018) used augmented reality to extend the display space of a smartphone and additionally presented new mid-air interaction techniques. The results of their study indicate that the extended display space was superior to using the smartphone alone. Additionally, input on the phone performed better than the proposed mid-air interaction techniques. Le et al. (2021) presented VXSlate, combining head tracking and a tablet to perform fine-tuned manipulations on a large virtual display. A virtual representation of the users hand and the tablet is presented on the large display. Kern et al. (2021) introduced a framework for 2D interaction in 3D including digital pen and paper on physically aligned surfaces, and a study ($n = 10$) showed that the technique resulted in low task load and high usability.

Biener et al. (2020) investigated the joint interaction space of tablets and immersive VR HMDs for supporting the interaction of knowledge workers with and across multiple 2D windows embedded in a 3D space (see Fig. 3). Specifically, they designed techniques, including touch and eye gaze, and therefore combined indirect and direct techniques. The goal was to be unobtrusive and compatible with small physical spaces within everyday environments like trains and planes. Using physical devices like tablets or pens can also minimize motions and provide hand support for long hours of work and therefore reduce fatigue. For example, Gesslein et al. (2020) proposed pen and gaze-based interaction techniques for supporting interaction with spreadsheets in VR. Aside from the large display space, they also made use of the 3D view to show additional information above the 2D screen. Einsfeld et al. (2006) also presented a semantic information visualization of documents in a 3D interface, which visualizes documents, meta-data, and semantic relations between documents. Dengel et al. (2006) extended this work through interaction techniques for searching and navigating large document sets with a stereoscopic monitor and a data glove.

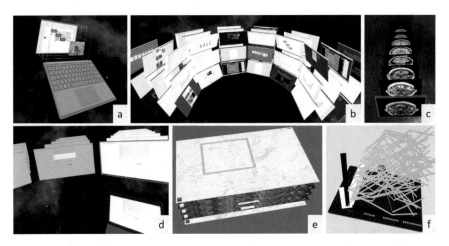

Fig. 3 Applications proposed by Biener et al. (2020) using the joint interaction space of tablets and immersive VR HMDs for tasks like presentation editor (**a**), window manager (**b**), medical imaging (**c**), code version control (**d**), map navigation (**e**), and information visualization (**f**)

Evaluating these techniques indicated that they are fun and enable an efficient interaction. Further, Deller et al. (2008) introduced interaction techniques for managing 2D documents within a virtual work desk.

As has been seen, many proposed techniques include a touch surface (Normand and McGuffin 2018; Biener et al. 2020; Gesslein et al. 2020; Le et al. 2021), which enables fine grained sensing of writing and touch, while supporting the users fingers or stylus, and has found to perform better than mid-air techniques (Normand and McGuffin 2018; Gesslein et al. 2020; Romat et al. 2021; Kern et al. 2021).

The large display space of XR enables display of more data than typical physical displays, yet the need to manipulate data over such large space efficiently without generating fatigue of the user is a challenge. Indirect input has been shown to perform equally to direct while inducing less fatigue (Brasier et al. 2020). The user may execute smaller gestures, and may support their hands to enable long hours of work, and maps their action to the large display space. This is not a new concept for information workers, used for indirect mapping of mouse inputs.

2.2 System Control

While many techniques have been proposed for task such as object manipulation (for a recent survey we refer to Mendes et al. (2019)), research on system control has not been as much in the focus of attention. Within the context of seated virtual reality, Zielasko et al. (2019a), studied the effects of passive haptic feedback on touch-based menus. They found a mid-air menu with passive haptic feedback to outperform desk-

a

b

c

Fig. 4 Stacked radial menu in the spreadsheet application presented in Gesslein et al. (2020)

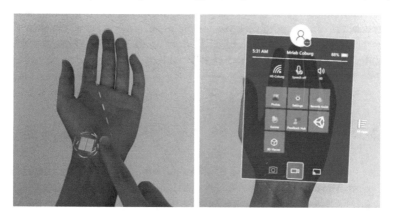

Fig. 5 Touching a wrist with a finger is used to summon a menu in HoloLens2 HMD

aligned alternatives (with and without haptic feedback). However, they also noted hardware requirements for supporting passive haptic feedback in VR, which might be challenging to achieve in everyday environments. Bowman and Wingrave (2001) compared a menu system using pinch gloves (TULIP) with floating menus and pen and tablet menus. They found that users had a preference for TULIP although pen and tablet was significantly faster. This was due to the TULIP interface providing less affordances (Fig. 4).

In current HMDs system, control is usually realized via gestures, controllers and pointing. For example, the Oculus Quest opens a rectangular menu-window upon pressing the menu-buttons on the controller; then, the user can navigate through the menu using raycasting and the controllers trigger. Alternatively, a hand gesture mode is available where the user can open the menu by performing a pinch gesture and navigate using raycasting originating from the hand and pinch gestures to select. Tapping with a finger on the wrist of the other hand will open the menu in a HoloLens 2. Navigation is then done by tapping directly on the buttons on the interface, similar to a touchscreen (see Fig. 5).

The work by Zielasko et al. (2019a) shows that mid-air menus are preferred over menus aligned with the desk. This is also reflected in implementations of current HMDs that present the menu vertically in front of the user. It is also beneficial to have haptic feedback which is also given in pen and tablet techniques that have shown to be usable for system control.

Many of the works mentioned above focus on special gestures for summoning a system control window when interacting with 3D space around the user. The gestures for summoning are quite large, sometimes using two hands, and they are mostly context-free. Information workers, working mostly sitting next to a desk and using small supported hand motions, may not be able to use some of these gestures. Furthermore, it is of interest to use very small gestures that can help the user to summon menus within the context of the data. Gesslein et al. (2020) uses the depth display of HMDs to separate between the planar display of a tablet as the location of the original data and the space above the plane as the place for meta-data and menus. The researchers render multiple layers of pie menus in context of 2D spreadsheets (follow the radial menus design of Gebhardt et al. (2013)) when displayed in VR. The motion of the user's pen above the 2D tablet screen is used to access stacked radial menus (see Fig. 4).

2.3   Text Entry

Text entry and editing is a major task of information work, which is a spatial challenge for XR users. The use of near-eye displays can block the view on physical peripherals such as physical keyboards or touch keyboards and may interfere with the view of the users own palms and the hand-eye coordination, required for efficient typing.

2.3.1   Representing Keyboards and Hands

The best and most popular way to enter text is the full-scale physical keyboard that has hardly changed in the last century and a half since its introduction. The keyboard supports the user's fingers and gives haptic feedback, as the user presses each key. To leverage on the massive install base of physical keyboards for XR users, there is a need to track its position and orientation in space and represent it inside the HMD display, as well as the user's hands.

Jiang et al. (2018) present a technique called HiKeyb. The keyboard is being recognized in the depth video and is represented in the virtual space by a corresponding virtual model, while the user's hands are segmented from the depth video and included in the virtual environment as a planar billboard. Users using this technique were measured reaching typing speed of 23.1 words per minute. McGill et al. (2015) used a color video input and blend the real-time video of the user's hands over the physical keyboard, as a window within the HMD display, showing that users were able to type using this input although their typing speed was slower compared to their natural typing speed in the real world. Part of this difference might be due to the novelty of the XR environment, and part maybe due to inherent latency or inaccuracies of the system.

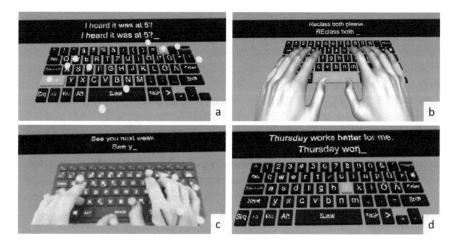

Fig. 6 Different representations of the user's hands for typing in a virtual environment (Grubert et al. 2018a), including representing fingertips as spheres (**a**), using an inverse kinematic model (**b**), video stream (**c**), and no hand representation (**d**)

Capturing a video of the real-world hands may not be a solution that fits every application. Its styling may break the immersion of a VR experience, and it is limited by the ability to capture the real hands (real-world illumination, real-world visibility). Researchers have explored other ways of sensing the user's hands actions, from 3D scanning to none at all.

Walker et al. (2017) rendered a virtual keyboard in the HMD's virtual environment and did not render the user hands at all. Upon a finger pressing a key on the physical keyboard, the corresponding virtual key lights up. They combined this approach with an auto-correction algorithm and showed that users could reach a speed of 40 words per minute. A similar approach by Otte et al. (2019) used touch-sensitive keyboards enabling highlighting touched keys in virtual displays prior to pressing them. They compared fingertip visualization with a touch-sensitive keyboard and found that they are similarly efficient.

Researchers looked at reconstructing the user's hands geometry and render them in the HMD virtual space as 3D models that follow the user's hand motions and position. Knierim et al. (2018) present a system that tracks the physical keyboard and the users hands. They compared different renderings of the hand's models from a realistic rendering, abstract and fingertip rendering both as full opaque objects as well as semi-transparent objects. The performance of experienced typists, which less rely on view of their hands, was not significantly influenced by the visualizations, while inexperienced typists needed some kind of visualization and transparency had no significant influence. For all typists realistic rendering of their hands resulted in higher presence and lower workload.

Grubert et al. (2018a) compared four different hand representation techniques in the context of text entry: no representation and video inlay (following the work of McGill et al.), and using tracking of fingertips in 3D space, they rendered two types of 3D models: A minimalist model of the fingertips only, leaving most of the user palm transparent, and a full 3D animated model of the palms. Since the researchers tracked only the fingertips positions, an inverse kinematics technique was used to animate the finger's joints (see Fig. 6). Their study showed no significant differences in typing speed between different renderings. However, using video inlay and fingertip visualization resulted in significantly lower error rates compared to the other two techniques. Surprisingly, using fully animated models increased the error rate of typing, almost as much as using no visualization of the hands at all, probably due to the accumulated effects of small latency and differences between the recovered model and the real hands. Interesting, the actual speed of typing was not affected by the representation; only, the error rate, however, the representation can influence subjective measures like presence and workload.

Other works looked at the effect of the keyboard peripheral and the way they are rendered on the text entry quality. The use of XR also opens new possibilities that were not possible in the physical world. For example, since the user does not see their own hands and the keyboard, those may be rendered to the user in new locations, for example, closer to the document or the gaze direction of the user. Dube and Arif (2020) explored the effect of rendering virtual keyboards' keys shapes and choose 3-dimensional square keys. Grubert et al. (2018b) visualized the keys of a physical keyboard in VR and the fingertips of the user. The researchers also studied the ability to relocate the keyboard and user hands from their physical location to a position in front of the user's gaze. While physical keyboards performance, where the user's fingertips stays lying on the physical keyboard, where not affected by the relocation, soft keyboards, requiring the user's fingertips to raise above the touch surface showed some reduction in speed yet kept a reasonable performance.

Another way to sense and render the user hands is to use point clouds, generated by depth cameras and LiDARs. While displaying a 3D representation of the hands which might improve hand-eye-coordination, they do not require computational heavy and error-prone processes of recovery like for a full 3D-articulated model of the hands. Pham and Stuerzlinger (2019) compared visualizations for typing on a physical keyboard in VR. They compared no VR with the following: no keyboard representation, hand represented as point cloud; keyboard represented as rectangular frame, hand represented as point cloud; virtual model of keyboard, hand represented as point cloud; keyboard and hands shown as video; keyboard and hands represented as point cloud. Authors concluded that the video-see-through is the best option because it is easy to implement and achieves a good entry speed. The point-cloud solution was also found to be competitive; however, it is more complex to implement.

Even though using a physical keyboard for text entry in XR allows for efficient text entry, it demands that there is a physical keyboard available. This might not be suitable for some scenarios like mobile applications or in limited spaces.

2.3.2 Mobile Text Entry

While most large text entry tasks are still best to be done near a working desk, using a full-size keyboard, the use of wearable HMDs enables the users to enter text also on the go without the constraints of a physical environment and a physical keyboard. Researchers looked at using phones as text entry devices for XR users that are common and mobile. One challenge of current phone keyboards is being based on touch, so they require the user's visual sense to guide the fingertips before they touch keys on the phone's screen. To overcome this difficulty, Kim and Kim (2017) use a phone with hovering sensing (sensing finger tips at some distance prior to touching the phone's screen) to visualize both the phone's keyboard and the nearby user's fingertip. Son et al. (2019) used two touch pads with hover function for typing in VR with two thumbs, resulting in a typing speed of 30 WPM. Knierim et al. (2020) focused on a portable solution and compared the on-screen smartphone keyboard with a desktop-keyboard connected to a smartphone and with a VR-HMD that shows the physical keyboard via video-pass-through. Results indicate a higher input speed in the HMD condition compared to smartphone only, but lower speed compared to a smartphone combined with a physical keyboard. This shows that HMDs with physical keyboards perform better than virtual touchscreen keyboards but worse than physical keyboards without HMDs.

2.3.3 Gaze-Based Text Entry

Using XR HMDs opens the possibilities to use new modalities to aid text entry. In recent years, several commercial AR and VR HMDs have introduced integrated eye-tracking functionality. Ahn and Lee (2019) and Kumar et al. (2020) combined gaze and touch to input text and Rajanna and Hansen (2018) combined gaze and a button click. The additional touch modality is used to select a key and speeding up eye tracking for text entry, usually using dwell time over a key to confirm inputs. Lu et al. (2020) explored a hands-free text input technique and compared sensing blinking and neck movements as alternatives to dwell time. Results showed that blinking performed best. Ma et al. (2018) added a brain–computer interface as a selection mechanism.

To date, these approaches allow much slower entry speeds compared to physical keyboards and are currently not the first choice for extensive text entry tasks.

2.3.4 On-Surface and Mid-air Text Entry

As XR modifies the user senses, it is possible to render virtual keyboards and turn any physical surface in the environment into a keyboard, enjoying the support and haptic feedback of the surface. Richardson et al. (2020) present a technique which combines hand tracking and a language model to decode text from the hand motions using a temporal convolutional network. Participants of a study reached a speed of 73 words per minutes (WPM), comparable to using physical keyboards. To achieve such speed, the current system was trained for each user for about an hour. Fashimpaur et al. (2020) also used a language model to disambiguate text entered by pinching with the finger that would normally be used to type a character. This approach, however, achieved a much lower performance (12 WPM).

Typing on a virtual keyboard in mid-air lacks haptic feedback. Gupta et al. (2020) explored different tactile feedback techniques for a mid-air keyboard in VR. In their study, they compared audio–visual feedback to vibrotactile feedback on the fingers, as well as spatialized and non-spatialized feedback on the wrist. Performance of the four techniques was comparable, but participants preferred tactile feedback. Results also indicated a significantly lower mental demand, frustration, and effort for the tactile feedback on fingers. Participants also preferred the spatial feedback on the wrist over the non-spatial. Dudley et al. (2019) compared typing in mid-air to typing on a physical surface (Fig. 7), both using only the index finger or all ten fingers and found that users are significantly faster when typing on a surface compared to mid-air. They also reported that participants could not effectively use all ten fingers in the mid-air condition, resulting in a lower speed than the index finger condition.

Other text entry techniques in XR use purely virtual keyboards. This offers higher mobility because no extra hardware needs to be carried around. Xu et al. (2019b) and Speicher et al. (2018) evaluated different pointing methods for typing on virtual keyboards, including controllers, head and hand pointing. Both concluded that controllers are usually the best choice. Research was also done in evaluating different keyboard layouts for virtual keyboards. For example, using a circular keyboard that can be controlled via head-motion (Xu et al. 2019a) or a pizza-layout using dual thumbsticks (Yu et al. 2018). Instead of keyboards, different devices for text entry were explored, like a cube with keys (Brun et al. 2019), a ring worn on the index

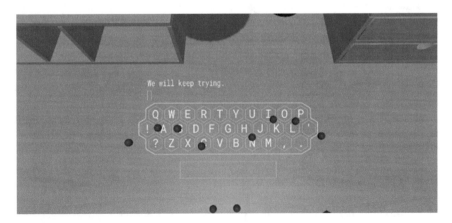

Fig. 7 Keyboard and hand visualization as presented by Dudley et al. (2019). In their study, the keyboard was once positioned in mid-air and once on the table. In both cases, the fingers were visualized as purple spheres

finger (Gupta et al. 2019), a circular touchpad (Jiang and Weng 2020) or a glove that uses chords to represent letters. Also González et al. (2009) compared six text input techniques for VR and found that the mobile phone resulted in the highest typing speed, followed by pen-based QWERTY and pinch keyboard.

However, the performance of such techniques is much lower than for physical keyboards which makes it less suited for longer text entries. Yet, they can still be useful in a mobile scenario, when, for example, writing short messages.

2.3.5 Speech Input

Speech input is another option for text entry in XR. It is already used with many everyday devices today, for example, on phones. Using speech input in XR has also been explored in previous work and Bowman et al. (2002) even found it outperforms a pinch keyboard, a one-hand chord keyboard and a pen on tablet technique with regards to speed. Yet, none of the examined techniques resulted in high levels of performance or usability. Hoste et al. (2012) present a multimodal approach for text entry combining speech input with body gestures for error corrections. In a user study, participants have rated it the most efficient technique compared to controller input, pure speech input, and pure gesture input. However, with 11.5 WPM, it was not the fastest of the compared techniques. Even though speech input can be faster than some other techniques, there are several drawbacks of using it for knowledge work in everyday environments. Common use cases for speech input like voice assistants at home or in a car, which use speech input mainly for commands, are very different from use cases for knowledge work where it is very common to write longer texts. Use of speech input can issue privacy concerns whenever the users are not located in a private space on their own. For example, when entering a password or handling sensitive data, speech input can not be used without revealing this data to any bystanders. Regardless of the content, speech input can also be disturbing to other people, for example, colleagues in an office or other passengers when using the system in public transportation. Another more fundamental problem is the distinction between commands and transcription which is problematic in all speech input systems, not just in VR. The system needs to figure out which words belong to a command like "open new document" and which words should be transcribed in said document. A similar problem also arises in collaborative settings like in a meeting, where it can be difficult for the speech input system to discern between words that should be transcribed and words that are just part of the discussion with colleagues. Such situations could be disambiguated by a mode switch, for example, only transcribe words while pressing a certain button. Another concern is that speech might interfere with productivity.

2.3.6 Using Keyboards Beyond Text Entry

Additionally, combining a keyboard with VR can open up new possibilities not available in real world. Schneider et al. (2019) explored different input and output

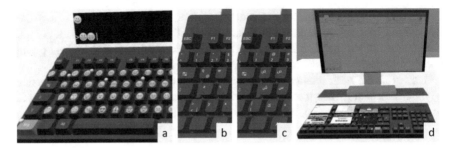

Fig. 8 Reconfiguring the layout of a physical keyboard in VR. Examples are enabling emoji input (**a**), input characters from different languages (**b**, **c**), and window manager (**d**)

mappings enabling different keyboard layouts and functionalities like emoji entry, text processing macros, secure password entry by randomizing the keys, window manager or entering characters from different languages (see Fig. 8).

3 Collaboration

XR as immersive technology has a great potential to connect remote coworkers as if they are immersed in the same space. XR's need to track the user's head and hands can be used to animate their avatars, representing their body language.

On the other hand, XR generates a unique challenge for communication between coworkers by physically occluding the users faces, their gaze, and facial expression by the head-mounted display. While we are optimistic that in long term, HMDs are going to look like regular prescription glasses and not occlude important parts of the users faces; collaboration software has to bridge this current gap, while using the unique abilities of the immersive displays. Next, we discuss approaches for collaboration in VR and AR.

3.1 Collaboration in Virtual Reality

Virtual reality blocks the full view of users and replaces them with a virtual world, generating a special challenge to combine coworkers in the same physical space. Without exact representation of the other users and any geometry in the environment, users may accidentally hit them.

Programming in a pair, working together at the same time on the same code, has shown several advantages, such as increased knowledge transfer, generation of higher quality code, increased code comprehension, and team bonding. Lately, Dominic et al. (2020) compared the use of a state-of-the-art remote video sharing to a VR system that represented the avatars of programmers, as well as their keyboard and mice. They found the VR system enables participants to find twice as much bugs and reduce the time needed to solve them. Programmers may have been more focused thanks to reduction of external distractions, and they might also have been affected by the immersive feeling of sharing the same space. The authors suggest to further explore the physical and mental demands of collaboration in VR and the effects on productivity and frustration. Sharma et al. (2011) developed the *VirtualOffice* system to connect virtually between remote workers along the full work day, including awareness of side conversations, social happening, and additional opportunities to generate informal communication. The system supported different alert mechanism from text to 3D displays of the virtual office. The authors used Greenhalgh and Benford's concept of an "aura" attached to each operation to publicized actions and attract coworkers to get involved. The system was designed to use real offices as a base, so it was limited to connected remote workers that work in remote physical offices. Nguyen et al. (2017a) present CollaVR which enables collaborative reviewing of VR videos using VR HMDs. In addition to watching the video, it allows the users to take notes and exchange feedback. In a preliminary study, experts were positive about using VR for such tasks. In the study, only up to three people worked together; therefore, the authors proposed to do further research on awareness visualizations that are scalable. Additionally, it would be helpful to explore asymmetric hardware setups to include collaborators without access to specific hardware.

While most of the works we discuss in this chapter are focused on enabling collaborations in the context of specific tasks, the office environment enables more than a designed environment for performing work tasks. The joining of coworker together enables generation of informal interactions through chance conversations that are not well supported by current pre-planned teleconferencing. Chow et al. (2019) investigated asynchronous interaction in a virtual office environment through virtual recoding and replay of one's action. They also identified and addressed challenges in such a setting such as intrusion of personal space or awareness of actions.

In summary, it has been shown that VR has the ability to increase productivity in collaboration tasks, which is potentially caused by reduced distractions and a feeling of sharing the same space. A benefit of using VR in knowledge work is to connect workers at remote locations and enable natural, informal interactions that are not possible via teleconferencing systems.

3.2 Collaboration in Augmented Reality

Butscher et al. (2018) present ART, a tool for collaboratively analyzing multidimensional data in augmented reality. The visualization is placed on a touch-sensitive tabletop to facilitate existing interaction techniques. They evaluated their design using expert walkthroughs which revealed that AR can support collaboration, a fluid analysis process and immersion in the data. Dong and Kamat (2011) present another tool for collaboration using augmented reality and tabletops. They developed ARVita where collaborators can observe and interact with simulations in the context of construction planning. AR HMDs were also used alongside a tabletop display by Ens et al. (2020) to support casual collaborative visual analytics. They evaluated their prototype, uplift, with expert users and concluded that systems like that have the potential to support collaborative discussions, presenting models or analyses to other high-level stakeholders.

Pejsa et al. (2016) used projection-based spatial AR to generate a life size view of collaborators, rendered from the point of view of each participant (called Room2Room). Avoiding the use of HMDs, enabled to present the participants in a natural view, life size, using hand gestures that related to the room and using face expressions as part of the communication. As the system did not support stereo rendering, the view of the collaborators was set to align with 3D objects in the room, such as sofas or walls. While the presence enabled by Room2Room has not reached that of a physical face to face meeting, the participants reported much more presence than using video conferencing and were able to finish physical arrangement task faster, aided by expressive direction pointing and hand gestures.

Park et al. (2000) examined a CAVE-based approach for collaboratively visualizing scientific data. They found that users mostly work alone and used localized views to test things without disturbing the overall view and then global views to discuss results with the others. An open question was how the number of participants effects collaborative visualizations. Jing et al. (2019) presented a handheld AR application to support synchronous collaborative immersive analytics tasks such as querying information about content depicted on a physical whiteboard.

Cordeil et al. (2016) compared HMD and CAVE for collaboratively analyzing network connectivity. They found that HMDs were faster than CAVE in tasks like searching for the shortest path or counting triangles. But, no differences in accuracy or communication were found. Additionally they stress the fact that HMDs are less expensive and more readily available.

These works show that AR increases immersion and presence and can support collaborative analyses and presentations. It has also been shown that users value private spaces before sharing their work with others to not clutter the shared space.

3.3 Hybrid Collaboration

We have seen examples of collaboration in VR and AR. However, specific devices are not always available to all collaborators. In the following, we present approaches that combine different technologies.

If collaborators do not have access to an XR device or are in situations where using them might be inappropriate, it is useful to enable collaboration between XR and standard applications on desktops or phones. Reski et al. (2020) presented a system for synchronous data exploration using a hybrid interface. It consists of an immersive virtual reality application and a non-immersive Web application. They validated the approach in a user study representing a real-world scenario. They concluded that the system fostered experiences of shared discovery and therefore has potential for collaborative data exploration tasks. Future work could have a closer look at the collaborative and communicative behavior of coworkers inside and outside of VR.

Norman et al. (2019) presented a study involving collaboration between two local mixed reality users and one remote desktop user. They found that the remote user was more engaged while in the role of a coordinator. Therefore, it is suggested that remote users have specific roles to increase their participation.

Fender and Holz (2022) presented a system that allows synchronous collocated and remote collaboration, as well as asynchronous collaboration. They demonstrate scenarios in which a VR user interacts with another user represented in VR as a live 3D reconstruction either collocated or remotely. Additionally, they also present a asynchronous scenario, where the VR user blocks out everything from the real environment, but all events are recorded and can be replayed later, showing, for example, a 3D reconstruction of a coworker dropping something off. The asynchronous method, however, raises the question such as how the VR user can respond appropriately, if the coworker is no longer present when the event is replayed.

Tang et al. (2010) explored the communication channels during a three-way collaborative meeting. The channels include the person space, the reference space using hand shadows, and the shared task space. Although in this work the setup was not studied in hybrid setting, it can inform how to create hybrid experiences with XR where participants in XR could see virtual hands as reference space and participants without XR could see hand shadows displayed over the task space.

In some cases, different technologies were also combined to construct new environments. Cavallo et al. (2019) presented a co-located collaborative hybrid environment for data exploration. This means they combine high-resolution displays, table projections, augmented and virtual reality HMDs, and mobile devices like laptops. Their evaluation results indicate that integrating AR can increase the speed of the analysis process. However, they also state that there are still limiting factors like resolution and field of view of current HMDs.

It can be seen that collaboration is also viable between collaborators using different technologies. In such cases, it has found to be useful to assign roles to increase participation. Combining different technologies like HMDs, mobile devices and displays provide possibilities to include collocated users with different devices. Yet, the behavior of collaborators in different environments needs further research.

4 Environments

XR has the potential to change the work environment of users, beyond the limitations of their physical environment, and to be designed to reduce stress and increase productivity which are important factors in everyday work as stress has been found to affect physical (Heikkilä et al. 2020; Eijckelhof et al. 2013) and mental health (Stansfeld and Candy 2007). We will discuss the importance of including parts of the physical world into the virtual environment (*VE*) and how this can be achieved.

This also leads to social implications, which can be caused by not being aware of people outside the virtual environment or because bystanders are not aware of what the XR user is doing.

4.1 Managing Stress and Productivity

Ruvimova et al. (2020) evaluated the use of VR to reduce distractions induced by open office environments. They compare four different environments for a task of visual programming: a closed office without VR, an opened office without VR, a VR beach environment while the participant was located in a real open office (see Fig. 9), a VR open office environment while the participant was located in a real open office. Results indicated that both the closed physical office and the VR beach virtual environment were equally successful in reducing distraction and inducing flow and were preferred over the two open office environments. This suggests that VR can be used to stay focused in open offices and the VR environment can be customized to every user's needs. This study focused on single person tasks; the effect of using VR on social interactions between colleagues who share the space is still an open question. Anderson et al. (2017) and Thoondee and Oikonomou (2017) showed that their VR application, showing a nature environment, can reduce stress at work and improve mood. Pretsch et al. (2020) showed that using VR to experience natural landscapes can significantly reduce stress as perceived by participants and has a significantly higher effect than video streaming similar images. Valtchanov et al. (2010) immersed users after stress-induction task in an explorable VR nature settings and showed that interactive VR nature reduces stress and has positive effect beyond passive VR nature displays.

Li et al. (2021) investigated the influence of physical restraints in a virtual working environment in a study where participants did a productivity task in a car while being exposed to different environment. Their findings suggest that users perform better in familiar working environments like an office but prefer secluded unlimited nature environments. They also showed how virtual borders can guide the user to touch the cars interior less.

Lee et al. (2019) used augmented reality as visual separators in open office environments to address visual distractions. The results of their study suggest that this technique reduces visual distractions and improves the experience of shared workspace by enabling users to personalize their environment.

Pavanatto et al. (2021) compared physical monitors with virtual monitors displayed in augmented reality and concluded that it is feasible to use virtual monitors for work, yet technically they are still inferior to physical ones. They suggest mixing physical and virtual displays to utilize the enlarged space of the virtual reality and the familiarity of the physical monitors.

All this research shows that XR has the potential to improve the work space of a knowledge worker, by increasing productivity and reducing distractions and stress. XR allows the user to create an optimal working environment which can be easily

Fig. 9 VR replaces the working environment of a worker in an open place to a beach scene, helps the worker stays focused

adapted to different situations and requirements. VR may currently be ahead of AR in this aspect, as it replaces the entire environment of the user, while AR displays are compared to the real-world quality, yet both can be used to optimize the workplace, by adding additional displays or visual separators. Multiple studies have shown how stress can be reduced by immersing oneself in a computer-generated nature in VR. It has been shown to outperform 2D displays, and interactions with the display increase immersion and relaxation performance. However, it is not totally clear how it compares to conventional relaxing methods.

4.2 Including Reality

Virtual reality replaces the visual and audio sensing of the users with a new virtual environment. As seen above, this new environment may help users to better focus or relax. However, there are objects in the physical environment of the worker that might be of importance for her, like tea cups, desks, or coworkers. This subsection looks at research that examines how much of the physical environment users should be aware of while in a virtual environment.

McGill et al. (2015) stated that VR users have problems when interacting with real-world elements and being aware of the real-world environment. They addressed these issues in three studies. As already mentioned in Sect. 2.3, they showed that typing performance can be significantly improved when enabling a view of reality instead of showing no hands and no keyboard. In another study, they investigated how much reality can be shown and still enable the user to feel present in the virtual environment. They concluded that it was optimal to present the user with reality when the user is currently interacting with real-world objects. Then, they studied how this approach could be applied to people instead of objects in social environments to make the user aware of the presence of others. They concluded that it is important to include some aspects of the physical environment into the virtual. Otherwise, the usability of HMDs in everyday life would be reduced. Therefore, they propose to blend in relevant parts of reality to preserve immersion while allowing the user to accomplish important actions in the physical environment, like using certain objects, drinking, or being aware of other people.

OneReality (Roo and Hachet 2017) looks at blending objects over the continuum of virtuality and describe it as a design space. RealityCheck (Hartmann et al. 2019) takes McGill's approach further by doing real-time 3D reconstruction of the real world that is combined with existing VR applications for the purposes of safety, communication, and interaction. The system allows users to freely move, manipulate, observe, and communicate with people and objects situated in their physical space without losing the sense of immersion or presence inside their VR applications.

O'Hagan and Williamson (2020) presented "Reality-aware VR headsets" that can identify and interpret elements in the physical environment and respond to them. They evaluated four different notification methods to inform users about the presence of bystanders. Two methods only reported the existence of a bystander and the other two also indicated the position. They detected that some participants were uncomfortable when informed about a bystander with no position information. In a second study, they explored dynamic audio adjustment to react to the real world. They either decreased volume to direct attention to a sound in the physical environment or increased volume to block-out noise. Results showed that decreasing the volume was effective, but not increasing.

Simeone (2016) used a depth camera to detect bystander's positions and show the information to the user in a "VR motion tracker" which indicated bystanders as a dots in a triangular area that represented the Kinect's field of view. Participants of a preliminary study considered it useful and not distracting.

In addition to showing a live 3D reconstruction of a bystander in VR, Fender and Holz (2022) presented a different approach, namely asynchronous reality, which allows the user to enter a "Focus Mode" that blocks all distractions from the environment. However, events like a coworker dropping something off are recorded and can be played back later, so the user does not miss important events.

Zielasko et al. (2019b) compared how substituting a physical desk during a seated task in the virtual environment influences cyber-sickness, performance, and presence. They did not find a difference between showing and not showing a desk.

However, they argue that showing a desk allows seamless integration of other elements like a keyboard, for which we have seen in Sect. 2.3 that it is useful to visualize them.

Knowledge worker use phones regularly. Phones are an important connection to distant coworkers and may be even more important in a virtual reality, where users are completely isolated from their surroundings. However, phones, like other physical objects, are usually not included in the virtual environment. Several studies considered enabling using mobile phones in VR. Desai et al. (2017) presented a system (SDSC) that can detect a smartphone in a video stream, embed it into the virtual environment and fit screenshots sent from the smartphone onto it, allowing VR users to interact with their smartphones while being immersed in the virtual environment. Alaee et al. (2018) use depth-based video segmentation to show a smartphone and the user's hands as video-pass-through blended in to the virtual environment (NRAV). They compared the technique with SDSC and concluded that using NRAV participants could perform several tasks with the same efficiency as when not wearing a HMD and were faster with NRAV than with SDSC. Some users preferred to remove HMDs, but the authors argue that acceptance of the technology will further increase with technological improvements. Bai et al. (2021) presented a technique that brings a virtual representation of the phone and the users hand into VR. Evaluating this technique showed that it successfully connected the real phone with the virtual world, but the experience differed from using a phone in the physical world, with decreased usability caused by hardware and software limitations.

Previous research has shown that it can be very helpful to include parts of the reality in the virtual environment. This is especially true for knowledge workers being immersed for extended periods of time where they need to interact with physical objects like phones or a water bottle or with other people in their surroundings. There are different possibilities to achieve this, similar to including physical keyboards, from virtual replicas to blending in a video stream. For including smartphones, however, the current hardware of HMDs is a limiting factor, as the resolution is not high enough to properly display the content. Regarding collocated people, it has been shown to be important to not only indicate their presence but also their position to make the XR user feel comfortable.

4.3 Social Implications

When working in everyday environments, there are, in many cases, other people around. Therefore, it is important to also have a look at social implications. This includes how the knowledge worker feels when using XR devices, but also how people around the XR user feel and behave because it could potentially keep people from using XR in public, if they know bystanders are uncomfortable. Just looking at the XR user does not provide a realistic evaluation of everyday scenarios.

Bajorunaite et al. (2021) conducted two surveys to explore passenger needs in public transportation that might prevent them from using VR devices. One survey was aimed at an airplane scenario ($n = 60$) and one at ground public transportation, like buses or trains ($n = 108$). For both scenarios, participants expressed concerns about accidental interactions with other passengers and loss of awareness of their surrounding. They suggest to provide cues from the reality and find ways to achieve an engaging experience with less movement. This is in line with the findings presented in Sect. 4. The results from the surveys also indicate that participants are very conscious of their self-image and how they are perceived by other passengers while using a VR device. They express concerns about being judged because they block out reality.

George et al. (2019) had a closer look at bystanders and explored their ability to identify when HMD users switch tasks by observing their gestures. This could help them find good moments for interruptions. In their study, there was a set of tasks that the HMD user performed (authentication, reading, manipulation, typing, watching video). The bystanders, who were aware of the task set, in the study could identify the task type in 77% of the time and recognize task switches in 83% of the time. The authors suggest future work to find out if it has a positive effect on social acceptability when bystanders are able to retrieve meaning from the interactions of the HMD user.

O'Hagan et al. (2020) studied how comfortable bystanders are in interrupting VR users. Their results indicate that the level of comfort and the acceptability of the interruption strategy is more influenced by the relationship to the VR user than the setting.

Hsieh et al. (2016) presented techniques for socially acceptable text entry, scrolling, and point-and-select realized through hand orientation and finger movement detected by a sensor-equipped haptic glove which can independently track mid-air hand gestures. These interaction techniques were considered unobtrusive and socially acceptable.

Research shows that XR users are self-concious of the social aspect of their work, and the fear of being judged can limit their use of XR, which may be a subject for future research. It has also been indicated that it could be helpful if bystanders can retrieve some meaning from the behavior of XR users. This would allow them to better understand them, just like it helps the XR user to be aware of some aspects of the reality to avoid conflicts that disturb bystanders.

We believe that HMDs could be socially acceptable when they become almost not noticeable like regular glasses. Then, the issue might be that when the HMDs looks like glasses and become unnoticeable, if the user is sitting at a cafe and doing strange gestures in the air it could look awkward and not acceptable. This is were having subtle indirect gestures from another device such as a tablet could be more socially acceptable (and also require less energy and be more appropriate on crowded space like inside an airplane). However, some tasks may require large gestures that can not be hidden. Then, this is an issue of the population getting used to it, similarly to how we accept people talking to mid-air when using an ear piece. If more people use VR HMDs in public, it will probably become more accepted, like using a laptop.

In addition, the progress in display resolution could contribute to create HMDs experiences where the main display at the front of the user can contain most of the information in it thus require less head turning on the side or minimize the head turning angle.

Another social implication is the fact that HMDs have cameras that could violate the privacy of others. If we can built HMDs that look like glasses (HoloLens is a step in that direction), we should learn from the privacy lessons from Google Glass.

5 Extended Exposure

In recent years, we have seen a surge in research of knowledge work in XR (AR and VR), showing the possibilities provided by the immersive space. Different works are aimed at enabling users to work in XR for longer periods of time. For example, one possibility of VR, which hides the user's own body from her sight, includes the ability to use smaller physical motions, while the self-avatar completes a full motion (CoolMoves 2021), reducing fatigue while enabling large interaction spaces.

However, research on the effect of long-term immersion over full work days, multiple days a week, is very limited.

Earlier works on eye strain caused by physical displays (Stewart 1979; Jaschinski et al. 1998) suggest individuals are affected differently. Stewart (1979) argued that eye strain results from different factors (i.e., visual, postural, environmental, personal) and that these problems can be solved by considering ergonomics when designing visual displays, suggesting the design of HMDs can be improved to reduce potential problems.

Later research on long periods of using XR has been focusing on the context of manufacturing; therefore, we address these works here, even though they do not actually cover knowledge work. Grubert et al. (2010) conducted a study with 19 participants doing an order picking task for 4 h with and without AR support. Results showed that using AR does not increase the overall objective and subjective strain. However, some participants perceived higher eye discomfort in AR. This was more likely for users with visual deficiencies. They also reported a higher work efficiency in AR compared to non-AR.

Wille et al. (2014) conducted several studies comparing the work with HMDs over several hours with other technologies like tablets or monitors. Objective measures indicated no physiological effects on the visual system and only limited influence of the HMDs weight on the neck muscles which contrasts with the subjective ratings. The authors speculate that the unfamiliar technology influences the subjective ratings.

Funk et al. (2017) studied an industrial assembly task with instructions projected directly on workpiece, and using a depth camera (Kinect v2) to verify assembly correctness. All participants used the system for at least 3 full working days. The results showed that the instructions were helpful for untrained workers; however, it also slowed down the performance and increased cognitive load, especially for expert workers.

Steinicke and Bruder (2014) conducted a 24-h self-experiment in virtual reality (using Oculus Rift DK1 HMD) with one participant, who worked, ate, slept and entertained himself with music or movies. They reported higher simulator sickness after periods involving many movements and lower values when resting. The participant reported limitations of the HMD due to latency when moving and a limited resolution when working. It was also reported that the participant was sometimes confused about whether he was in VR or a real environment and that the perceived accommodation seemed to vary after a few hours.

Nordahl et al. (2019) had two participants using VR HMDs for 12 h. They used Oculus Rift CV1 HMD for 6 h and the HTC Vive HMD for the rest. They only took the HMDs off for switching them after 6 h. While in VR, the participants used different applications. The reported results indicate that simulator sickness symptoms were mild with a peak after 7 h that is difficult to explain because the experiment was not fully controlled.

The most extensive research on long-term immersion has been conducted by Guo et al. (2019a, b, 2020) and Shen et al. (2019). They applied Maslows Hierarchy of Needs to guide the design of a VR office. First, they conducted a short-term study ($n = 16$) (Guo et al. 2019b) using a text input and image processing task which was done in the virtual and a physical environment. They concluded that the designed VR office was comfortable and efficient and therefore, in a next step, used it for a long-term study.

In the long-term experiment (Guo et al. 2019a), 27 participants were in the virtual and physical office for 8 h each, doing knowledge worker tasks like document correction, keyword searching, text input, and image classification. They compared the results with the short-term study and concluded that physiological needs like drinking, belongingness needs like communication, temporal presence, and self-presence are important for long-term immersion but can be ignored for short term. Safety needs and emotional needs on the other hand must be met in both conditions.

This 8-h experiment was also used to investigate mental fatigue differences between the virtual and physical work spaces (Shen et al. 2019). Participants performed a psycho-motor vigilance task (PVT) 6 times during the experiment, and results showed that there were significantly less PVT lapses in the physical environment, and the reaction times were slower in VR, indicating a higher mental fatigue in VR. The authors propose two explanations. Either the additional visual information processing in VR occupies more attention resources, or that VR can increase attention of participants more effectively which lets them allocate higher attention resources.

The same experimental setup was also used to explore the difference in visual discomfort between working in VR and physical environment (Guo et al. 2020). The results showed that subjective visual fatigue, pupil size, and accommodation response changes with time in both conditions. They also detected a gender difference suggesting that female participants suffer more from visual fatigue in VR than male participants. However, this could be caused by male participants in the sample having more experience with VR than the female participants. There was also no significant difference in nausea which can be explained by the static content. The authors recorded no significant eye strain difference between VR and the physical environment, yet focus difficulty was significantly higher in VR which might be caused by the accommodation vergence conflict.

These studies showed only mild simulator sickness symptoms which can be explained by displaying relatively static content in knowledge worker tasks. A large part of physical discomfort is due to the weight and form factor of HMDs, which will hopefully become much more comfortable in the near future.

Shen et al. (2019) reported higher mental fatigue in VR compared to a physical environment. Additionally, in VR, the reaction time significantly increased over time but not in the physical environment. The authors propose two explanations. Either the additional visual information processing in VR occupies more attention resources, or VR can increase attention of participants more effectively which lets them allocate higher attention resources.

From those studies, it can be concluded that simulator sickness symptoms are rather mild (Nordahl et al. 2019; Guo et al. 2020) which can be explained by the relatively static content in knowledge worker tasks. A large part of physical discomfort is clearly due to the weight and form factor of HMDs. As HMD hardware is being improved, mainly on resolution, frame rate, weight and even dynamic focal distance, we expect the VR experience become more comparable to physical environment one, and more such long-term studies will be required. Existing research points to important directions when designing applications for long-term use like latency (Steinicke and Bruder 2014), physiological needs, emotional needs, safety, presence, and belongingness (Guo et al. 2019a). Experience can be heavily influenced by personal traits like impaired vision or XR past experience. Therefore, longer studies are needed, so the participants get accustomed to the new technology which will make it much more comparable to a physical environment.

6 Applications

This section will have a closer look at examples of applications that support knowledge work in XR.

There are several application examples involving data analysis. Zielasko et al. (2017) discussed the potentials and benefits of using VR HMDs in a desktop configuration, i.e., when being seated in front of a table. They described scenarios and use cases in the domain of data analysis. A similar proposal was made by Wagner Filho et al. (2018) and Wagner Filho et al. (2019). On both instances, users interacted with data using mid-air interaction using their hands.

Another application scenario that benefits from XR is programming. Elliott et al. (2015) presented concepts for supporting software engineering tasks such as live coding and code reviews using VR HMDs in conjunction with mouse and keyboard interaction. Dominic et al. (2020) compared remote pair programming and code comprehension in VR against a standard shared display. In their study ($n = 40$), the average time to solve a bug was lower in VR, and they solved nearly twice as many. Authors explain this difference through reduced distractions in VR and a sense of being collocated with the collaborator.

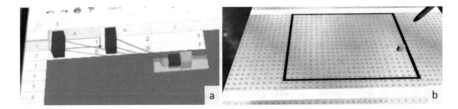

Fig. 10 The left image shows relations between cells. A function is applied to the cells at the top which results in the value shown in the bottom cell. The right image shows how the spreadsheet is visualized beyond the boundaries of the tablet used for interaction which is outlined in black

XR has also been explored for creative tasks, for example Nguyen et al. (2017b), proposed a video editing system for VR.

As the resolution, size and weight of HMDs evolves to more consumer-oriented glasses-like form factor; HMDs becomes an attractive alternative to physical monitors (Pavanatto et al. 2021), being more mobile, large, and private. In recent years, we see research that looks at ways that common 2D office tasks may be enhanced when done via near-eye displays.

Gesslein et al. (2020) enhanced a spreadsheet application in VR which enabled new functionalities not possible in 2D, like visualizing relations between cells above the screen or extending large sheets beyond what is possible on physical screens (see Fig. 10). O'Brien et al. (2019) presented a virtual environment for browsing wikipedia content. Biener et al. (2020) propose many different applications that leverage the possibilities of VR in the context of mobile knowledge workers. For example, they present an array of layered screen arranged around the user that expands the users small portable display and an application that visualizes 3D data on top of a touchscreen device (Fig. 3). Dengel et al. (2006) and Deller et al. (2008) presented applications for working with documents on a stereoscopic display.

There are also commercially available solutions that support knowledge work in virtual reality, such as Oculus Infinite Office (Oculus 2021) where the user can open virtual browser windows and interact with them using a controller, gestures or a physical keyboard which is included in the virtual environment as a 3D model and a video-pass-through visualization of the hands while typing. An example for AR would be spatial.io Spatial.io (2021) which allows collaborative meetings by representing remote coworkers as avatars.

7   Challenges

Informed by the presented review of literature, we see several challenges that need to be addressed in the future to make every day virtual and augmented reality a compelling experience that every knowledge worker wants to use and possibly prefer over a real office. This includes evolving HMDs, by also embracing other devices and peripherals around the user and improving the overall user experience in XR.

7.1 Challenges in the Next Generation of HMDs

The technology of consumer available XR HMDS has progressed by leap and bounds in recent years. It is possible nowadays to see HMDs with a resolution of 5K, and refresh rates of up 144 Hz. However, for being good monitor replacements for information workers, there is a need to display text at quality that is comparable to 2D monitors. Current lenses that are used in commercial HMDs are simple Fresnel lenses that reduce the display quality further away from the center of the display, many times to a level where text is unreadable. Multilayered lenses and other optic solutions that are able to generate sharper displays might still be too expensive for current HMDs that are used mostly for entertainment. Also, the combination of eye tracking and changeable focal distance of the display or light field display can reduce fatigue originated from inaccurate convergence/focus rendering.

Another aspect that limits the everyday use of XR HMDs, especially for longer periods of time, is the form factor which can impact comfort and social acceptability. It has been seen in Sect. 5 that a great part of users discomfort during the use of HMDs is the weight. As manufacturers are working on lighter and thinner HMDs, we hope they will be comfortable for extended use. Glasses-like form factors may also help with social acceptability as it is less disconnecting workers from their environment and make them easier to communicate and collaborate.

As has been mentioned in Sect. 4, when using XR for longer periods, there is more importance for sensing around the headset, from the structure of the environment around the user, enabling the user to move around and use different physical resources, to interacting with coworkers, and updating of the XR space and applications according to the changing conditions around the worker. Detection of peripherals such as physical keyboards (e.g., supported by Oculus Quest 2) enables representation of them in the HMD display, where XR applications can use them and even modify them for their needs (Schneider et al. 2019). Better environment sensing via cameras and depth sensors enables users to move naturally in virtual offices while being in an uncontrolled dynamic environment and avoiding obstacles (Cheng et al. 2019; Yang et al. 2019). And precise and responsive hand tracking also supports a range of interaction possibilities like pointing, gesturing, or text entry.

7.2 Challenges in Future XR Experience for Knowledge Worker

There are also several design challenges that need to be addressed to make XR experience appealing to knowledge workers.

One of the advantages of using XR for work is the independence of the physical conditions in the user's environment. When workers travel or as they work from home, they might find themselves in physical environments that are less than optimal.

In many cases, users need to limit themselves to small spaces, such as an airplane seat, while they are expected to work at their best capability. Working applications should be aware of the user's limitations and display a virtual working environment that is fully controlled by the users given their limited input space. While current XR applications require users to prepare an empty physical environment to enable uninterrupted and safe working spaces, future applications will have to be flexible and adaptable to a variety and dynamically changing environments (Gal et al. 2014; Yang et al. 2019).

Given the possibly limited input space and the need to reduce fatigue of the worker, new mappings will enable users to execute small motions, mostly supported, according to their or the environments limitations, and have them mapped to large effects in the virtual space (Ahuja et al. 2021; Wentzel et al. 2020). The environment around the user may exhibit the change of tasks and enable fast switching of context. It should help relax the users when it is needed and keep them aware of the presence of other people in the work vicinity both physical and remote. The representation of the users should bridge the difference in presence between local and remote users, for example, by representing physical affordances such as white boards and meeting rooms in the virtual domain too. Workers without XR displays need also to be aware of the presence of remote users, with range of methods, from large displays and representation robots to projections (Pejsa et al. 2016).

8   Summary and Conclusion

In this chapter, we have presented an overview of interaction techniques that can support knowledge workers in XR.

Techniques for interacting with 2D content in 3D included controllers, gloves, hand tracking, tablets, eye gaze, pens, and more. Studies have shown that it can be beneficial to use indirect input which reduces fatigue while preserving performance. Researchers are already working on socially acceptable techniques, and future research should also keep that in mind because this is an important aspect in everyday environments. It has also been found that touch surfaces perform better than mid-air which is in line with the findings from exploring text entry techniques. In that context, it has also been shown that users prefer tactile feedback, for example, provided by a physical surface, over mid-air typing. For text entry, it is very popular to include physical keyboards in the virtual environment and different visualizations for keyboards and hands have been explored like video-pass-through, point clouds, virtual models, and abstract representations. It has been shown that the type of visualization influenced workload and presence, but not performance, as long as there is some kind of visualization. Typing on any physical surface has also been shown to be effective when combined with language models and convolutional networks. However, currently, such techniques need to be calibrated for each user which decreases usability. Additionally, many other techniques and devices have been explored including eye-gaze-typing and phones, usually resulting in much lower entry speeds. While this could be negligible for some use cases, it is an important factor for knowledge workers. Future research on interaction techniques for knowledge work in XR could focus on how the system can adapt to changes in the physical environment, by providing appropriate input techniques for different scenarios.

We also presented approaches on how collaboration can be supported in XR for tasks like pair programming, video reviewing, or exploring information. It has been shown that such systems can perform better than standard video tools and increase presence. A problem that arises is how the presented systems can be scaled to allow collaboration of more people, as usually the studies only involved two or three users. We also presented solutions for including users without XR devices, for example, via a Web application. However, it is important to design such applications in a way that engage participation from the non-VR user.

Research on virtual environments has shown that VR can be used to reduce distractions in office environments because the virtual environment can be customized to the user's needs. VR has also been found to be able to reduce stress, for example, by showing natural scenes and that users prefer such scenes even though they perform better in familiar environments like offices. Future work could investigate which environments are suited best for which situations. Research also suggests to include some parts of the physical environment in the virtual environment. This can be done by blending in relevant parts, like tables or objects on the table. They can be included as video stream or as virtual replicas while preserving immersion. Similar to keyboards this can also be done for phones. However, the limited resolution of today's HMDs makes it hard to use such small devices. Besides objects, it is also helpful to include information about bystanders, like presence or position. This can help the VR user to avoid undesired bahavior like accidental interactions. However, further research is needed on how VR user and bystanders feel and how they are affected.

We have shown that some research has been conducted on the effects of extended usage of XR devices such as VR and AR HMDs. Unsurprisingly, a main issue is physical discomfort caused by weight and form factor of HMDs which will hopefully improve as technology advances. Studies also suggest that the experience can be influenced by factors like latency, safety, presence, impaired vision, or experience. To date, the longest study was 24 h; therefore, more research is needed on longer even periods of time.

Finally, we presented some applications that show the value of using XR for knowledge work. Several works show that XR can be beneficial in the area of data analysis, including spreadsheet applications. XR has also been shown to support collaborative programming, and it can be utilized to increase limited screen space in mobile scenarios.

References

Ahn S, Lee G (2019) Gaze-assisted typing for smart glasses. In: Proceedings of the 32nd annual ACM symposium on user interface software and technology, pp 857–869

Ahuja K, Ofek E, Gonzalez-Franco M, Holz C, Wilson AD (2021) Coolmoves: user motion accentuation in virtual reality. Proc ACM Interact Mob Wearable Ubiquitous Technol 5(2). https://doi.org/10.1145/3463499

Alaee G, Deasi AP, Pena-Castillo L, Brown E, Meruvia-Pastor O (2018) A user study on augmented virtuality using depth sensing cameras for near-range awareness in immersive VR. In: IEEE VR's 4th workshop on everyday virtual reality (WEVR 2018), vol 10

Anderson AP, Mayer MD, Fellows AM, Cowan DR, Hegel MT, Buckey JC (2017) Relaxation with immersive natural scenes presented using virtual reality. Aerosp Med Hum Perform 88(6):520–526

Andujar C, Argelaguet F (2007) Virtual pads: decoupling motor space and visual space for flexible manipulation of 2d windows within VEs. In: 2007 IEEE symposium on 3D user interfaces. IEEE

Bai H, Zhang L, Yang J, Billinghurst M (2021) Bringing full-featured mobile phone interaction into virtual reality. Comput Graph 97:42–53

Bajorunaite L, Brewster S, Williamson JR (2021) Virtual reality in transit: how acceptable is VR use on public transport? In: 2021 IEEE conference on virtual reality and 3D user interfaces abstracts and workshops (VRW). IEEE, pp 432–433

Biener V, Schneider D, Gesslein T, Otte A, Kuth B, Kristensson PO, Ofek E, Pahud M, Grubert J (2020) Breaking the screen: interaction across touchscreen boundaries in virtual reality for mobile knowledge workers. arXiv preprint arXiv:2008.04559

Billinghurst M, Clark A, Lee GA (2015) A survey of augmented reality. Found Trends Hum Comput Interact 8:73–272

Bowman DA, Wingrave CA (2001) Design and evaluation of menu systems for immersive virtual environments. In: Proceedings IEEE virtual reality 2001. IEEE, pp 149–156

Bowman DA, Rhoton CJ, Pinho MS (2002) Text input techniques for immersive virtual environments: an empirical comparison. In: Proceedings of the human factors and ergonomics society annual meeting, vol 46. SAGE Publications Sage CA, Los Angeles, CA, pp 2154–2158

Bowman D, Kruijff E, LaViola JJ Jr, Poupyrev IP (2004) 3D user interfaces: theory and practice. Addison-Wesley, CourseSmart eTextbook

Brasier E, Chapuis O, Ferey N, Vezien J, Appert C (2020) Arpads: mid-air indirect input for augmented reality. In: 2020 IEEE international symposium on mixed and augmented reality (ISMAR). IEEE, pp 332–343

Brun D, Gouin-Vallerand C, George S (2019) Keycube is a kind of keyboard (k3). In: Extended abstracts of the 2019 CHI conference on human factors in computing systems, pp 1–4

Butscher S, Hubenschmid S, Müller J, Fuchs J, Reiterer H (2018) Clusters, trends, and outliers: how immersive technologies can facilitate the collaborative analysis of multidimensional data. In: Proceedings of the 2018 CHI conference on human factors in computing systems, pp 1–12

Cavallo M, Dolakia M, Havlena M, Ocheltree K, Podlaseck M (2019) Immersive insights: a hybrid analytics system for collaborative exploratory data analysis. In: 25th ACM symposium on virtual reality software and technology, pp 1–12

Cheng L-P, Ofek E, Holz C, Wilson AD (2019) Vroamer: generating on-the-fly VR experiences while walking inside large, unknown real-world building environments. In: 2019 IEEE conference on virtual reality and 3D user interfaces (VR), pp 359–366. https://doi.org/10.1109/VR.2019.8798074

Chow K, Coyiuto C, Nguyen C, Yoon D (2019) Challenges and design considerations for multimodal asynchronous collaboration in VR. Proc ACM Hum Comput Interact 3(CSCW):1–24

Cordeil M, Dwyer T, Klein K, Laha B, Marriott K, Thomas BH (2016) Immersive collaborative analysis of network connectivity: cave-style or head-mounted display? IEEE Trans Vis Comput Graph 23(1):441–450

Deller M, Agne S, Ebert A, Dengel A, Hagen H, Klein B, Bender M, Bernardin T, Hamann B (2008) Managing a document-based information space. In: Proceedings of the 13th international conference on intelligent user interfaces, pp 119–128

Dengel A, Agne S, Klein B, Ebert A, Deller M (2006) Human-centered interaction with documents. In: Proceedings of the 1st ACM international workshop on human-centered multimedia, pp 35–44

Desai AP, Pena-Castillo L, Meruvia-Pastor O (2017) A window to your smartphone: exploring interaction and communication in immersive VR with augmented virtuality. In: 2017 14th Conference on computer and robot vision (CRV). IEEE, pp 217–224

Dominic J, Tubre B, Ritter C, Houser J, Smith C, Rodeghero P (2020) Remote pair programming in virtual reality. In: 2020 IEEE international conference on software maintenance and evolution (ICSME). IEEE, pp 406–417

Dong S, Kamat VR (2011) Collaborative visualization of simulated processes using tabletop fiducial augmented reality. In: Proceedings of the 2011 winter simulation conference (WSC). IEEE, pp 828–837

Drucker P (1966) The effective executive harper & row. New York, NY

Dube TJ, Arif AS (2020) Impact of key shape and dimension on text entry in virtual reality. In: Extended abstracts of the 2020 CHI conference on human factors in computing systems, pp 1–10

Dudley J, Benko H, Wigdor D, Kristensson PO (2019) Performance envelopes of virtual keyboard text input strategies in virtual reality. In: 2019 IEEE international symposium on mixed and augmented reality (ISMAR). IEEE, pp 289–300

Eijckelhof B, Huysmans M, Bruno Garza J, Blatter B, Van Dieën J, Dennerlein J, Van Der Beek A (2013) The effects of workplace stressors on muscle activity in the neck-shoulder and forearm muscles during computer work: a systematic review and meta-analysis. Eur J Appl Physiol 113(12):2897–2912

Einsfeld K, Agne S, Deller M, Ebert A, Klein B, Reuschling C (2006) Dynamic visualization and navigation of semantic virtual environments. In: Tenth international conference on information visualisation (IV'06). IEEE, pp 569–574

Elliott A, Peiris B, Parnin C (2015) Virtual reality in software engineering: affordances, applications, and challenges. In: 2015 IEEE/ACM 37th IEEE international conference on software engineering, vol 2. IEEE, pp 547–550

Ens B, Goodwin S, Prouzeau A, Anderson F, Wang FY, Gratzl S, Lucarelli Z, Moyle B, Smiley J, Dwyer T (2020) Uplift: a tangible and immersive tabletop system for casual collaborative visual analytics. IEEE Trans Vis Comput Graph

Fashimpaur J, Kin K, Longest M (2020) Pinchtype: text entry for virtual and augmented reality using comfortable thumb to fingertip pinches. In: Extended abstracts of the 2020 CHI conference on human factors in computing systems, pp 1–7

Fender AR, Holz C (2022) Causality-preserving asynchronous reality. In: CHI conference on human factors in computing systems, pp 1–15

Funk M, Bächler A, Bächler L, Kosch T, Heidenreich T, Schmidt A (2017) Working with augmented reality? A long-term analysis of in-situ instructions at the assembly workplace. In: Proceedings of the 10th international conference on pervasive technologies related to assistive environments, pp 222–229

Gal R, Shapira L, Ofek E, Kohli P (2014) Flare: fast layout for augmented reality applications, pp 207–212. https://doi.org/10.1109/ISMAR.2014.6948429

Gebhardt S, Pick S, Leithold F, Hentschel B, Kuhlen T (2013) Extended pie menus for immersive virtual environments. IEEE Trans Vis Comput Graph 19(4):644–651

George C, Janssen P, Heuss D, Alt F (2019) Should I interrupt or not? Understanding interruptions in head-mounted display settings. In: Proceedings of the 2019 on designing interactive systems conference, pp 497–510

Gesslein T, Biener V, Gagel P, Schneider D, Kristensson PO, Ofek E, Pahud M, Grubert J (2020) Pen-based interaction with spreadsheets in mobile virtual reality. In: 2020 IEEE international symposium on mixed and augmented reality (ISMAR). IEEE, pp 361–373

González G, Molina JP, García AS, Martínez D, González P (2009) Evaluation of text input techniques in immersive virtual environments. In: New trends on human-computer interaction. Springer, Berlin, pp 109–118

Grubert J, Hamacher D, Mecke R, Böckelmann I, Schega L, Huckauf A, Urbina M, Schenk M, Doil F, Tümler J (2010) Extended investigations of user-related issues in mobile industrial AR. In: 2010 IEEE international symposium on mixed and augmented reality. IEEE, pp 229–230

Grubert J, Witzani L, Ofek E, Pahud M, Kranz M, Kristensson PO (2018a) Effects of hand representations for typing in virtual reality. In: 2018 IEEE conference on virtual reality and 3D user interfaces (VR). IEEE, pp 151–158

Grubert J, Witzani L, Ofek E, Pahud M, Kranz M, Kristensson PO (2018b) Text entry in immersive head-mounted display-based virtual reality using standard keyboards. In: 2018 IEEE conference on virtual reality and 3D user interfaces (VR). IEEE, pp 159–166

Guo J, Weng D, Zhang Z, Jiang H, Liu Y, Wang Y, Duh HBL (2019a) Mixed reality office system based on Maslow's hierarchy of needs: towards the long-term immersion in virtual environments. In: 2019 IEEE international symposium on mixed and augmented reality (ISMAR). IEEE, pp 224–235

Guo J, Weng D, Zhang Z, Liu Y, Wang Y (2019b) Evaluation of maslows hierarchy of needs on long-term use of HMDs–a case study of office environment. In: 2019 IEEE conference on virtual reality and 3D user interfaces (VR). IEEE, pp 948–949

Guo J, Weng D, Fang H, Zhang Z, Ping J, Liu Y, Wang Y (2020) Exploring the differences of visual discomfort caused by long-term immersion between virtual environments and physical environments. In: 2020 IEEE conference on virtual reality and 3D user interfaces (VR). IEEE, pp 443–452

Gupta A, Ji C, Yeo H-S, Quigley A, Vogel D (2019) Rotoswype: word-gesture typing using a ring. In: Proceedings of the 2019 CHI conference on human factors in computing systems, pp 1–12

Gupta A, Samad M, Kin K, Kristensson PO, Benko H (2020) Investigating remote tactile feedback for mid-air text-entry in virtual reality. In: 2020 IEEE international symposium on mixed and augmented reality (ISMAR). IEEE, pp 350–360

Hartmann J, Holz C, Ofek E, Wilson AD (2019) RealityCheck: blending virtual environments with situated physical reality. Association for Computing Machinery, New York, NY, USA, pp 1–12

Heikkilä K, Pentti J, Madsen IE, Lallukka T, Virtanen M, Alfredsson L, Bjorner J, Borritz M, Brunner E, Burr H et al (2020) Job strain as a risk factor for peripheral artery disease: a multi-cohort study. J Am Heart Assoc 9(9):e013538

Hoppe AH, van de Camp F, Stiefelhagen R (2020) Enabling interaction with arbitrary 2d applications in virtual environments. In: International conference on human-computer interaction. Springer, Berlin, pp 30–36

Hoste L, Dumas B, Signer B (2012) Speeg: a multimodal speech-and gesture-based text input solution. In: Proceedings of the international working conference on advanced visual interfaces, pp 156–163

Hsieh Y-T, Jylhä A, Orso V, Gamberini L, Jacucci G (2016) Designing a willing-to-use-in-public hand gestural interaction technique for smart glasses. In: Proceedings of the 2016 CHI conference on human factors in computing systems, pp 4203–4215

Huang Y-J, Fujiwara T, Lin Y-X, Lin W-C, Ma K-L (2017) A gesture system for graph visualization in virtual reality environments. In: 2017 IEEE Pacific visualization symposium (PacificVis). IEEE, pp 41–45

Jaschinski W, Heuer H, Kylian H (1998) Preferred position of visual displays relative to the eyes: a field study of visual strain and individual differences. Ergonomics 41(7):1034–1049

Jiang H, Weng D (2020) Hipad: text entry for head-mounted displays using circular touchpad. In: 2020 IEEE conference on virtual reality and 3D user interfaces (VR). IEEE, pp 692–703

Jiang H, Weng D, Zhang Z, Bao Y, Jia Y, Nie M (2018) Hikeyb: high-efficiency mixed reality system for text entry. In: 2018 IEEE international symposium on mixed and augmented reality adjunct (ISMAR-adjunct). IEEE, pp 132–137

Jing A, Xiang C, Kim S, Billinghurst M, Quigley A (2019) Snapchart: an augmented reality analytics toolkit to enhance interactivity in a collaborative environment. In: The 17th international conference on virtual-reality continuum and its applications in industry, pp 1–2

Kern F, Kullmann P, Ganal E, Korwisi K, Stingl R, Niebling F, Latoschik ME (2021) Off-the-shelf stylus: using XR devices for handwriting and sketching on physically aligned virtual surfaces. Front Virtual Reality 2:69

Kim YR, Kim GJ (2017) Hovr-type: smartphone as a typing interface in VR using hovering. In: 2017 IEEE international conference on consumer electronics (ICCE). IEEE, pp 200–203

Knierim P, Schwind V, Feit AM, Nieuwenhuizen F, Henze N (2018) Physical keyboards in virtual reality: analysis of typing performance and effects of avatar hands. In: Proceedings of the 2018 CHI conference on human factors in computing systems, pp 1–9

Knierim P, Kosch T, Groschopp J, Schmidt A (2020) Opportunities and challenges of text input in portable virtual reality. In: Extended abstracts of the 2020 CHI conference on human factors in computing systems, pp 1–8

Kumar C, Hedeshy R, MacKenzie IS, Staab S (2020) Tagswipe: touch assisted gaze swipe for text entry. In: Proceedings of the 2020 CHI conference on human factors in computing systems, pp 1–12

Le K-D, Tran TQ, Chlasta K, Krejtz K, Fjeld M, Kunz A (2021) Vxslate: exploring combination of head movements and mobile touch for large virtual display interaction. In: Designing interactive systems conference, pp 283–297

Lee H, Je S, Kim R, Verma H, Alavi H, Bianchi A (2019) Partitioning open-plan workspaces via augmented reality. Pers Ubiquit Comput 1–16

Li J, George C, Ngao A, Holländer K, Mayer S, Butz A (2021) Rear-seat productivity in virtual reality: investigating VR interaction in the confined space of a car. Multimodal Technol Inter 5(4):15

Lu X, Yu D, Liang H-N, Xu W, Chen Y, Li X, Hasan K (2020) Exploration of hands-free text entry techniques for virtual reality. In: 2020 IEEE international symposium on mixed and augmented reality (ISMAR). IEEE, pp 344–349

Ma X, Yao Z, Wang Y, Pei W, Chen H (2018) Combining brain-computer interface and eye tracking for high-speed text entry in virtual reality. In: 23rd International conference on intelligent user interfaces, pp 263–267

McGill M, Boland D, Murray-Smith R, Brewster S (2015) A dose of reality: overcoming usability challenges in VR head-mounted displays. In: Proceedings of the 33rd annual ACM conference on human factors in computing systems, pp 2143–2152

Mendes D, Caputo FM, Giachetti A, Ferreira A, Jorge J (2019) A survey on 3d virtual object manipulation: from the desktop to immersive virtual environments. Comput Graph Forum 38(1):21–45

Nguyen C, DiVerdi S, Hertzmann A, Liu F (2017a) Collavr: collaborative in-headset review for VR video. In: Proceedings of the 30th annual ACM symposium on user interface software and technology, pp 267–277

Nguyen C, DiVerdi S, Hertzmann A, Liu F (2017b) Vremiere: in-headset virtual reality video editing. In: Proceedings of the 2017 CHI conference on human factors in computing systems, pp 5428–5438

Nordahl R, Nilsson NC, Adjorlu A, Magalhaes E, Willemsen S, Andersson NS, Wang J, Serafin S (2019) 12 hours in virtual reality: two cases of long-term exposure to consumer-grade virtual reality. In: 2019 IEEE conference on virtual reality and 3D user interfaces (VR)

Norman M, Lee GA, Smith RT, Billingurst M (2019) The impact of remote user's role in a mixed reality mixed presence system. In: The 17th international conference on virtual-reality continuum and its applications in industry, pp 1–9

Normand E, McGuffin MJ (2018) Enlarging a smartphone with AR to create a handheld vesad (virtually extended screen-aligned display). In: 2018 IEEE international symposium on mixed and augmented reality (ISMAR). IEEE, pp 123–133

O'Brien E, Jacquouton B, Moineau A, Campbell AG (2019) Wikipedia in virtual reality and how text-based media can be explore in virtual reality. In: Proceedings of the 2019 international conference on artificial intelligence and advanced manufacturing, pp 1–9

Oculus. http://www.oculus.org. Accessed: 28 July 2021

O'Hagan J, Williamson JR (2020) Reality aware VR headsets. In: Proceedings of the 9th ACM international symposium on pervasive displays, pp 9–17

O'Hagan J, Williamson JR, Khamis M (2020) Bystander interruption of VR users. In: Proceedings of the 9th ACM international symposium on pervasive displays, pp 19–27

Otte A, Schneider D, Menzner T, Gesslein T, Gagel P, Grubert J (2019) Evaluating text entry in virtual reality using a touch-sensitive physical keyboard. In: 2019 IEEE international symposium on mixed and augmented reality adjunct (ISMAR-adjunct), pp 387–392

Park KS, Kapoor A, Leigh J (2000) Lessons learned from employing multiple perspectives in a collaborative virtual environment for visualizing scientific data. In: Proceedings of the third international conference on collaborative virtual environments, pp 73–82

Pavanatto L, North C, Bowman DA, Badea C, Stoakley R (2021) Do we still need physical monitors? An evaluation of the usability of AR virtual monitors for productivity work. In: 2021 IEEE virtual reality and 3D user interfaces (VR). IEEE, pp 759–767

Pejsa T, Kantor J, Benko H, Ofek E, Wilson A (2016) Room2room: enabling life-size telepresence in a projected augmented reality environment. In: Proceedings of the 19th ACM conference on computer-supported cooperative work and social computing (CSCW'16)

Perelman G, Serrano M, Raynal M, Picard C, Derras M, Dubois E (2015) The roly-poly mouse: designing a rolling input device unifying 2d and 3d interaction. In: Proceedings of the 33rd annual ACM conference on human factors in computing systems, pp 327–336

Pham D-M, Stuerzlinger W (2019) Hawkey: efficient and versatile text entry for virtual reality. In: 25th ACM symposium on virtual reality software and technology, pp 1–11

Pretsch J, Pretsch E, Saretzki J, Kraus H, Grossmann G (2020) Improving employee well-being by means of virtual reality-realex: an empirical case study. Eur J Econ Bus Stud 6(1):95–105

Rajanna V, Hansen JP (2018) Gaze typing in virtual reality: impact of keyboard design, selection method, and motion. In: Proceedings of the 2018 ACM symposium on eye tracking research & applications, pp 1–10

Reski N, Alissandrakis A, Tyrkkö J, Kerren A (2020) "oh, that's where you are!"—towards a hybrid asymmetric collaborative immersive analytics system. In: Proceedings of the 11th Nordic conference on human-computer interaction: shaping experiences, shaping society, pp 1–12

Richardson M, Durasoff M, Wang R (2020) Decoding surface touch typing from hand-tracking. In: Proceedings of the 33rd annual ACM symposium on user interface software and technology, pp 686–696

Romat H, Fender A, Meier M, Holz C (2021) Flashpen: a high-fidelity and high-precision multi-surface pen for virtual reality. In: 2021 IEEE virtual reality and 3D user interfaces (VR). IEEE, pp 306–315

Roo JS, Hachet M (2017) One reality: augmenting how the physical world is experienced by combining multiple mixed reality modalities. In: Proceedings pf UIST 2017, UIST'17. Association for Computing Machinery, New York, NY, USA, pp 787–795. https://doi.org/10.1145/3126594.3126638

Ruvimova A, Kim J, Fritz T, Hancock M, Shepherd DC (2020) "transport me away": fostering flow in open offices through virtual reality. In: Proceedings of the 2020 CHI conference on human factors in computing systems, pp 1–14

Schneider D, Otte A, Gesslein T, Gagel P, Kuth B, Damlakhi MS, Dietz O, Ofek E, Pahud M, Kristensson PO et al (2019) Reconviguration: reconfiguring physical keyboards in virtual reality. IEEE Trans Vis Comput Graph 25(11):3190–3201

Sharma G, Shroff G, Dewan P (2011) Workplace collaboration in a 3d virtual office. In: 2011 IEEE international symposium on VR innovation. IEEE, pp 3–10

Shen R, Weng D, Chen S, Guo J, Fang H (2019) Mental fatigue of long-term office tasks in virtual environment. In: 2019 IEEE international symposium on mixed and augmented reality adjunct (ISMAR-adjunct). IEEE, pp 124–127

Simeone AL (2016) The VR motion tracker: visualising movement of non-participants in desktop virtual reality experiences. In: 2016 IEEE 2nd workshop on everyday virtual reality (WEVR). IEEE, pp 1–4

Slater M, Sanchez-Vives MV (2016) Enhancing our lives with immersive virtual reality. Front Robot AI 3:74

Son J, Ahn S, Kim S, Lee G (2019) Improving two-thumb touchpad typing in virtual reality. In: Extended abstracts of the 2019 CHI conference on human factors in computing systems, pp 1–6

Spatial.io. https://spatial.io. Accessed: 29 July 2021

Speicher M, Feit AM, Ziegler P, Krüger A (2018) Selection-based text entry in virtual reality. In: Proceedings of the 2018 CHI conference on human factors in computing systems, pp 1–13

Stansfeld S, Candy B (2007) Psychosocial work environment and mental health-a meta-analytic review. Scand J Work Environ Health 32:443–462. https://doi.org/10.5271/sjweh.1050

Steinicke F, Bruder G (2014) A self-experimentation report about long-term use of fully-immersive technology. In: Proceedings of the 2nd ACM symposium on spatial user interaction, pp 66–69

Stewart T (1979) Eyestrain and visual display units: a review. Displays 1(1):17–24

Tang A, Pahud M, Inkpen K, Benko H, Tang JC, Buxton B (2010) Three's company: understanding communication channels in three-way distributed collaboration. In: Proceedings of the 2010 ACM conference on computer supported cooperative work, CSCW'10. Association for Computing Machinery, New York, NY, USA, pp 271–280. https://doi.org/10.1145//1718918.1718969

Thoondee KD, Oikonomou A (2017) Using virtual reality to reduce stress at work. In: 2017 Computing conference. IEEE, pp 492–499

Valtchanov D, Barton KR, Ellard C (2010) Restorative effects of virtual nature settings. Cyberpsychol Behav Soc Networking 13(5):503–512

Wagner Filho JA, Freitas CMDS, Nedel L (2018) Virtualdesk: a comfortable and efficient immersive information visualization approach. Comput Graph Forum 37(3):415–426

Wagner Filho JA, Freitas CM, Nedel L (2019) Comfortable immersive analytics with the virtualdesk metaphor. IEEE Comput Graph Appl 39(3):41–53

Walker J, Li B, Vertanen K, Kuhl S (2017) Efficient typing on a visually occluded physical keyboard. In: Proceedings of the 2017 CHI conference on human factors in computing systems, pp 5457–5461

Wentzel J, d'Eon G, Vogel D (2020) Improving virtual reality ergonomics through reach-bounded non-linear input amplification. Association for Computing Machinery, New York, NY, USA, pp 1–12

Wille M, Adolph L, Grauel B, Wischniewski S, Theis S, Alexander T (2014) Prolonged work with head mounted displays. In: Proceedings of the 2014 ACM international symposium on wearable computers: adjunct program, pp 221–224

Xu W, Liang H-N, Zhao Y, Zhang T, Yu D, Monteiro D (2019) Ringtext: dwell-free and hands-free text entry for mobile head-mounted displays using head motions. IEEE Trans Vis Comput Graph 25(5):1991–2001

Xu W, Liang H-N, He A, Wang Z (2019b) Pointing and selection methods for text entry in augmented reality head mounted displays. In: 2019 IEEE international symposium on mixed and augmented reality (ISMAR). IEEE, pp 279–288

Yang JJ, Holz C, Ofek E, Wilson AD (2019) Dreamwalker: substituting real-world walking experiences with a virtual reality. In: Proceedings of the 32nd annual ACM symposium on user interface software and technology, UIST'19. Association for Computing Machinery, New York, NY, USA, pp 1093–1107. https://doi.org/10.1145/3332165.3347875

Yu D, Fan K, Zhang H, Monteiro D, Xu W, Liang H-N (2018) Pizzatext: text entry for virtual reality systems using dual thumbsticks. IEEE Trans Vis Comput Graph 24(11):2927–2935

Zielasko D, Weyers B, Bellgardt M, Pick S, Meibner A, Vierjahn T, Kuhlen TW (2017) Remain seated: towards fully-immersive desktop VR. In: 2017 IEEE 3rd workshop on everyday virtual reality (WEVR). IEEE, pp 1–6

Zielasko D, Krüger M, Weyers B, Kuhlen TW (2019a) Passive haptic menus for desk-based and HMD-projected virtual reality. In: 2019 IEEE 5th workshop on everyday virtual reality (WEVR). IEEE, pp 1–6

Zielasko D, Weyers B, Kuhlen TW (2019b) A non-stationary office desk substitution for desk-based and HMD-projected virtual reality. In: 2019 IEEE conference on virtual reality and 3D user interfaces (VR). IEEE, pp 1884–1889

The Use of Augmented Reality for Temporal Coordination in Everyday Work Context

Lisa Thomaschewski, Nico Feld, Benjamin Weyers, and Annette Kluge

Abstract Augmented reality (AR) has been used in a large variety of scenarios from assembly support over gaming to collaborative work. Teamwork is a specific type of collaborative work and emerges in numerous everyday contexts. It is characterized (in addition to other aspects) by specific needs in terms of time-related synchronization of team members to enable them to coordinate the team task. This is specifically relevant in situations where team members are spatially dispersed, such that direct communication (orally and visually) is not possible. These restrictions reduce task-related communication and coordination, which are key for successful teamwork. AR has the potential to enable coordination in spatially dispersed teamwork by enhancing each team members' view with information of the current status of the team task and additional feedback if needed, all adapted to the specific needs of the team members. As a key element of AR, this digital information is registered to the team member's individual perspective on the work object in question. This chapter will first give an introduction to collaborative work, teams, teamwork, and taskwork followed by a broad overview of existing AR-based team-supportive methods. We will first present a taxonomy for the development and implementation of AR-based support systems and give a short example on its usage in the context of a user-centered design followed by a review of the current research conducted by the authors of the chapter and a discussion of future work.

L. Thomaschewski (✉) · A. Kluge
Department of Work, Organizational and Business Psychology, Ruhr University Bochum, Bochum, Germany
e-mail: lisa.thomaschewski@ruhr-uni-bochum.de

A. Kluge
e-mail: annette.kluge@ruhr-uni-bochum.de

N. Feld · B. Weyers
Human-Computer Interaction, University of Trier, Trier, Germany
e-mail: feldn@uni-trier.de

B. Weyers
e-mail: weyers@uni-trier.de

© The Author(s), under exclusive license to Springer Nature Switzerland AG 2023
A. Simeone et al. (eds.), *Everyday Virtual and Augmented Reality*, Human–Computer Interaction Series, https://doi.org/10.1007/978-3-031-05804-2_3

57

1   Collaborative Work, Teams, Teamwork, and Taskwork

The relevance of joint work or division of work in groups, organizations, or teams is becoming more and more important in everyday work and organizational context. Assigning the completion of a task to several entities can have immense benefits, especially with complex tasks that require a wide range of different subject matter experts, knowledge, or skills to complete (Higgs et al. 2005). Thus, joint work is not limited to the level of individuals, but can occur between groups, organizations, or teams (e.g., joint work of an environmental organization with a city or a government). The purpose of joint work is the mutual pursuit of one or more specific goals. To reach this common goal, all entities must actively engage in joint activities. This evolving process between social entities is defined as collaboration (Bedwell et al. 2012). Collaboration can therefore take place between individuals, groups, organizations, teams, and so on. In contrast, teamwork only includes the joint work between individuals in teams and thus represents a specific form of collaboration (Bedwell et al. 2012).

The label "team" usually refers to the association of at least two individuals who are pursuing one or more common goals, often within an organizational framework. To achieve these goals, teams must interact dynamically and adaptively (Kluge 2021; Morgan et al. 1986; Salas et al. 1992, 2015). This interaction is characterized by a high degree of interdependence among the team members, since achieving the common goals requires the execution of several subtasks, work steps, actions, or operations that have been distributed among different team members. In organizational contexts, teams are usually formed to perform specific tasks.

Thereby, one can distinguish between actions that are concretely directed toward the task execution and actions or processes that are not directly addressing the actual task execution but are indispensable for several people working together effectively. Actions that specifically address the task execution, such as interacting with tools, machines, or other equipment to process a workpiece (or similar), or the execution or adherence to procedures and rules to complete a sales process (or similar) are generally referred to as taskwork (Kluge 2021). Therefore, taskwork describes and encompasses all the functions that each team member must perform to reach the common team goal(s) (Mathieu et al. 2008). When several people work together, it is not only about performing tasks. In order to work effectively as a team, the team members must interact with each other and "share knowledge, coordinate behaviors, and trust one another" (Salas et al. 2015, p. 600). These interactions, relationships, and interdependencies among the members of the team are generally referred to as teamwork (Kluge 2021). Obviously, taskwork and teamwork are intertwined, so that their effectiveness mutually benefits each other (Salas et al. 2015): For instance, imagine a pilot/co-pilot team whose goal was to land safely at the destination airport. If both only focused on operating their assigned instruments (taskwork) without interacting with each other or the tower (teamwork), the goal, including landing, would be at risk for failure, as compared to if the team had worked together. If the team focused solely on teamwork, it would also likely lead to disaster. As this example shows, teamwork is essential "for effective team performance, as it defines how tasks and goals are accomplished in a team context" (Salas et al. 2015, p. 600).

Teamwork encompasses a variety of processes, including communication, cooperation, and coordination: three essential processes for team behavior (Hagemann and Kluge 2017; Kozlowski and Ilgen 2006) that are strongly linked to team effectiveness (Brannick et al. 1995). Broken down to its essence, communication describes the exchange of information between two persons, most commonly called sender and receiver. In relation to team communication, this definition may need to be broadened to include that an information exchange can have a shaping and changing influence on team attitudes, behaviors, and cognitions (Salas et al. 2015). Since, as already outlined, teams pursue one or more common goals, they may need to work purposefully and cooperate. Thereby, team cooperation is decisively influenced by the attitudes, beliefs, and feelings of each team member (Salas et al. 2015) that determine whether or not the team member will engage in and support the collective goals (Sinclair 2003). Cooperation can be proactive, in that the team member intentionally does something that is conducive for attaining the common team goal (e.g., offer support to the team members). The latter could be also more implicit, in that the team member refrains from doing certain things that could impede the attainment of the common goal (e.g., put own interests aside in favor of team success) (Sinclair 2003). However, in order to work together effectively and efficiently as a team, it is not enough to communicate and cooperate together; all related processes must also be adequately coordinated, meaning that all team- and taskwork-related actions, operations, processes, work steps, subtasks, etc., must be orchestrated in sequence and time (Marks et al. 2001). This can be done either explicitly, in that team members intentionally use processes such as communication for coordination purposes, or implicitly, by anticipating the team needs "and dynamically adjusting their behaviors accordingly without having to be instructed" (Rico et al. 2008, p. 164). The aforementioned processes, communication, cooperation, and coordination, are central to taskwork and teamwork, as they determine how the team inputs (e.g., resources and knowledge) are converted into team outputs (e.g., satisfaction, performance, quality, and accuracy) (Driskell et al. 2018).

To consider it from another perspective: For a team to be content and perform successfully, good communication, cooperation, and coordination are prerequisite. Therefore, these processes have been studied in team research extensively, and many scientifically based training and development approaches exist (for an overview of existing training approaches, see Goldstein and Ford (2002)). In addition, optimizing the aforementioned processes by means of training, various tools, and, above all, technologies can support team communication, coordination, and cooperation. For example, one of the simplest technologies we have used for decades, and still use, is the telephone to simplify communication channels (not only) between and among team members. Currently, teams also have the option of using more advanced technologies such as email, messaging, or video conferencing systems as standard, depending on the communication requirements. A relatively recent approach to support teams in their teamwork processes is the use of augmented and mixed reality (AR/MR) although the development of this technology for the multi-user context started more than 20 years ago (Sereno et al. 2020). The next section provides a broad overview of existing possibilities to support teams using AR.

2 Supporting Teams Using AR—An Overview

By the late 90s, the first researchers had identified the potential of AR and MR technology in terms of their application in the research area of computer-supported cooperative work (CSCW). In CSCW, collaboration is often classified by means of four categories allocated to the dimensions of time and place following the CSCW matrix (Fig. 1), as introduced by Johansen (1998). The time dimension can either be denoted as synchronous or asynchronous. In synchronous interaction, the information exchange (as outlined above) happens instantaneously, whereas asynchronous interaction takes place at a certain time delay. An example of synchronous collaboration may be direct interaction via speech (also including telephone or video calls), and the use of emails represents an example of asynchronous collaboration. In the place dimension, the actual spatial location of each collaborator is denoted. In remote collaboration, collaborators are in different geographical locations, as compared to a co-located situation, where the collaborators work together in the same physical space (e.g., the pilot/co-pilot example).

As AR allows a seamless merging of the users' real and virtual environments (Billinghurst et al. 2014), researchers considered the potential in collaboration by

- integrating the user's real environment in remote collaboration and
- enhancing co-located collaboration by integrating virtual content.

As synchronous collaboration appears to benefit the most from these two enhancements, most research concerning AR in collaboration has addressed synchronous scenarios with only a few exceptions, such as the work presented by Irlitti et al. (2016), who proposed alternative opportunities for asynchronous collaboration using AR.

	synchronous	asynchronous
co-located	face to face interactions	continuous task
remote	remote interactions	communication & coordination

Fig. 1 CSCW matrix, as introduced by Johansen (1998)

The factor of place has been represented equally in research. One of the first examples of a co-located application was the "Studierstube" by Szalavári et al. (1998a), an application that used AR to display the same 3D graph for both team members. The application allowed both collaborators to interact via a 3D mouse and showed that this application was superior to a traditional desktop environment. Kuzuoka (1992) evaluated a system in 1992 that used AR to share the view between two remote team members and would allow a seamless collaboration by not only ensuring verbal communication but also sharing the gestures of the team members.

Apart from time and space, symmetry is another factor in AR-supported collaboration describing the team members' authority or role, as defined by Feld and Weyers (2019). If every team member has the same authority and role, the collaboration is denoted as "symmetric." An early example was the already mentioned "Studierstube," as well as another work by Szalavári et al. (1998b), who proposed a concept where multiple users could have a high-quality video-game experience using AR, such as for playing mah-jongg, which was well accepted by the users.

In contrast, Bauer et al. (1999) evaluated an asymmetric AR teleconference system in 1999, where one expert guided a field worker through a wiring task using a shared pointer and found an increased efficiency in the collaboration task.

In general, the early research considered solving technical challenges and system architecture for possible AR-collaboration applications, and when the hardware became less of an obstacle, the focus shifted more to the development of techniques and applications. A recent example was the work by Piumsomboon et al. (2018a), in which a small avatar (i.e., "Mini-Me") of another team member was displayed and dynamically positioned in case the team member was not in view. This avatar was found to improve the performance of the collaboration and increased the social presence for the team member assisted by the avatar. This work was also aligned with another recent topic in AR collaboration: the virtual representation of remote team members. For example, Yoon et al. (2019) investigated a possible effect of different avatar representations on social presence in a remote collaboration application using AR. This topic was not exclusive to AR but was also important for VR collaboration.

Due to the increasing power of the available hardware, the concept of sharing a user's real environment in 3D and real time was investigated. For example, in their work Superman versus Giant, Piumsomboon et al. (2018b) investigated the concept of sharing a user's real environment via an unmanned aerial vehicle (UAV) to a remote VR user. This user could then traverse this reconstructed environment either via flying or increasing their size to increase the remote user's spatial awareness and assist the local user more efficiently.

In their literature review, Ens et al. (2019) identified five research opportunities they expected to play a major role in future research:

- complex collaboration structures in time, space, and symmetry
- convergence and transitional interfaces
- empathic collaboration
- collaboration beyond physical limits
- social and ethical implications

Most research today is investigating or proposing solutions for a single factor of the dimensions time, space, and symmetry. However, it is likely that future research will surpass these boundaries and investigates supporting synchronous and asynchronous collaboration at the same time or allows for co-located, as well as remote, team members to collaborate. Furthermore, a mixture of various user roles should be expected, such as a virtual conference, where the current session chair, the presenter, and the audience all have different user roles that can change over the course of the conference. This work at hand focuses specifically on these three aspects and presents a use case, concept, and solution for such issues.

Due to the limits of current devices, users are usually bound to one technology (e.g., AR or VR) throughout the collaboration. This, however, is likely to change in near future, as the industry is developing devices that support AR and VR simultaneously, such as the Lynx R1 (https://www.lynx-r.com/) or the Meta Quest devices (https://www.oculus.com/). This would then not only allow the user to use a single device for both AR and VR, but also to seamlessly traverse between those during the collaboration.

For perception of other team members, current research has often considered direct task-related cues, such as pointing gestures and gaze direction. Due to additional hardware, such as heart-rate sensors and face cameras, various emotions of a user could be recorded and shared with the team members, which could allow for higher empathy among team members.

Another research opportunity is expanding collaboration beyond the physical limits, where researchers do not recreate physical, co-located collaboration, but implement features that would be impossible in a real collaboration. For example, the aforementioned Superman versus Giant concept by Piumsomboon et al. (2018b) allowed to scale the user in a virtual representation of a real environment or allowed them to fly, both of which are not possible without the usage of AR or VR.

Finally, an opportunity for future research includes the social and ethical implications of using AR and VR in collaborations, but not exclusively in collaboration. One major aspect of this is the privacy concerns when using these technologies. For example, in the Superman versus Giant concept, the environment was streamed to a remote user. However, there may be people in this environment who do not agree to be part of the streamed content, or there may be places being streamed that the users do not have the appropriate broadcast rights to visually transmit. Therefore, it is important to consider how to handle sensitive data in such a setting. This agrees with another aspect, the social acceptance of using AR and VR. One example is Google Glass, from 2012. These glasses allowed the wearer to display basic information on the glasses as well as to capture photos and videos. These glasses were rejected by most users as bystanders could be recorded unwillingly by the wearer. They were even banned in some places, such as in hospitals or banks.

These opportunities show not only that AR has the potential to enhance collaboration between team members, but also that there are still future research areas to consider. Therefore, the following section highlights the role of taxonomies to provide a tool for decision-making and how to proceed in research and application development.

3 Where to Start and What to Support? Considering Team, Task, and Technology in the Selection and Development of AR-Based Support

In the literature, a number of taxonomies have been presented that consider the classification of AR applications, their design, and/or their deployment (e.g., Feld and Weyers (2019)). Most taxonomies have been either technique-, user-, information-, or interaction-centered (Normand et al. 2012). Yet, if AR applications are to be implemented in an organization, which can be understood as an integral element of everyday contexts, it is particularly important not to consider people (user), technology (technique), and the organization independently, but rather holistically and as interacting entities in the sense of the socio-technical system design approach (Schweiß et al. 2019). According to this approach, the deployment of technology and the organization must be subject to joint optimization (Ulich 2013), meaning that it is not sufficient to develop technology or the organization without also adapting or optimizing the other part at the same time. This perspective was also reflected by the (hu-)man–technology–organization (MTO) concept, which emerged from this approach and further placed the work task as primary in the center of the socio-technical system (Ulich 2013). From this perspective, the technical and social subsystems of the organization are linked by the work task, that is, the work task creates the connection between people and the structure of the organization (Ulich 2013).

Since AR technologies in organizational contexts represent a form of socio-technical systems, their development (or selection) and implementation should follow the socio-technical system and the MTO concept, in that social aspects (e.g., team requirements, team capabilities), work tasks (or processes), and technological aspects (i.e., the system to be deployed) should be regarded as mutually interacting factors (Ulich 2013). Neglecting one of these factors (or their mutual interaction) in the development or selection of AR technologies could significantly impede the intended system benefits (Salas et al. 2008; Schweiß et al. 2019).

The use of AR technologies in an organizational team context is typically implemented due to a specific goal. The aim is mostly to support or improve one or more specific teamwork process(es) (as outlined in the introduction of this chapter). Therefore, before defining system capabilities, one should consider the respective team skills and requirements as well as the requirements of the task or teamwork process(es) to be supported (Salas et al. 2008; Schweiß et al. 2019). Such task-and-team analysis would provide the data to design a system where the technology fit the team needs and requirements (team-technology fit, Schweiß et al. (2019), Thomaschewski et al. (2019, 2021)) as well as the team task and process(es) (task-technology fit, Goodhue and Thompson (1995a), Thomaschewski et al. (2021)).

Therefore, the authors have proposed a theory-driven taxonomy for the support of teams using AR, which provides a task analytical basis for the selection and design of AR assistance in teamwork (Thomaschewski et al. 2019). The taxonomy is intended to describe specific situations of teamwork and to select conducive augmentation possibilities. It can support the design of the teamwork processes where AR technologies would be used. For example, the taxonomy could be used as a checklist to anticipate and define different user groups and their needs before the development of the prospective AR technology. Furthermore, the taxonomy could be used in the very early developmental stages of AR technologies to evaluate whether all relevant constellations or potentials of AR application have been considered. The taxonomy could also serve to evaluate existing AR technologies in the research context, such as by identifying influencing factors (independent variables) or target (dependent) variables and varying or observing their expressions (Thomaschewski et al. 2019).

Based on contemporary as well as established findings from CSCW and organizational psychology research, we defined four dimensions in accordance with the MTO concept: (1) social aspects (representing the social system component), (2) technical aspects (representing the technical system component), (3) teamwork processes (representing the work task as a link between the social and technical aspects, and the dimension), and (4) teamwork benefits due to AR utilization (representing assumed and intended benefits resulting from AR use). The taxonomy is shown in Fig. 2.

The first dimension, social aspects, can be used to determine the specific social context. The focus is on the supported team's constellation, needs, and skills. This dimension serves to determine (1) how the team is qualitatively constructed (e.g., an expert-only team, or a mixed team of novices and experts), (2) how many team

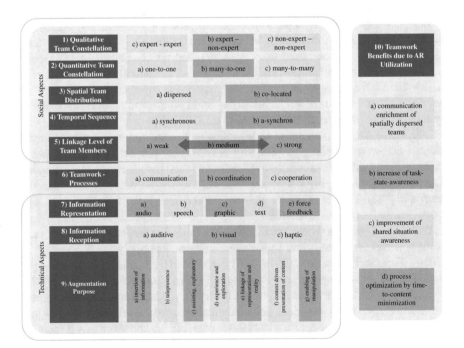

Fig. 2 Teamwork taxonomy (Thomaschewski et al. 2019)

members (or users) will interact (e.g., one-to-one or many-to-one), (3) if the team will work co-located or spatially dispersed, (4) the synchronicity of the different team tasks (do the team members work synchronously or asynchronous), and (5) the degree of coupling between the team members (e.g., level of team member familiarity and collaborative history). Altogether, this dimension considers the team composition as well as other contextual factors.

The work task, and therefore, the teamwork process, links the social and technical aspects. The second dimension, teamwork processes, serves for defining the specific work tasks and teamwork processes that shall be supported or enhanced using AR. In accordance with the MTO concept and human-centered design approaches, the dimensions social aspects and teamwork processes should be regarded first and serve as a baseline for defining the technical requirements of the system.

The third dimension, technical aspects, considers the design of the actual AR tool, based on the previously defined social aspects. With the support of information representation (7), the augmentation(s) could be planned (e.g., audio or graphic, or both). Using the class (8) on characterizing information reception along with (7), the perception of the augmentation(s) can be predicted. Finally, with category (9), the function of the augmentation could be determined (e.g., whether the tool was intended to create telepresence or be capable of inserting information/annotations).

In addition, the taxonomy offers a fourth dimension; teamwork benefits due to AR utilization, on the vertical axis, which is intended to specifically derive the assumed and intended benefits of the to-be-developed or deployed AR technology (e.g., whether the tool would increase the situation awareness in the team or enrich communication). Actively anticipating the intended benefits could assist in evaluating whether the technology could achieve this goal, along with the previously defined categories.

Altogether, the taxonomy is specifically focused on the design of AR-supported teamwork. Based on user- and task-centered development approaches, it could be used to describe teamwork and to select appropriate team- and task-specific augmentation(s). Schweiß et al. (2019) presented a possible approach by applying the presented taxonomy in a user-centered design process. They discussed the role of the taxonomy as specifically used in the requirement analysis step in an iterative user-centered design process. Not only could it be used to gather initial requirements at a very early stage of the process, but also at later stages, in which the first prototypes had been investigated by the user, and potential adaptions to the requirements were identified. Additionally, the taxonomy could be used to gather relevant use cases to the actual scenarios in the development process, suitable for the design and evaluation process. Finally, the taxonomy enables not only the application of design guidelines via its classification but also the creation of new guidelines if it identified the user-centered design process itself.

4   Make It Special: Spatially Dispersed Teams

Some work teams are spatially dispersed teams. This is a type of team that is becoming increasingly popular in companies and organizations (e.g., Boos et al. (2017)). These teams work in a remote, synchronous or asynchronous setting, which may be either asymmetric (as in case of remote guidance, e.g., Bauer et al. (1999)) or symmetric as in the use case outlined below. In the literature, spatially dispersed teams have been examined within the context of office work and mostly are referred to as virtual teams. Therefore, the focus has been on their advantages (e.g., the possibility to access experts worldwide) and disadvantages (e.g., forced asynchrony due to time differences), adequate support interventions, and leadership. However, in other fields, there are often teams that do not work in one place. Examples can be found in a variety of high reliability organizations and production settings, such as the military, aviation, fire departments, nuclear power plants, and refineries (Hagemann et al. 2012).

Due to the spatial dispersion, members of these teams do not have a mutual visual context or workspace and cannot communicate immediately without technological support. This can impede their team performance, especially when these teams execute interdependent team tasks, several team tasks in parallel or simultaneous team and individual tasks (Bardram 2000; LePine et al. 2008; Marks et al. 2001). The lack of virtual and synchronous communication can lead to discordant assumptions concerning the current team task status in relation to the end goal, which is according to Kraut et al. (2002) referred to as task state awareness. Therefore, spatially dispersed teams often show a poor task state awareness, which, as a consequence, negatively affects the temporal coordination of the subtasks of their team task.

Temporal coordination, specifically relevant in synchronous scenarios, encompasses three main components: (1) the correct sequencing of the subtasks (Bardram 2000), (2) the correct timing of the subtasks (e.g., Hollnagel (1998)), and (3) the ability to adapt dynamically to variables in the team's context (Kluge et al. 2018). To show a preferably good temporal coordination, teams have to orchestrate their subtasks according to the aforementioned components. Due to the spatial dispersion, these teams are prone to scheduling errors (e.g., synchronization problems, inaccurate judging of duration, and low levels of shared temporal cognitions; McGrath (1991)), which leads to not being "on the same temporal page" (Mohammed and Nadkarni 2014, p. 405), creating discord regarding when subtasks should be started and finished as well team members adhering to different schedules and pacing (Gevers et al. 2009).

One possibility to counteract poor temporal coordination is the use of coordination artifacts, such as clocks, specific software, schedules, checklists, and so on (Bardram 2000). These are suitable for supporting the temporal coordination, as they provide reliable information about the team process state and thus contribute to enhancing the task state awareness of the team. Therefore, it appears reasonable to use AR for supporting spatially dispersed teams in their temporal coordination since AR can provide information about the process state of the team task (e.g., by means

Fig. 3 Research assumption: how AR can enhance temporal team coordination

of graphical annotations). Moreover, head-mounted AR displays (AR-HMDs), in particular, are well-suited to provide information in the visual periphery of the user and thus create an ambient awareness of the augmented information (Schmalstieg and Hollerer 2016). By using the peripheral instead of focal attention of the user (Cadiz et al. 2002), less attention is required (Downs et al. 2012), and fewer cognitive resources are used, so that the user has access to more cognitive capacities for the execution of the actual team tasks.

Altogether, we assume that AR technology allows for superimposing information about the teamwork process state in an ambient manner, which generates ambient awareness of the process state and in turn improves the task state awareness of spatially dispersed teams with the result of an optimized temporal coordination (Fig. 3). To test this assumption, the authors have conducted several laboratory studies. The next sections provide an overview of that research.

5 Setting Up an Experimental Team Task Context

Our overall objective is to increase task state awareness of spatially dispersed teams with the help of AR. Therefore, the authors wanted to build and empirically investigate the effects of temporal coordination artifacts that support the temporal coordination of teamwork of spatially dispersed teams in a production setting by enhancing the team's task state awareness.

To test a corresponding tool, a suitable test environment and use case were required. A corresponding test environment that encompasses a production setting and can be realized as teamwork context is WaTrSim (i.e., **wa**stewater **tr**eatment plant **sim**ulation; for previous studies with WaTrSim, please see Burkolter et al. (2009), Frank et al. (2017), Thomaschewski et al. (2021), Weyers et al. (2015)). WaTrSim is a digital simulation of a realistic wastewater treatment plant (Fig. 4, left panel) that is fully controllable via a graphical user interface (Fig. 4, right panel).

The simulated scenario in WaTrSim is to initiate the plant with the goal of generating a high production outcome (e.g., maximizing the amount of purified water and gas, minimizing the amount of wastewater). To achieve this goal, a sequence of 13 fixed steps has to be executed in the right order and a preferably good timing. The steps consist of adjusting the settings at different parts of the plant (heaters, valves, and tanks). Thereby, the users are supported by the gaze guiding tool (GGT, for further description, pretest and evaluation, please see Frank et al. (2017), Kluge et al. (2013), Weyers et al. (2015)), which is a digital manual that guides the users gaze

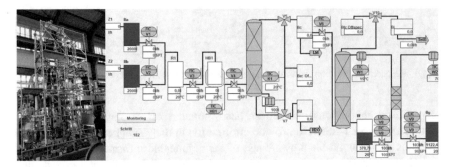

Fig. 4 Real facility of the WaTrSim located at TU Dresden (left panel) and part of the WaTrSim interface (right panel)

to the part of the plant where the setting has to be changed and displays the exact change specification. As shown in Fig. 5, the GGT is a semi-transparent overlay with a cutout highlighting the area to be controlled. The cutout/plant area is identified by a red–orange rectangle. Adjacent to the cutout, there is an additional info box that directs the user on their task.

Since we aimed at supporting spatially dispersed teams, this setting was extended to a team context (Fig. 6). Therefore, three instances of WaTrSim were used, so that two instances could be ran as individual task (IT, task was controlled by a single user) and one instance as team task (TT, task was controlled by two users as a team; each user must perform a predefined subset of the 13 fixed steps to initiate the WaTrSim). To simulate spatial dispersion, both team members were located in separate rooms, so that they had no mutual (physical) workspace and no possibility to communicate (Fig. 7). Both rooms were equally equipped with two on-wall projections representing the IT and TT, respectively. The projections were positioned on separate walls at a 90° angle, so that the user had to actively turn to see the process state of the other task. Both team members were equipped with AR glasses (HoloLens 1), which displayed the GGT. Additionally, the AR interface displayed information about the

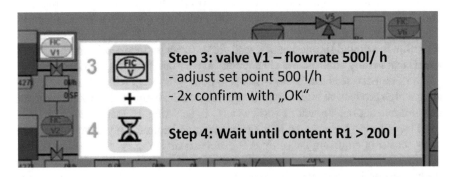

Fig. 5 Gaze guiding tool (GGT). *Note:* The original GGT is in German and has been translated for this chapter

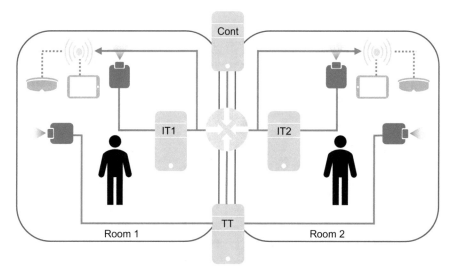

Fig. 6 System architecture of the general study setup for the team context: connection between AR glasses, tablets (for controlling WaTrSim), and PCs (running the simulation and handling the communication) have been implemented via local Ethernet. *IT_1* PC providing individual task for participant in room 1, *IT_2* PC providing individual task for participant in room 2, *TT* PC providing team task for both participants. *Cont* server used to remotely start and control the ITs and TT. HoloLens and tablet are connected via local Wi-Fi connections provided by local access points

process state of the task the user was not currently working on. The latter is the ambient-awareness tool (AAT). The AAT is intended to increase the team's task state awareness by implicitly presenting team members with ambient information about the current state of the task they not currently working on and consists of iconic representations of the next three steps that must be performed in the respective task. The simulations were controlled via a tablet. AR glasses, tablets (used for controlling WaTrSim), and PCs (running the simulation and handling the communication) were connected via the local Ethernet network, as shown in Fig. 6.

6 Pre-study I: Does Gaze Guiding Help?

During a first pretest in 2018, the general study setting and the functionality of the tools were to be tested as a proof-of-concept. Therefore, we used a first prototype of the AAT (Fig. 8). For the representation of the next three steps, we used colored symbols that were displayed in the periphery of the AR interface. While working on the IT, the symbols representing the process state of the TT were presented on the left side of the projected simulation surface of the IT. The symbols representing the IT while working on the TT were presented to the right side of the simulation surface of the TT (Fig. 8).

Individual Task (IT)   **Individual Task (IT)**

Team Task (TT)

Fig. 7 General laboratory study diagram with WaTrSim

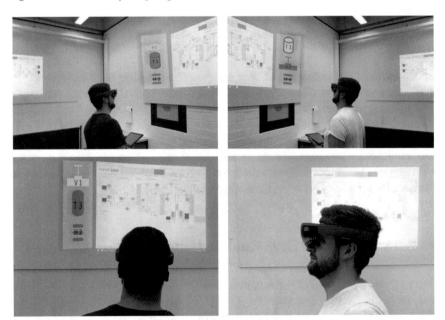

Fig. 8 Pre-study 2018. Left panels: team member A working on the IT; the symbols left to the simulation surface represent the AR-based symbols, showing the next three steps in the TT. Right panels: team member B, working on the TT; the symbols right to the simulation surface represent the AR-based symbols, showing the next three steps in the IT

In total, 11 participants (all students, 9 female) participated in the pretest. The dyadic team was formed by one participant and one female student assistant each, who had a high level of expertise in controlling the WaTrSim. Thus, we have tested a total of 11 teams. One study session lasted approximately 60 min and consisted of 15 min HoloLens usage training, 15 min WaTrSim operation training (IT only), and 30 min actually operating WaTrSim (IT and TT; for further explanation of the task please refer to *Setting up an experimental team task context*).

6.1 Results

The pretest showed that the implemented study design worked stably. Furthermore, additional questionnaire data showed that the participants had considered the devices for the AAT attractive and helpful as well as perceived the HoloLens as supportive for the specific task (WaTrSim initialization); and working with the HoloLens did not require high mental effort.

To summarize, the preliminary study showed that the concept of the AAT could be successfully applied in a spatially dispersed interdependent production tasks. Since AR superimpositions are not effective per se, we conducted a further study that evaluated different interface arrangements of the AAT to identify the most supportive interface design. This step was necessary from our perspective, as different aspects such as perceptual issues (Drascic and Milgram 1996; Kruijff et al. 2010), the cluttering of superimpositions (Rosenholtz et al. 2007), the misleading of attentional cues (Veas et al. 2011), or information overload (Doswell and Skinner 2014; Irlitti et al. 2016; Irizarry et al. 2013; Krevelen and Poelman 2010) had to be considered. The next section describes our approach to identify the final AAT interface.

7 Pre-study II—How and What to Superimpose?

To determine the most suitable interface, we conducted a two-part study with a paired sample in which we examined the usability and user experience (UX) of several interface configurations (see Thomaschewski et al. (2021)). The first part of the study was conducted in the laboratory and focused on evaluating different display options of several object properties for the ambient awareness objects (AAOs), considering their anticipated usability in the context of the interface. The objective of the first part of the study was to derive possible interface configuration clusters, which would also be evaluated for UX in the second part of the study. Since this study was focused on the evaluation of different interface designs and not on the coordination between team members, we did not invite dyadic teams but individuals for the evaluation.

In total, 22 participants (3 female) that were familiar with operating WaTrSim participated in the study. Due to one participant withdrawing over the course of the second part of the study, the analyses were based on the data of 21 participants.

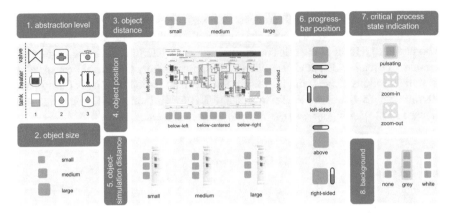

Fig. 9 AAO properties that were evaluated in the first part of the study. Following a predefined hierarchy, evaluation started with choosing a display mode for *abstraction level*, followed by *object size*, *object distance*, *object position*, *object-simulation distance*, *progress-bar position*, *critical process state indication* and ended with choosing a *background* for the AAOs

As shown in Fig. 8 (and the final version in Fig. 13), the AAT consists of three icons (depending on the next step tank, heater, or valve) and indicates the next three steps for the task, the user is currently not looking at. In order to configure an interface with a possible high usability, eight object properties (Fig. 9) were predefined that would influence the usability of the interface, depending on their visualization (display mode). For example, placing the AAOs at a distance too far from the simulation surface could result in the objects not being in the field of view (FOV) and thus impair usability; too close, and it could distract the user.

7.1 Pre-study II, Part I: Usability Evaluation

For the usability evaluation, the authors developed an instrument, the usability cluster questionnaire (UCQ), which was specifically suited to the evaluation of the interface. Using a hierarchical forced-choice paradigm (HFC), the UCQ directs the participant to select different display modes in the AAO properties, so that each execution leads to an individual interface configuration per participant. As illustrated in Fig. 9, the choice hierarchy was defined from *1. abstraction level of the AAOs* to *8. background*, meaning, that each participant chose a display mode for the abstraction level in the first step (1, 2, or 3), the display mode for object size in the second step (small, medium, or large), up to the display mode for background in the last step (none, grey, or white). For each AAO property, the participants were asked to select the subjectively "most helpful or appropriate display mode" (Thomaschewski et al. 2021). A more detailed description of the UCQ can be found in Thomaschewski et al. (2021).

To allow the participants to evaluate the AAO properties using the UCQ, the simulation surfaces of the WaTrSim were projected onto two different walls at a 90°

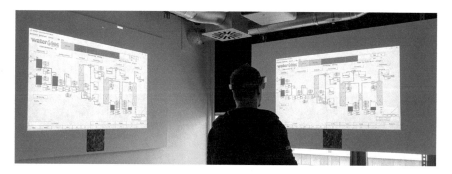

Fig. 10 Pre-study II, part one

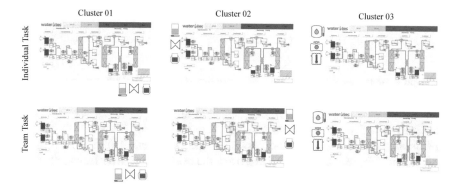

Fig. 11 AAT configurations as result of pre-study part I

angle, as in the pre-study (see above). However, in contrast to the pre-study, only, images of the simulation surface were used, so that the simulation could not actually be controlled (Fig. 10). AAO properties were displayed via HoloLens 1.

To investigate whether the individual interface configurations could be assigned to specific patterns, a divisive hierarchical cluster analysis was subsequently performed. The results indicated the formation of three clusters, so that three interface configurations could be derived. The results are shown in Fig. 11.

7.2 Pre-study II, Part II: User Experience Evaluation

Part II was conducted as an online study. Therefore, the participants from Part I were invited via email to evaluate the three interface configurations according to their UX in a follow-up online survey. To evaluate the UX, the participants were shown video mock-ups of the three inferred interface configurations from study Part I (Fig. 11) and asked to evaluate the UX using the AttrakDiff (Hassenzahl et al. 2003) and

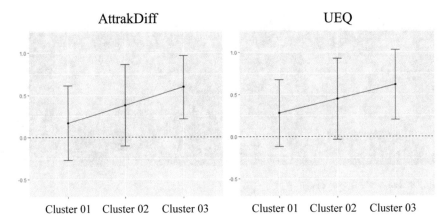

Fig. 12 Visualization of the UX total score means. Left panel: results from the AttrakDiff. Right panel: results from the UEQ. Error bars indicate the 95% confidence interval

five scales of the user experience questionnaire (UEQ; attractiveness, perspicuity, dependability, stimulation, novelty; Laugwitz et al. (2006)).

Subsequent replicated ANOVAs did not show significant differences among the perceived UX of the three interface configurations. However, the results did appear to indicate a minor preference for cluster 3 (Figs. 11, 12, and 13). A more detailed elaboration of the results can be retrieved from the work presented by Thomaschewski et al. (2021).

According to these results, the interface for the main study would be designed, in which we would finally investigate the impact of the AAT on the temporal coordination of spatially dispersed teams. The next section outlines the design of the main study.

8 Main Study: Design to Evaluate the Impact of the AAT on the Temporal Coordination of Spatially Dispersed Teams

Based on the proposed assumption in the introduction (Fig. 3), the main study investigated whether the developed AAT could positively affect the temporal coordination of spatially dispersed teams. In this context, not only the main effect of the AAT on the temporal coordination is investigated. In addition, different design components of the AAOs were examined for differences in their supportive effect.

To this end, 110 dyadic teams were studied in five different groups, among which the factors of dimensionality (2D vs. 2.5D) and dynamics (static = without progress bar vs. dynamic = with progress bar) of the AAOs had been varied (Fig. 14).

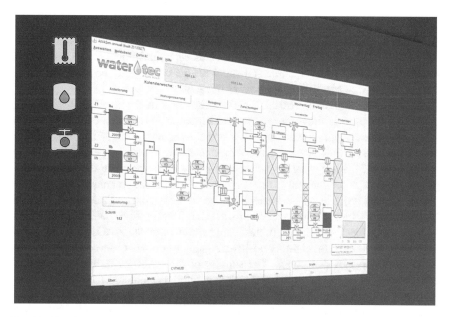

Fig. 13 Simulation surface of WaTrSim and the final AAT left sided to the simulation surface

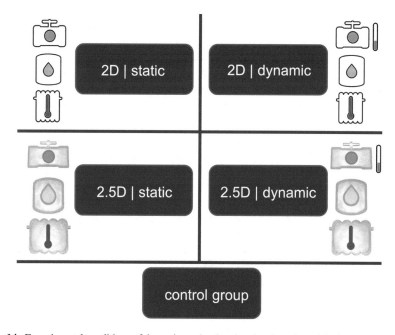

Fig. 14 Experimental conditions of the main study, showing the alteration of the factors (1) dimensionality (2D vs. 2.5D) and (2) dynamics (static = without progress bar vs. dynamic = with progress bar). *Note:* The GGT (see section *Setting up an experimental team task context*) was available to all groups (including control group)

The authors' intention to report this study here has the focus of outlining existing research concepts and to give a most complete picture possible of our research agenda. At the time of chapter writing, the evaluation of the effectiveness of the AAT is still being completed. However, some statistical results can already be made regarding the participants' subjective assessment of the AAO:

Apart from the measure of the general usefulness of the AAOs for starting up WaTrSim, all of the following reported outcomes were recorded on a Likert-scale of 1 to 5, where 1 corresponds to a low and 5 to a high rating. First, it should be noted, that the participants rated the AAOs as rather attractive (single item, $M = 3.38$, $SD = 1.21$, no significant differences in the rating between the experimental groups) and in general useful for starting up WaTrSim (single binary item, 72.25% yes vs. 27,43% no). The user experience of the whole system (including AAOs, Gaze Guiding Tool, tablet control, and WaTrSim GUI; 3 items, $M = 3.48$, $SD = 0.95$) as well as the subjective meaningfulness and relevance of the AAOs (7 items, $M = 3.43$, $SD = 0.84$) was rated rather positive. Again, we did not observe any significant differences between the groups. The support of the AAOs regarding the temporal coordination of team and individual task was rated as mediocre (single item, $M = 2.56$, $SD = 1.40$), whereby significant differences between the groups ($F(3, 170) = 4.452$, $p = 0.005$) resulted. Post-hoc tests showed that the group with 2DD AAOs rated the supportiveness significantly higher in comparison to the group with 2DS AAOs ($p = 0.02$) as well as to the group with 3DS AAOs ($p = 0.025$). The support of the AAOs in terms of remembering the steps for the start-up procedure was rated rather low (single item, $M = 2.02$, $SD = 1.24$).

Taken together, the AAOs are perceived as attractive and comfortable in use. Additionally, the participants rated the AAOs as meaningful, relevant, and generally useful for operating WaTrSim, but rather mediocre supportive in terms of the temporal coordination between individual and team task. With respect to memorizing the steps of the start-up procedure, the AAOs were perceived as rather low supportive.

The previous sections explained the development and deployment of an AR-based support tool that uses graphical and abstract icons for the interface design to support spatially dispersed teams. The preliminary work suggests that productivity and accuracy in teams could be supported by such tools. However, what about the overall team feeling and experience? When team members work in different spaces, this can lead to a lack in the team feeling/experience (for an overview, see Morrison-Smith and Ruiz (2020)). Apart from the socio-emotional components that should be taken into account in terms of good work design, a lack of feeling of community can again have negative impacts on team performances.

A possible approach to maintain the team feeling/experience despite (long) distances between team members may be the use of AR-based avatars. The next section presents another of our preliminary study where an AR-based assistance system was developed that used avatars to support geographically distant teams.

9   A Within-Subject-Study: Development of an AR-Based Avatar Assistance System to Support Spatially Dispersed Teams

The ongoing study could be regarded as an extension to the aforementioned studies and was intended to provide evidence regarding how interaction and communication, and thus the team experience, could be enabled for spatially dispersed team partners using AR-based avatars.

Research already exists on the use of avatars in collaborative work processes. For instance, Piumsomboon et al. (2018a) investigated the deployment of an AR-based "Mini-Me" avatar in two different mixed-reality (AR and VR) collaboration scenarios and showed that social presence and the collaboration experience could be enhanced using avatars. Yoon et al. (2019) investigated the effects "of avatar appearance on social presence and user's perception in AR" (p. 1) for collaborative tasks and showed that a realistic, full-body avatar was considered best suited for remote collaboration. Furthermore, Waldow et al. (2019) reported feedback from subjects, suggesting that visual cues to the avatar's gaze direction may be relevant, but this has not been empirically evaluated.

Based on these findings and the study results previously described for the present work, further follow-up studies will aim at investigating the deployment of avatars in symmetric (team members assigned to equal roles (Ens et al. 2019; Feld and Weyers 2019)) and spatially dispersed team scenarios in regard to the teams' temporal coordination. Therefore, in a first step, a feasibility study was conducted to investigate whether the behavior of a full-body avatar as a representation of the spatially dispersed team member including context cues, could influence task performance (accuracy and processing time) and the perception of co- and social presence in the context of a collaboration task.

9.1   Study Design

Again, the WaTrSim was adopted for the study, and this time the participant's task was to read certain states (e.g., tank levels, heater temperatures, etc., hereinafter region of interest (ROI)) on the wall-projected simulation surface. These would be subsequently reported (verbally) to the spatially dispersed team member (which in this case was the investigator, who was located in a different room). The support consisted of the participant seeing the team partner as an AR-based avatar through the HoloLens 1 (Fig. 15). The avatar controlled by the investigator used a full-body tracking system based on a combination of a Microsoft Kinect Azure as well as head and finger tracking by the MS HoloLens 2. The investigator and participant were able to communicate verbally via microphone and speakers using Skype. Figure 16 depicts the technical layout in detail.

Fig. 15 Study design. Left panel: investigator controlling the avatar. Right panel: participant's view of the WaTrSim surface and the AR-based avatar

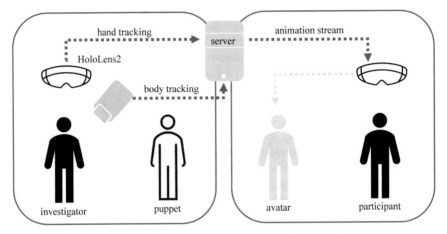

Fig. 16 Technical design: for the full-body tracking of the investigator, we used a combination of Microsoft Azure Kinect for upper and lower body with additional tracking data from Microsoft HoloLens2 for hand and head tracking. The so generated animation stream was provided via server to the HoloLens1 the participant wore to animate the avatar. For spatial registration (positioning of investigator, avatar and participant), a puppet was used giving the investigator orientation where the participant was located, the participant needed to stand in one specific position in the room

The avatar control was handled by the experimenter and realized through an external tracking system, which tracked the movements of the experimenter and mapped them to the avatar. In order to have a reference point for the physical orientation, gaze direction, and pointing gestures, a mannequin was used (Fig. 16), which represented the relative position of the participant.

To observe the effects, the factors (1) avatar behavior (avatar actively pointing to the ROI vs. avatar not pointing to the ROI) and (2) contextual cues (additional highlighting of the ROI vs. no additional highlighting of the ROI) were varied in a within-subject design (Fig. 17). As dependent variables, co- and social presence as well as processing time and accuracy were measured for each condition. Therefore, each

Avatar pointing	ROI highlighted	Experimental condition
✗	✗	no support condition
✗	✓	highlight condition
✓	✗	avatar condition
✓	✓	avatar + highlight condition

Fig. 17 Experimental conditions showing the alteration of the factors (1) avatar behavior and (2) contextual cues

participant underwent all experimental conditions, with each condition consisting of five trials that were randomized to counterbalance learning and memory effects.

9.2 Results

For analysis, the data of 23 students (12 female, mean age: 24.09 ($SD = 3.27$)) were used. A total of 30.43% of them indicated that they had prior VR or AR experience, and 43.48% indicated prior experience with avatars but not in a vocational context.

Social presence was measured with the 5-item scale by Bailenson et al. (2003), to survey co-presence, we applied the co-presence subscale by Harms and Biocca (2004). Team performance was operationalized by measuring the time the participants needed to orally read the ROI. To measure accuracy, error rates were calculated.

For co-presence, a one-way ANOVA indicated a significant difference between the groups ($F(3, 66) = 11.048, p < 0.001, \eta^2 = 0.179$). Post-hoc tests showed significant differences between the (a) no support condition and avatar condition ($p = 0.009$), (b) no support condition and avatar + highlight condition ($p < 0.001$), (c) highlight condition and avatar condition ($p = 0.016$), and (d) highlight condition and avatar + highlight condition (see Fig. 18). Comparing the groups regarding social presence, a one-way ANOVA showed no significant differences ($F(2.02, 44.35) = 4.19, p = 0.021, \eta^2 = 0.058$). Processing time appeared enhanced by additional highlighting of the upcoming state: A one-way ANOVA indicated significant differences between the groups ($F(3, 66) = 6.167, p < 0.001, \eta^2 = 0.167$). Subsequently, post-hoc tests revealed significant differences between highlight condition and avatar condition ($p = 0.007$), and between avatar condition and highlight + avatar condition ($p = 0.033$)

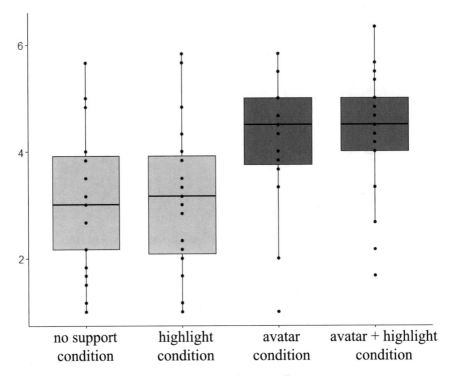

Fig. 18 Boxplots for the co-presence measure. Scale range 1:7

(see Fig. 19). Processing errors were so few that a comparison of the accuracy was not meaningful.

9.3 Discussion

The ongoing study may be the first study to examine the role of an avatar in a team collaboration task in a simulated work environment. Though the expressiveness of the data were limited, the insights could provide guidance for designers. First, co-presence has been shown to be effective and that it is higher when the avatar is actively engaged in the task. Second, highlighting of specific regions of interest has a positive influence on processing time. Third, AR-based support enabled the participants to perform almost error-free. These findings provide a foundational direction for the design of AR-based avatar interfaces. The publication of the ongoing study's results is currently in preparation.

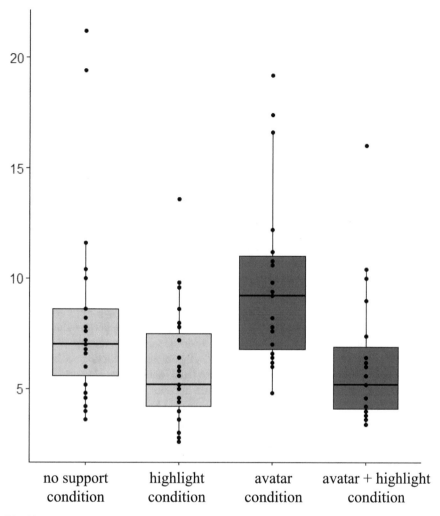

Fig. 19 Boxplots for the processing time. Y-axis shows processing time in seconds

10 General Discussion and Conclusion

In this chapter, we introduced the topics of collaborative work, teams, teamwork, and task work and showed the potential of AR applications for the support of teams. We reviewed the state of the research concerning team-supportive AR applications and presented a self-developed taxonomy for the use and/or the implementation of AR applications in teamwork environments. Furthermore, we provided insights into past and current research in the field of team support by means of AR. Thereby, the focus was on the AR-based support of spatially dispersed teams. Our intention for writing the chapter at hand was to outline our research agenda of the past years. To discuss our findings to this point, we summarize the topics covered in the chapter below. Thus, the focus is on our experience-based conclusions. Additionally, we outline the contribution we believe our research allows us to provide.

Already in 1995, Goodhue and Thompson proposed that the technology used must have a good fit to the task it is supposed to support (Task-Technology Fit) (Goodhue and Thompson 1995b). However, what we can conclude from our ongoing studies so far is that it is not only of great importance to establish a fit between the task and the technology that is as good as possible. It is also of great importance to consider the fit between the team to be supported and the respective technology used (team-technology fit, Thomaschewski et al. (2019, 2021)). Nevertheless, from the view of current research presented in this chapter, we were able to infer that during the development of AR-based assistance systems, the task is still in the focus. When it comes to the support of spatially dispersed teams, the specifics of the team to be supported are not considered (e.g., experience level of the team members, number of team members, team history, etc.).

In the context of the aforementioned research review, we have only been able to identify one paper (Piumsomboon et al. 2018a) in which the team aspect was at least considered, but the application was then discussed more from a task, interaction technique, and technical communication perspective. Neglecting the needs of and demands on the team to be supported can negatively affect the performance as well as the well-being of single team members and/or the general team experience.

Therefore, we would like to encourage developers and researchers to draw attention not only on the respective task, but on the team that shall be supported. In order to also take these person-related variables into account, we advocate that the focus in the development of AR-based support tools should be more on the experience and behavior of the team members. To assist developers, researchers, and users in this regard, we have presented a taxonomy in this chapter. This taxonomy is intended to be used to consider both task and team-related factors when developing and/or deploying AR-based technologies.

We demonstrated how team and task can be taken into account as reciprocally dependent and equally significant factors in the development of AR-based applications with the presentation of pre-study II. To this end, we based our interface config- uration on UX as well as usability measures, that we derived from assessing partic- ipants, who were familiar with the actual task (operating WaTrSim). The reported results for the main study confirmed the effectiveness of this approach: On the one hand, we showed that the superimpositions used in the interface were perceived as attractive, relevant, and generally supportive for starting up WaTrSim. On the other hand, the supportiveness of the superimpositions in relation to the temporal coor- dination of individual and team task was rated as rather mediocre. In relation to remembering the next steps of the start-up procedure, the support level was rated as rather low. However, the reported results are based on the subjective perception of the participants. Further, analysis of objective-assessed performance markers will shed more light on the actual effectiveness of the developed tool.

To demonstrate a further approach for supporting spatially dispersed teams, we additionally outlined a study in which we developed an AR-based avatar assistance system. Here, we showed that guiding the gaze by means of AR-based highlighting of relevant interface parts can significantly reduce processing time in a search task. Furthermore, we showed that the perception of co-presence could be significantly increased by an active avatar behavior, whereas we found no significant influence on the perception of social presence. By primarily focusing on the avatars influence on co- and social presence, we could show that avatars can positively contribute to the team feeling and teamwork experience. Regarding limitations, it should be noted that the influence of the avatars' sex on the participants' perception of the team experience was not evaluated. Here, preliminary work showed that the avatars' sex can have a significant influence on help-seeking behavior. Lehdonvirta et al. (2012) showed that female avatars were more likely to be asked for help in comparison to male avatars.

Our research of the past few years led to the notion that physiological differences between male and female users should be considered in AR-related research much more. For instance, on average, women have a smaller interpupillary distance (Dodgson 2004) as well as a less strong muscular system in the head and neck region (Côté 2012), which might lower the usability of head-mounted displays for them significantly. Additionally, recent research has shown that, on average, women are also more prone to different types of motion sickness (Garcia et al. 2010), which might be related to the female hormonal cycle (Matchock et al. 2008). Taken together, from our point of view, we highly recommend to draw more attention on possible effects of the avatar's sex as well as on sex-related differences in the users in future AR research. Against this background, in our future research, we will focus on the avatars' sex as well as on gender identification as an influencing factor in AR-related research. Considering these differences will generate results that can be generalized to a broader, more diverse (and thereby more realistic) population.

In conclusion, the chapter at hand provides several contributions to AR-related team research: By reviewing the state of research in relation to AR-based support of spatially dispersed teams, we provide an up to date overview of current and past developments, which might serve as a framework including the provided taxonomy. This framework can be helpful for guiding future developments in the context of AR-based support of spatially dispersed teams. We further illustrated the implementation of that framework by outlining a set of empirical studies. These studies cover the topics of AR-based interface design, visual guidance technology, as well as the implementation of AR-based avatars for spatially dispersed teams.

Still, more research is needed in the field of supporting spatially dispersed teams, as they are becoming increasingly prevalent due to their high potential. However, since the behavior and experience, and accordingly the performance, of those teams can differ from teams working on-location, more research is needed to develop and offer adequate support methods/applications for spatially dispersed teams.

Acknowledgements This work was partly supported by the DFG (Deutsche Forschungsgemein-schaft/German Research Foundation) [grant number KL2207/7-1 & WE5408/3-1].

References

Bardram JE (2000) Temporal coordination–on time and coordination of collaborative activities at a surgical department. Comput Support Coop Work (CSCW) 9(2):157–187

Bailenson J, Blascovich J, Beall A, Loomis J (2003). Interpersonal distances in virtual environments. Pers Soc Psychol Bull 29(7):819–833. https://doi.org/10.1177/0146167203029007002

Bauer M, Kortuem G, Segall Z (1999) "Where are you pointing at?" A study of remote collaboration in a wearable videoconference system. In: Third international symposium on wearable computers, pp 151–158

Bedwell WL, Wildman JL, DiazGranados D, Salazar M, Kramer WS, Salas E (2012) Collaboration at work: an integrative multilevel conceptualization. Hum Resour Manag Rev 22(2):128–145

Billinghurst M, Clark A, Lee G (2014) A survey of augmented reality. Found Trends Hum-Comput Interact 2014:73–272

Boos M, Hardwig T, Riethmüller M (2017) Führung und Zusammenarbeit in verteilten Teams. Hogrefe Verlag

Brannick MT, Prince A, Prince C, Salas E (1995) The measurement of team process. Hum Factors 37(3):641–651

Burkolter D, Kluge A, German S, Grauel B (2009) Waste water treatment simulation (WaTr-Sim): validation of a new process control simulation tool for experimental training research. In: Proceedings of the human factors and ergonomics society 53rd annual meeting. Sage, pp 1969–1973

Cadiz JJ, Venolia G, Jancke G, Gupta A (2002, Nov) Designing and deploying an information awareness interface. In: Proceedings of the 2002 ACM conference on computer supported cooperative work, pp 314–323

Côté JN (2012) A critical review on physical factors and functional characteristics that may explain a sex/gender difference in work-related neck/shoulder disorders. Ergonomics 55(2):173–182

Dodgson NA (2004, May) Variation and extrema of human interpupillary distance. In: Stereoscopic displays and virtual reality systems XI, vol 5291. SPIE, pp 36–46

Doswell JT, Skinner A (2014, June) Augmenting human cognition with adaptive augmented reality. In: International conference on augmented cognition. Springer, Cham, pp 104–113

Downs J, Plimmer B, Hosking JG (2012, June) Ambient awareness of build status in collocated software teams. In: 2012 34th International conference on software engineering (ICSE). IEEE, pp 507–517

Drascic D, Milgram P (1996, April). Perceptual issues in augmented reality. In: Stereoscopic displays and virtual reality systems III, vol 2653. SPIE, pp 123–134

Driskell JE, Salas E, Driskell T (2018) Foundations of teamwork and collaboration. Am Psychol 73(4):334

Ens B, Lanir J, Tang A, Bateman S, Lee G, Piumsomboon T, Billinghurst M (2019) Revisiting collaboration through mixed reality: the evolution of groupware. Int J Hum Comput Stud 131:81–98

Feld N, Weyers B (2019) Overview of collaborative virtual environments using augmented reality. In: Gesellschaft für Informatik e.V. (Hrsg.) Mensch und computer 2019-workshopband, pp 185–191

Frank B, Kluge A (2017) Cued recall with gaze guiding—reduction of human errors with a gaze-guiding tool. In: Hale KS, Stanney KM (eds) Advances in neuroergonomics and cognitive engineering. Springer, Heidelberg, pp 3–16

Garcia A, Baldwin C, Dworsky M (2010, Sept) Gender differences in simulator sickness in fixed-versus rotating-base driving simulator. In: Proceedings of the human factors and ergonomics society annual meeting, vol 54, no 19. SAGE Publications, Sage CA; Los Angeles, CA, pp 1551–1555

Gevers JM, Peeters AG, M. (2009) A pleasure working together? The effects of dissimilarity in team member conscientiousness on team temporal processes and individual satisfaction. J Organ Behav Int J Ind Occup Organ Psychol Behav 30(3):379–400

Goldstein IL, Ford JK (2002) Training in organizations. needs assessment, development, and evaluation, 4th edn. Wadsworth, Belmont, USA

Goodhue DL, Thompson RL (1995a) Task-technology fit and individual performance. MIS Q 19(2):213–236

Goodhue DL, Thompson RL (1995b) Task-technology fit and individual performance. MIS Q 213–236

Hagemann V, Kluge A (2017) Complex problem solving in teams: the impact of collective orientation on team process demands. Front Psychol 8:1730

Hagemann V, Kluge A, Ritzmann S (2012) Flexibility under complexity: work contexts, task profiles and team processes of high responsibility teams. Empl Relat

Harms C, Biocca F (2004) Internal consistency and reliability of the networked minds measure of social presence. In: Seventh annual international workshop: presence. Universidad Politecnica de Valencia, Valencia

Hassenzahl M, Burmester M, Koller F (2003) AttrakDiff: Ein Fragebogen zur Messung wahrgenommener hedonischer und pragmatischer Qualität. In: Mensch & computer 2003. Vieweg+ Teubner Verlag, pp 187–196

Higgs M, Plewnia U, Ploch J (2005) Influence of team composition and task complexity on team performance. Team Perform Manag Int J

Hollnagel E (1998) Cognitive reliability and error analysis method (CREAM). Elsevier

Irlitti A, Smith RT, Von Itzstein S, Billinghurst M, Thomas BH (2016) Challenges for asynchronous collaboration in augmented reality. In: IEEE International symposium on mixed and augmented reality (ISMAR-adjunct), pp 31–35

Irizarry J, Gheisari M, Williams G, Walker BN (2013) InfoSPOT: a mobile augmented reality method for accessing building information through a situation awareness approach. Autom Constr 33:11–23

Johansen R (1998) Groupware: computer support for business teams. The Free Press

Kluge A (2021) Arbeits- und Organisationspsychologie. Kohlhammer Verlag

Kluge A, Grauel B, Burkolter D (2013) Job aids: how does the quality of a procedural aid alone and combined with a decision aid affect motivation and performance in process control? Appl Ergon 44:285–296

Kluge A, Borisov N, Schüffler A, Weyers B (2018) Augmented reality to support temporal coordination of spatial dispersed production teams. In: Dachselt R, Weber G (eds) Mensch und computer 2018—workshopband. Gesellschaft für Informatik e.V., Bonn, pp 293–300. https://doi.org/10.18420/MUC2018-WS07-0350

Kozlowski SW, Ilgen DR (2006) Enhancing the effectiveness of work groups and teams. Psychol Sci Public Interest 7(3):77–124

Kraut R, Gergle D, Fussel S (2002) The use of visual information in shared visual spaces: informing the development of virtual co-presence. In: Churchill EF, McCarthy J, Neuwirth C, Rodden T (eds) Proceedings of the 2002 ACM conference on computer supported cooperative work—CSCW'02. ACM Press, New York, USA, pp 31–40. https://doi.org/10.1145/587078.587084

Kruijff E, Swan JE, Feiner S (2010, Oct) Perceptual issues in augmented reality revisited. In: 2010 IEEE international symposium on mixed and augmented reality. IEEE, pp 3–12

Kuzuoka H (1992) Spatial workspace collaboration: a shared view video support system for remote collaboration capability. In: Proceedings of the SIGCHI conference on Human factors in computing systems—CHI'92, pp 533–540

Laugwitz B, Schrepp M, Held T (2006) Konstruktion eines Fragebogens zur Messung der User Experience von Softwareprodukten. In: Mensch & computer, pp 125–134

Lehdonvirta M, Nagashima Y, Lehdonvirta V, Baba A (2012) The stoic male: how avatar gender affects help-seeking behavior in an online game. Games Cult 7(1):29–47

LePine JA, Piccolo RF, Jackson CL, Mathieu JE, Saul JR (2008) A meta-analysis of teamwork processes: tests of a multidimensional model and relationships with team effectiveness criteria. Pers Psychol 61(2):273–307

Marks MA, Mathieu JE, Zaccaro SJ (2001) A temporally based framework and taxonomy of team processes. Acad Manag Rev 26(3):356–376

Matchock RL, Levine ME, Gianaros PJ, Stern RM (2008) Susceptibility to nausea and motion sickness as a function of the menstrual cycle. Womens Health Issues 18(4):328–335

Mathieu J, Maynard MT, Rapp T, Gilson L (2008) Team effectiveness 1997–2007: a review of recent advancements and a glimpse into the future. J Manag 34(3):410–476

McGrath JE (1991) Time, interaction, and performance (TIP) a theory of groups. Small Group Res 22(2):147–174

Mohammed S, Nadkarni S (2014) Are we all on the same temporal page? The moderating effects of temporal team cognition on the polychronicity diversity–team performance relationship. J Appl Psychol 99(3):404

Morgan BB Jr, Glickman AS, Woodward EA, Blaiwes AS, Salas E (1986) Measurement of team behaviors in a Navy environment. Rep. No. 86-014. Naval Training Systems Center, Orlando, FL

Morrison-Smith S, Ruiz J (2020) Challenges and barriers in virtual teams: a literature review. SN Appl Sci 2:1096. https://doi.org/10.1007/s42452-020-2801-5

Normand JM, Servières M, Moreau G (2012, Mar) A new typology of augmented reality applications. In: Proceedings of the 3rd augmented human international conference, pp 1–8

Piumsomboon T, Lee GA, Hart JD, Ens B, Lindeman RW, Thomas BH, Billinghurst M (2018a, Apr) Mini-me: an adaptive avatar for mixed reality remote collaboration. In: Proceedings of the 2018a CHI conference on human factors in computing systems, pp 1–13

Piumsomboon T, Lee G, Ens B, Thomas B, Billinghurst M (2018b, Sept) Superman vs giant: a study on spatial perception for a multi-scale mixed reality flying telepresence interface. IEEE Trans Visual Comput Graphics, pp 1–1

Rico R, Sánchez-Manzanares M, Gil F, Gibson C (2008) Team implicit coordination processes: a team knowledge-based approach. Acad Manag Rev 33(1):163–184

Rosenholtz R, Li Y, Nakano L (2007) Measuring visual clutter. J vis 7(2):17–17

Salas E, Dickinson TL, Converse SA, Tannenbaum SI (1992) Toward an understanding of team performance and training. In: Swezey RW, Salas E (eds) Teams: their training and performance. Ablex, Norwood, NJ, pp 3–29

Salas E, Cooke NJ, Rosen MA (2008) On teams, teamwork, and team performance: discoveries and developments. Hum Factors 50(3):540–547

Salas E, Shuffler ML, Thayer AL, Bedwell WL, Lazzara EH (2015) Understanding and improving teamwork in organizations: a scientifically based practical guide. Hum Resour Manage 54(4):599–622

Schmalstieg D, Hollerer T (2016) Augmented reality: principles and practice. Addison-Wesley Professional

Schweiß T, Thomaschewski L, Kluge A, Weyers B (2019) Software engineering for AR-systems considering user centered design approaches. In: Mensch und computer 2019-workshopband

Sereno M, Wang X, Besançon L, Mcguffin MJ, Isenberg T (2020) Collaborative work in augmented reality: a survey. IEEE Trans Visual Comput Graphics

Sinclair AL (2003) The effects of justice and cooperation on team effectiveness. Small Group Res 34(1):74–100

Szalavári Z, Schmalstieg D, Fuhrmann A, Gervautz M (1998a) "Studierstube": an environment for collaboration in augmented reality. Virtual Reality 3(1):37–48

Szalavári Z, Eckstein E, Gervautz M (1998b) Collaborative gaming in augmented reality. In: Proceedings of the ACM symposium on virtual reality software and technology—VRST, pp 195–204

Thomaschewski L, Herrmann T, Kluge A (2019) Unterstützung von Teamwork-Prozessen durch Augmented Reality (AR): Entwurf einer arbeitspsychologisch fundierten Taxonomie. Arbeit interdisziplinär analysieren–bewerten–gestalten [Interdisziplinary analyzing, evaluating and designing work]

Thomaschewski L, Weyers B, Kluge A (2021) A two-part evaluation approach for measuring the usability and user experience of an augmented reality-based assistance system to support the temporal coordination of spatially dispersed teams. Cogn Syst Res 68:1–17

Ulich E (2013) Arbeitssysteme als soziotechnische Systeme–eine Erinnerung. J Psychol Alltagshandelns 6(1):4–12

Van Krevelen DWF, Poelman R (2010) A survey of augmented reality technologies, applications and limitations. Int J Virtual Reality 9(2):1–20

Veas EE, Mendez E, Feiner SK, Schmalstieg D (2011, May) Directing attention and influencing memory with visual saliency modulation. In: Proceedings of the SIGCHI conference on human factors in computing systems, pp 1471–1480

Waldow K, Fuhrmann A, Grünvogel SM (2019) Investigating the effect of embodied visualization in remote collaborative augmented reality. In: Bourdot P, Interrante V, Nedel L, Magnenat-Thalmann N, Zachmann G (eds) Virtual reality and augmented reality. EuroVR 2019. Lecture notes in computer science. Springer, Cham, pp 246–262

Weyers B, Frank B, Bischof K, Kluge A (2015) Gaze guiding as support for the control of technical systems. Int J Inf Syst Crisis Response Manag Spec Issue Hum Comput Interact Crit Syst 7(2):59–80

Yoon B, Kim HI, Lee GA, Billinghurst M, Woo W (2019, Mar) The effect of avatar appearance on social presence in an augmented reality remote collaboration. In: 2019 IEEE conference on virtual reality and 3D user interfaces (VR). IEEE, pp 547–556

Rotational and Positional Jitter in Virtual Reality Interaction in Everyday VR

Anil Ufuk Batmaz and Wolfgang Stuerzlinger

Abstract One element that affects 3D tracking performance in virtual reality (VR) systems is fluctuations in the signal, i.e., jitter, which occurs regardless of the sensor technology used. In real-life VR systems, positional and rotational jitter can be found in all tracked objects, including the headset, controllers, or other trackers. Previous work had identified that $\pm0.5°$ rotational jitter negatively affects user performance for distal pointing. Yet, they also found that even using a second controller to reduce the "Heisenberg effect" introduced by the button press does not address the problem completely. Moreover, with jitter on the position of a virtual object, user performance significantly decreases with jitter above one fourth of the size of that virtual object. Still, users preferred to have positional jitter on a virtual target rather than rotational jitter on a VR controller. In this chapter, we extended the previous literature by conducting a user study on angular jitter with controllers held with two different grip styles and targets at two different depth distances. The results revealed that user performance decreases (already) with $\pm0.25°$ additional jitter. Thus, we suggest that practitioners/developers who design 3D user interfaces, controllers, and interaction techniques for daily 3D VR usage should focus on reducing jitter. Decreasing jitter not only improves user performance but also decreases frustration, which improves the user experience.

1 Introduction

For 3D interaction with a virtual environment and its 3D objects through a virtual reality (VR) systems, selection plays a critical role in everyday VR. In VR systems, pointing is thus one of the first and most frequent tasks that a user executes.

A. U. Batmaz (✉)
Concordia University, Montreal, QC, Canada
e-mail: ufuk.batmaz@concordia.ca

W. Stuerzlinger
Simon Fraser University, Vancouver, BC, Canada
e-mail: w.s@sfu.ca

During 3D pointing, the user has to point toward the desired target. The pointing device has to be in the correct position and orientation to enable accurate pointing within the virtual world. To facilitate such pointing, the user is (usually) provided with some form of feedback, such as a color change, when they correctly point to a target. Once the cursor is on the desired target, then the user confirms the target selection, typically with a button click.

As mentioned above, there are two aspects to selection: the user points to the correct target, and the input system transfers the pointing pose from the real world to the virtual world. During this transfer, a signal is generated by the controller and sent to the end-user application or software. This generated signal also contains fluctuations, called jitter. Such jitter can be observed in all stages of pointing in everyday VR.

When the user points the cursor toward a target, hand tremor might affect the pointing performance, which is usually between 4 and 12 Hz (Ang 2004; Elble et al. 1990; Hefter et al. 1987; Stiles 1980). This type of unintentional hand movement is included as jitter in the signal measured by the input device. Other biological factors, such as body sway or breathing, can also add additional jitter.

The 3D tracking system used by the input device can also generate different types of jitter (Fang et al. 2017). For instance, most current VR controllers contain an Inertial Measurement Unit (IMU) to measure the acceleration and orientation of the device by using the data from accelerometers and gyroscopes. The digital signal generated by the accelerometer and gyroscopes typically contains jitter due to imperfections in the transformation of the world pose data into a digital form. This jitter is usually the result of a combination of different issues, such as thermal noise, electrical noise, and quantization noise. Moreover, this jitter value changes with environmental conditions, including temperature and humidity.

Another type of jitter is generated by different form of light sensors for 3D tracking, such as infrared or visible light cameras (Oh et al. 2016). It is possible to observe such jitter with the all kinds of VR trackers, including cameras on headsets, hand tracking systems such as Leap Motion (Guna et al. 2014), and the Kinect (Xi et al. 2018). These sensors aim to detect the absolute pose of the input device; which could be a VR controller of a commercial VR HMDs or the hands of the user for the Leap Motion. These sensors detect visually salient entities, including beacons, shapes, or markers, which allows the tracking algorithm to detect the pose of the device. However, these beacons, shapes, or markers might not be always fully visible to the sensors because of occlusion. In this case, the tracking algorithm might not always work properly and the user can observe a sudden change in the pose of the virtual VR controller. Even when all markers or beacons are fully visible, the output of the tracking algorithm can contain noise in the pose due to simplifying assumptions in the algorithm (such as local linearity) or sensor limitations.

When the pose data of the input device(s) is received by a software on a computer, this data is typically processed with a filtering algorithm, such as the One-Euro filter (Casiez et al. 2012) or Kalman Filter (Welch 2009). These filtering algorithms can also add (temporal) jitter due to the phase shift they introduce.

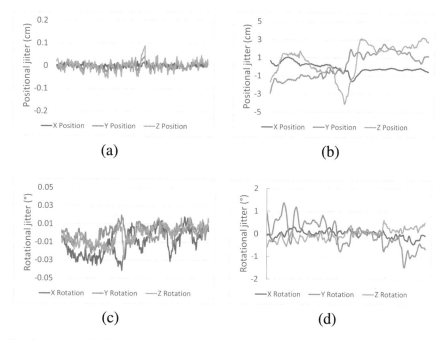

Fig. 1 An exemplar jitter recording on a VR Controller. Positional jitter in cm when the VR controller is **a** immobilized or **b** held in mid-air. Rotational jitter in degrees when the VR controller is **c** immobilized or **d** held in mid-air

Apart from these different types of jitter that impact user interaction even when the device is stably hovering in mid-air, different interaction actions can also add additional jitter. For instance, pulling a trigger or pushing a button on a VR controller can cause an unintentional pose changes. Such changes were previously investigated under the term "Heisenberg effect" for spatial interaction, and the results identified that user performance can decrease (Wolf et al. 2020).

Apart from all the information regarding input devices, such as a VR controller, jitter can be also observed in other parts of a VR system, such as the head-mounted display. Moreover, jitter can even be observed in input devices that are not attached to or held by the user. For instance, current tracking devices can be attached to static objects in the real environment, so that the real world objects' pose can be transferred into the VR system. Such tracking devices are also prone to exhibit jitter.

When a 2D mouse is left stable on a table, the amount of jitter recorded by the system is usually practically zero, due to the surface friction and high-resolution sensors. On the other hand, if a VR controller is left stable on a table, it is possible to observe tracking jitter in its pose (Fig. 1a, c). This jitter is even more visible when the user points a target on mid-air, as shown in Fig. 1b, d where there is then substantial movement even outside the human tremor band (4–12 Hz).

Previous work in the VR and AR literature focused on more precise and accurate interactions to eliminate the impact of jitter. For instance, the handlebar method supports more precise movement actions in mid-air, but requires bi-manual hand manipulation (Song et al. 2012). The 7-handle technique used triangle shaped widgets with seven points and subjects found this method less tiring and more efficient than the simple virtual hand (Nguyen et al. 2014). The MAiOR method used mid-air rails and widgets to increase the precision of object manipulation by separating DoFs (Mendes et al. 2016). Recent work presents a method that uses pivot points (Gloumeau et al. 2020) to further increase precision. All these techniques were proposed to decrease the detrimental impact of the jitter in state-of-the art systems.

With a series of experiments, we previously explored the change of user pointing performance due to jitter in VR systems (Batmaz et al. 2020b; Batmaz and Stuerzlinger 2019a, b). In our first experiment, we showed that user performance significantly decreases above $\pm 0.5°$ rotational jitter. In a second experiment reported in that work, we showed that using a second controller's trigger as an selection confirmation does not mitigate the jitter observable in a VR controller. In our final experiment, we showed that user performance also significantly decreases with jitter on the targets.

Here, we use the same terminology as in our previous work. We refer to "rotational jitter" as the orientation jitter that affects user performance with VR controllers. In VR environments, there are two common interaction methods, ray casting and virtual hand (Argelaguet and Andujar 2013). For VR controllers, rotational jitter has the most detrimental effect for one of the most common selection methods, ray casting, which works similar to a laser pointer. With the ray casting method, a small change in the rotation of the VR controller results in a larger change at a further distance. For instance, if a VR controller is rotated 5°, the cursor shifts 8.7 cm at 1 m but 17.4 cm at 2 m. Positional jitter at the controller has (relatively) less impact, as identified in previous work (Batmaz et al. 2020b). As jitter affects VR trackers attached to real world objects, which is particularly relevant for AR applications, we additionally explore "positional target jitter" as our second objective. This positional target jitter has a (relatively) larger impact on pointing, since rotational jitter at the center of a spherical target has (near to) zero impact during selection while positional jitter can change the object's center coordinates.

One major finding of our previous work on jitter was that our results identify potential explanations for other results of research on novel input devices. Pham and Stuerzlinger (Pham and Stuerzlinger 2019) showed that, compared to commercial VR controllers typically held in a power grip, using a pen-like device improves user performance in a 3D pointing task. However, another investigation of a pen-like device exhibited lower user performance (Batmaz et al. 2020a). When investigating several potential explanations for this difference, we realized that participants were complaining about hand tremor in the latter work. The analysis on the mid-air jitter data revealed that the pen-like device used in (Batmaz et al. 2020a) exhibited sufficiently large pose jitter to reduce user performance. Like in the previous studies, we use describe situations where it takes a user longer to execute a task, they make more errors, and/or their throughput reduces as a *decrease* in user performance.

We are investigating jitter levels observable in everyday VR/AR systems to make sure our results are directly applicable to current work. All electronic systems exhibit jitter, and jitter adds noise to signals during data transfer. On the other hand, 3D mid-air pointing is already an unusual interaction method—few things float in mid-air in the real world, e.g., (Stuerzlinger and Wingrave 2011)—and is thus more challenging than, e.g., 2D pointing, such as with a mouse. Thus, the additional jitter introduced by 3D tracking systems can affect user performance and their experience during interaction with everyday VR/AR systems relatively stronger. The impact of jitter in everyday VR/AR can be observed in various scenarios. For instance, drawing and writing is an important part in everyday VR/AR, and high levels of jitter in an input device can impact the communication between users and content annotation (Kern et al. 2021). Another example of the impact of jitter in everyday VR/AR is observable in VR shooting games, where the user has to aim toward to a target by pointing the controller. Any non-trivial level of jitter typically lowers the precision of the user in this task and thus affects the user experience negatively.

In this study, we investigated the effects of rotational and positional jitter on user performance with two different input devices, an HTC Vive Pro VR controller and a Logitech© VRInk pen, with targets placed at two different target depths. The position of the targets was chosen based on angular measures. Our results show that user performance significantly decreases with more than ±0.5° positional and rotational jitter.

2   Previous Work

In this section, we discuss previous work related to jitter and also to the experimental conditions that we investigated in our study. We first focus on the existing literature that is used to assess human motor performance in VR systems for different jitter levels. Then, we review previous research conducted on jitter in VR systems and the impact of jitter, including human motor performance assessment in VR systems.

2.1   Fitts' Law

Fitts' law (Fitts 1954) models human movement times for pointing. For Euclidean measures, Eq. 1 shows the Shannon formulation (MacKenzie 1992).

$$\text{Movement Time} = a + b * \log_2\left(\frac{A}{W} + 1\right) = a + b * \text{ID} \qquad (1)$$

In Eq. 1, a and b are empirical constants, typically identified by linear regression. A is the amplitude of the movement, which is the distance between two targets, and W the target width. The logarithmic term in Eq. 1 represents the task difficulty and is called the *index of difficulty*, ID.

For pointing tasks in 3D environments, several variations that use an angular ID have been proposed in the literature (Barrera Machuca and Stuerzlinger 2019; Cha

Table 1 Models proposed by previous work for 3D versions of Fitts's law

Paper	Model
Murata and Iwase (2001)	$MT = a + b\sin(\phi) + c(ID)$
Kopper et al. (2010)	$MT = a + bID_{DP}$
Stoelen and Akin (2010)	$MT = a + b(ID_{rotation} + ID_{translation})$
Vetter et al. (2011)	$MT = a \times d - \beta \times \log_2(TS) + \gamma \times \sin(2\theta) + \delta \times \sin(\theta) + c$
Cha and Myung (2013)	$MT = a + b\sin(\phi) + c\theta + dID$
Barrera Machuca and Stuerzlinger (2019)	$MT = a + b(ID) + c(CTD)$
Clark et al. (2020)	$MT = a + b(ID) + c(\theta) + d(\theta * TS)$

Fig. 2 Top view of angular pointing. A is the Euclidean distance between two targets, W is the target width and d is the distance from the user to the targets. Similarly, α represents the angular distance and ω the angular target width

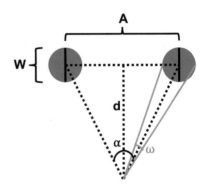

and Myung 2013; Clark et al. 2020; Kopper et al. 2010; Murata and Iwase 2001; Vetter et al. 2011; Stoelen and Akin 2010). These are shown in Table 1.

Our work does not aim to propose a novel angular ID equation. For simplicity, we thus used Kopper et al.'s angular ID formula:

$$ID_{angular} = \log_2\left(\frac{\alpha}{\omega^k} + 1\right) \qquad (2)$$

In Eq. 2, α represents the angular distance between targets and ω the angular target width. The constant k represents a relative weight between α and ω. For simplicity, we set $k = 1$. We used the same method to convert Euclidean distances to angular measures as Kopper et al. (2010), which is also illustrated in Fig. 2.

We also use throughput (based on effective measures), as defined in the ISO 9241-411:2012:

$$Throughput = \left(\frac{ID_e}{Movement\ Time}\right) \qquad (3)$$

In Eq. 3, movement time is the time between initiation of the movement and the selection of the target. The effective index of difficulty (ID_e) incorporates the user's accuracy in the task (ISO 2012):

$$\text{ID}_e = \log_2\left(\frac{A_e}{W_e} + 1\right) \tag{4}$$

In Eq. 4, A_e represents the effective distance, the actual movement distance to the target position, and W_e is the effective target width, the distribution of selection coordinates, calculated as $W_e = 4.133 \times \text{SD}_x$, where SD_x is the standard deviation of selection coordinates along the task axis. SD_x represents the precision of the task performance (MacKenzie and Isokoski 2008; MacKenzie and Oniszczak 1998).

2.2 3D Pointing Methods in VR

3D pointing is one of the essential components of interaction with the virtual environment through a VR system (LaViola et al. 2017). To select targets in a VR environment, the user has to first point at the target (and then confirm the selection). While pointing at targets is relatively easy within peri-personal space, i.e., within arm's reach, the task becomes more challenging for further targets.

To afford pointing at distal targets the most common solution is raycasting, which resembles a real-life task: using a laser pointer (LaViola et al. 2017). Nevertheless, as with laser pointing, ray casting is not very effective for accurate selection of small and/or distant targets. One simple method that aims to improve the accuracy and visibility of the cursor position with ray casting displays a virtual ray between the controller and the respective intersected surface of the virtual environment to give the user better visual feedback.

To facilitate the selection of distal targets various methods have been proposed, e.g. (Vanacken et al. 2007; De Haan et al. 2005; Liang and Green 1994), but none of these proposed methods support high-precision pointing at objects in distant dense object groups. This creates a need to understand the limitations for user performance when using the ray casting method.

2.3 Selection Methods

After the user points the cursor/ray at a target, a corresponding action is needed to activate the selection. Several multimodal methods to select a target in VR have been previously investigated, e.g., through voice or the blink of an eye (Vanacken et al. 2009). Current state-of-the-art VR controllers afford selection simply by pulling a trigger or pushing a button on the device. Since the VR controller hovers in mid-air, there is no physical feedback to counterbalance the force applied to the buttons or triggers. In this case, the VR controller's pose can be altered by the trigger/button press, and this error is called the "Heisenberg effect" of spatial interaction (Bowman et al. 2001).

The effect of the Heisenberg effect increases for farther targets, since even the slightest noise in the orientation of the VR controller magnifies with distance (Batmaz and Stuerzlinger 2019a). To eliminate the negative impact of the Heisenberg effect, previous studies used various bi-manual interaction methods, such as using the space bar of the keyboard or a second controller's trigger, both operated with the non-dominant hand (Batmaz and Stuerzlinger 2019b; Batmaz et al. 2020a).

2.4 Different Grip Styles in VR Systems

New VR controllers are being introduced with the aim of increasing the user's accuracy (Barber et al. 2018), precision (Romat et al. 2021), or the ergonomics (Kartick et al. 2020) of VR systems. Since previous work showed that arm, elbow, forearm, wrist, hand, finger, and fingertip position and rotation can play a crucial role in terms of user performance, the design of a VR controller is also critical (Yan and Downing 2001; Shih 2005; Schwarz and Taylor 1955; Liao 2014; Cutkosky and Wright 1986). This also includes the main design attributes of the controller, such as the size of the main handle. In addition, required grip strength, hand posture, and ergonomic factors all can affect user performance.

In current commercial VR systems, VR controllers support either one of two major grip styles. Our previous work (Batmaz et al. 2020a) used Napier's *prehensile movement* classification to anatomically and functionally categorize grip styles, and studied their effects in VR. The first major grip style is the precision grip, where the tool is pinched between multiple fingertips and the opposing thumb. The second one is the power grip: the object is held in the palm, while the fingers form a clamp position, with the thumb applying pressure counter to the fingers. HTC Vive's and Oculus' controllers are examples of controllers designed to be used in a power grip. The Massless and Logitech© VR Ink controllers are designed to be held in a precision grip.

Pham and Stuerzlinger's comparison of pointing performance with the precision and power grip showed that the precision grip significantly increased performance in terms of time, error rate, and throughput (Pham and Stuerzlinger 2019). Based on the Pham and Stuerzlinger's work, another study investigated the effects of the precision vs power grip with the Logitech© VRInk, which revealed that the power grip significantly decreased the error rate (Batmaz et al. 2020a). However, the throughput performance of the participants was lower compared to Pham and Stuerzlinger's work. More detailed analysis in the lead up to the current paper identified that the jitter exhibited by the pen controller in this second study was high enough to reduce the throughput performance of the participants. This motivated us to revisit jitter.

2.5 The Impact of Jitter in VR Systems

The adverse effect of jitter in VR systems was first analyzed by Teather et al. (2009), showing that an average of 0.3 mm spatial jitter in the input device decreased the user performance. A further study identified that the negative impact of a larger level of jitter increases with smaller targets (Pavlovych and Stuerzlinger 2009).

In the work discussed below in this section, all positional jitter mentioned was applied to the three positional axes of the targets objects and rotational jitter was applied to all three Euler axes of the VR controller used to point.

2.5.1 Effects of Jitter with a Uniform Distribution

Based on the results of the Teather et al. (2009), Batmaz and Stuerzlinger investigated the effects of jitter on user performance with a VR controller (Batmaz and Stuerzlinger 2019a). This study used an HTC Vive Pro system, which was one of the best tracking systems available on the market at that time. When the authors generated artificial jitter to add to the system, they used a uniform distribution, as uniformly distributed jitter is a simple way to characterize noise in complex systems.

In their study with 12 participants, Batmaz and Stuerzlinger focused on four levels of (added) rotational jitter: None, $\pm 0.5°$ jitter, $\pm 1°$ jitter and $\pm 2°$ jitter. To analyze the results with Fitts' law, they also used three target distances: 10, 20, and 30 cm and three target sizes: 1.5, 2.5, and 3.5 cm .

The researchers placed the targets 50 cm away from the user for distal pointing and placed the cursor 30 cm away from the controller. This setup allowed researchers to limit potential issues with the control-display ratio and potential confounds of visual depth and visibility for their initial results.

During the task execution, the authors asked participants to select a target by pulling the trigger on the VR controller. With this interaction method, the researchers aimed to include the negative impact of the "Heisenberg effect" in their results.

The results of this study showed that there is no significant difference between $\pm 0.5°$ jitter and none for execution time. On the other hand, their error rate significantly increased, and participants' throughput performance decreased significantly starting with $\pm 1°$ jitter. The researchers concluded that practitioners and designers must take care with systems above ± 0.5 ° jitter and test the user performance in terms of error rate.

In the detailed analysis of multiway interactions, the researchers investigated the effects of jitter on task difficulty. The authors used the task difficulty formula with the Euclidean target distance and target size (see Eq. 1). The results revealed that target distance does not have an impact on jitter. However, this approach is prone to errors: when the size of the target increased, the impact of the jitter was also (artificially) increased. Angular measures offer a better approach here.

While this study was the first step to analyze the negative impact of the rotational jitter, the authors used only a single depth distance, only uniform distribution noise, and the selection was subject to the "Heisenberg effect."

2.5.2 Effects of Different Selection Techniques and Discrete Uniform Distribution Noise on Rotational Jitter

In a subsequent study, Batmaz and Stuerzlinger analyzed the negative impacts of the jitter using White Gaussian Noise (WGN) and by eliminating the effects of the "Heisenberg effect" with a bi-manual selection techniques, again using an HTC Vive Pro setup (Batmaz and Stuerzlinger 2019b).

WGN is used to model random processes in information theory. Using WGN for jitter more closely models the cumulative impact of multiple sources of jitter on a controller in real life. To generate WGN, the authors used a standard normal distribution generator, the Marsaglia Polar Method (Marsaglia and Bray 1964), which yields random values with a mean of 0 and a standard deviation of 1.

Similar to the previous study (Batmaz and Stuerzlinger 2019a), the researchers used five different (added) levels of rotational jitter: None, $\pm 0.5°$ jitter, $\pm 1°$ jitter and $\pm 2°$ jitter and WGN. The authors also used the same three target distances: 10, 20, and 30 cm and three target sizes: 1.5, 2.5, and 3.5 cm to analyze the results. They also used the same depth distance (50 cm) with the same ray length (30 cm) to keep their study comparable with previous work (Batmaz and Stuerzlinger 2019a).

To mitigate the impact of the Heisenberg effect, the authors also investigated two different bi-manual selection techniques: participants selected the targets by pulling the trigger of the VR controller held in the non-dominant hand or by pressing the space bar key on the keyboard with their non-dominant hand. They compared the results with a condition that included the "Heisenberg effect," where the participants selected targets by pulling the trigger on the VR controller that is used to point targets.

The results showed that using a single controller to both point and select targets increased the error rate compared to bi-manual hand selection techniques. Yet, the time and throughput performance of the participants did not change when using a second controller or the space bar. However, the post-questionnaire results revealed that one-third of the participant preferred a single controller, one-third of the participants preferred two controllers, and one-third of the participants preferred one controller with the keyboard selection technique, which means that the selection technique is also subject to user preferences.

Batmaz and Stuerzlinger (2019b) also investigated the effects of different jitter values on user performance. The results were similar to their previous work (Batmaz and Stuerzlinger 2019a), where higher levels of jitter increased the participants' execution time and error rate, while also decreasing effective throughput performance. As in the previous work, the authors observed significant negative effects of jitter at and above $\pm 1°$ rotational jitter.

One of the interesting findings of this study concerned the speed accuracy trade-off of the participants under the impact of jitter. Subjects were taking longer with an increased amount of jitter, but their error rate did not decrease, and effective throughput results also did not increase. The authors observed that when the participants had to select a target with a VR controller with jitter, the participants were waiting for a "better moment" to select targets, i.e., when the cursor might have stabilized temporarily. Yet, since the jitter was generated continuously, the cursor never stabilized. Thus, the participants' strategy simply took longer to select targets, which explains why there were no performance improvements.

The study of Batmaz and Stuzerlinger (2019b) showed that using bi-manual selection techniques improves user performance in terms of error rate. Also, WGN exhibited a decrease in user performance compared to a constant, uniform distribution. However, this study work did not investigate the impact of depth distance on target selection with jitter nor the effect of positional target jitter.

2.5.3 Effects of Target Depth on Rotational Jitter and Target Jitter

To investigate the negative impact of target depth and positional target jitter, Batmaz et al. (2020b) ran a study with an HTC Vive Pro setup. As in their previous work, they invited 12 participants to their study but used only WGN in their artificially generated jitter. To analyze the results based on Fitts' law, they used three target distances, 10, 20 and 30 cm, and two target sizes, 1.5 and 2.5 cm.

Different from their other work (Batmaz and Stuerzlinger 2019a, b), the authors tested their approach with three depth distances, 0.75, 1.5 and 2.25 m, to analyze the impact of the control-display ratio.

Moreover, the authors used three different (added) levels of positional jitter relative to the target size. The first level was 1/4 of the first target size ($1.5\,cm/4 = \pm0.375\,cm$), and the second 1/4 of the second target size ($2.5\,cm/4 = \pm0.625\,cm$). The third level had no jitter on the target.

Apart from positional jitter, the authors also added rotational jitter to the VR controller and looked at the interaction between positional and rotational jitter. For rotational jitter, they used none, $\pm0.5°$ and $\pm1°$.

The results revealed that user performance significantly decreases when the depth distance increases in terms of time, error rate, and throughput. Similarly, the user performance decreases with increased target jitter.

The authors observed an interesting effect of positional jitter: the user performance significantly decreases for both positional jitter at 0.75 and 1.5 m, but at 2.25 m depth distance, they did not report a significant difference between positional jitter conditions. Since the targets are already far away and appear small beyond 1.5 m, no impact of positional jitter was observed – meaning that reducing the positional jitter at 2.25 m did not affect user performance.

Another finding of this study was the impact of jitter on fatigue. Except for a single person, all participants reported high fatigue after the experiment. Based on the questionnaire results, the study identified an overall negative impact of jitter on the user experience. Since one of their participant commented "No Jitter Please" in the questionnaire, the authors included this phrase in their title to highlight the severity of the problem. The authors did not report any significant interaction between positional and rotational jitter.

Even though (Batmaz et al. 2020b) investigated positional jitter and the impact of the depth distance on user performance, these values were based on Euclidean measures, i.e., all the target distances and target size were defined in centimeters, and the positional jitter was relative to target sizes.

In general, previous work on jitter revealed that

- Starting with $\pm 1°$ uniform and WGN jitter, user's error rate increases and throughput performance decreases.
- Changing the interaction style to bi-manual technique decreases the negative effect of jitter.
- When there is jitter in the system (either on a controller or target) (naive) participants wait for a "better moment" to select targets, which increases the execution time, but does not decrease the error rate. This might also increase fatigue and thus decrease the user experience.
- Reducing the positional jitter in far targets, such as 2.25 m, does not improve user performance.

3 Motivation and Hypotheses

Previous work investigated WGN rotational and positional jitter relative to the target size at different depth distances using different selection methods (Batmaz et al. 2020b; Batmaz and Stuerzlinger 2019a, b). However, all the target distances, target sizes and positional jitter ranges were based on Euclidean measures.

In this study, we decided to extend previous work and analyze rotational and positional jitter with *angular measures*. This enables us to correlate angular jitter with angular target size and target distances, i.e., make the results independent of the actual distances and sizes, which should enable a generalization of the outcomes to arbitrary target distances.

Based on the previous research, we investigated the following hypotheses:

H1. Angular size plays a critical role for user performance when jitter is present. Hypotheses in previous work were solely based on Euclidean measures (Batmaz et al. 2020b; Batmaz and Stuerzlinger 2019a, b). In this work, we define target sizes and target distances in terms of angles. Our previous work had identified that user motor performance in terms of time, error rate, and throughput decreases at $\pm 1°$ rotational jitter and with 1/4 of the target size (Batmaz et al. 2020b). Yet, we believe that user performance is affected by even lower levels of jitter and that the performance decrease really depends on the angular size of the targets - after all, ray casting involves (mostly) rotational movements.

H2. User performance depends on the depth distance used in the virtual environment. Even though we recast all the target sizes and distances into angular measures, we still believe that user performance will decrease with increased depth distances. Previous work identified that user performance can be negatively affected by visual depth cues conflicts in VR systems, such as the vergence and accommodation conflict (Batmaz et al. 2019; Barrera Machuca and Stuerzlinger 2018; Batmaz et al. 2022). Even though a constant target angle implies that the target size increases with further targets, visual depth cue conflicts would still impact user performance depending on target distance.

H3. A precision grip improves user performance when tracking jitter is present in the system. Previous work indicated that user performance significantly increases when a precision grip is used (Pham and Stuerzlinger 2019). However, other work claimed that the precision grip decreases user performance and explained their findings with the tracking issues related to the input device (Batmaz et al. 2020a). In this study, we used a more current version of the Logitech© VRInk pen, which does not suffer from tracking issues. Eliminating tracking issues should increase user accuracy and precision and thus improve the effective throughput of a participant. We believe that the increase in the precision and accuracy also increases the user performance when we add artificial jitter to the system.

4 User Study

To investigate our hypotheses, we conducted a user study using targets with different angular sizes at two different depth distances (1 and 2 m) with two different input devices that support two different grip styles (power grip and precision grip). We added three levels of jitter (None, 0.25° and 0.5°) to the controller for angular jitter and to the targets for positional jitter. All participants performed pointing tasks in all conditions.

Previous work on rotational and positional jitter used linear Euclidean measures, e.g., all target sizes and distances were characterized in (centi-)meters, and the findings were presented based on the corresponding metrics. In this work, we use angular measures rather than the Euclidean measures to make the findings more generalizeable. We still use the same Fitts' task as in previous work, to enable comparisons of our results with the literature.

4.1 Participants

Eight (8) right-handed participants (3 female and 5 male) attended our experiment. The average age was 28.62 (SD 4.56). All our participants were university students from the local department of the institution. They studied various disciplines, such as arts, engineering, computer science, or design. None of them had a prior experience with VR games or VR application development.

4.2 Apparatus

As in previous studies on jitter (Batmaz et al. 2020b; Batmaz and Stuerzlinger 2019a, b), we used an HTC Vive PRO VR system with three Lighthouses (trackers). The reason behind using a third Lighthouse was to increase the visibility of input devices to the tracking system and to increase the quality of the tracking data.

We used a PC with an Intel (R) Core (TM) i7-5890 CPU with 16 GB RAM and an NVIDIA GeForce RTX 1080 graphics card. Subjects used an HTC Vive Pro controller and a Logitech© VRInk pen controller as pointing devices, and the space bar of a Logitech desktop keyboard to indicate selection.

4.3 Procedure

After filling a demographic pre-questionnaire, participants were seated in a chair positioned (roughly) in the middle of the three HTC Vive Pro Lighthouses. Before starting the experiment, the experimenter explained and demonstrated the procedure to each participant and allowed participants to perform practice trials for a few minutes until they felt ready to start the experiment. After the main experiment, we asked participants to fill a post-questionnaire about their perceptions and insights.

In the virtual environment, subjects were placed in an empty room with pictorial depth cues. To assess user performance with 3D pointing, we used an ISO 92411-411 task (ISO 2012) with 11 targets distributed at equal distances in a circular arrangement. The first target was chosen randomly by the software for each repetition. The subjects experienced a clockwise and counter-clockwise target sequence, again selected randomly.

The eleven (11) potential target spheres, which are shown in Fig. 3, were gray at the beginning of each trial. We indicated the current target sphere by changing its color to orange. When the participant moved the ray/cursor using the controller, we

Fig. 3 Experimental environment view in the VR headset. Behind the experimental area, we showed the name of the input device that had to be used for the current round of trials as a text in the background

compared the distance between the target and cursor. If the cursor was inside of a sphere, we changed the color of that sphere to blue. If the participant selected the correct target while the cursor was inside of it, we changed the target's color to green and recorded a "hit." However, if the cursor was outside of the target upon selection, we showed the target in red, recorded a "miss," and played an error sound. As usual in Fitts' law studies, we asked participants to select targets as fast and as precise as possible.

In our study, participants used two different input devices with two different grip styles. As in previous comparisons of the precision grip and power grip, we asked participants to use a Logitech© VRInk pen with a precision grip and an HTC Vive Pro VR controller with a power grip, i.e., we investigated **Grip Style**, 2_{GS} = **precision grip and power grip**. This allowed us to investigate the impact of jitter on different grip styles (with different input devices). During the experiment, the name of the device that needed to be used to select targets was shown as text in the background, outside of the target area.

We also used two different **Depth Distances** (2_{DD} = **1 and 2 m**). We chose these depth distances based on previous work; we did not want targets within arm's length, i.e., closer than 70 cm and we wanted targets to be closer than 2.25 m, to be able to reliably observe the impact of jitter (Batmaz et al. 2020b).

We applied three different levels of rotational jitter on all three rotation axes of the controllers. For the first jitter level, the "none" condition, we did not add artificial jitter. For the second level of rotational jitter, we added $\pm WGN/4°$, and for the third, we applied $\pm WGN/2°$. In other words, the software generated WGN rotational jitter, and we multiplied this jitter with 0.25 for the second condition and 0.5 for the third one. For simplicity, we use only the coefficients for reporting **Rotational jitter**, 3_{RJ} = **None, $\pm 0.25°$, and $\pm 0.5°$**.

Similarly, we applied three different levels of positional jitter on all three positional axes of the targets. For the first level of positional jitter, we did not apply any artificial jitter, as the "none" condition. For the second level of positional jitter, we added $\pm WGN/4$ cm, and in the third, we applied $\pm WGN/2$ cm. Specifically, the software generated WGN positional jitter, and we multiplied this jitter value with 0.25 for the second condition and 0.5 for the third. As for rotational jitter, we refer to WGN coefficients for simplicity as **Positional jitter** 3_{PJ} = **None, ± 0.25 cm, and ± 0.5 cm**.

For positional and rotational jitter, we used the Marsaglia Polar Method (Marsaglia and Bray 1964) to generate WGN. We did not discard or cut off random values generated by this method.

For target distance, i.e., the diameter of the "circle of targets," we used two **Angular Target Distances** (2_{TD} = **5 and 20°**), and for each depth distance, we converted the angular measures to Euclidean target sizes and distances for Unity. We also used three different **Angular Target Sizes** (3_{TS} = **0.5, 1, and 1.5°**).

At the end of the experiment, we asked participants to fill a short questionnaire and asked about their insights for the experiment. We also asked participants about the perceived impact of jitter on their performance using 7-point Likert scale questions. Finally, we queried participants about their physical and mental fatigue.

4.4   Experimental Design

Since previous work on jitter did not report an interaction between positional and rotational jitter (Batmaz et al. 2020b), we decided to investigate the effects of these two forms of jitter independently. To mitigate the adverse effects of jitter, we decided to reduce the number of trials relative to previous work, taking also the potential impact of fatigue caused by jitter into account (Batmaz et al. 2020b). Thus, we prepared two separate studies for positional and rotational jitter.

For rotational jitter, all participants performed the experiment in three experimental conditions: two grip styles (2_{GS} = power grip and precision grip) at two different depth distances (2_{DD} = 1 and 2 m) with three different rotational jitter (3_{RJ} = none, $\pm 0.25°$, and $\pm 0.5°$) conditions. For positional jitter, the same participants performed the experiment in three experimental conditions: two grip styles (2_{GS} = power grip and precision grip) at two different depth distances (2_{DD} = 1 and 2 m) with three different positional jitter (3_{PJ} = none, ± 0.25 cm and ± 0.5 cm) conditions.

We counterbalanced rotational and positional jitter conditions across subjects to avoid learning effects. We collected data for movement time (s), error rate (%), and effective throughput (bits/s) as dependent variables to analyze user performance.

We also varied the index of difficulty (ID), by using three angular target sizes (3_{TS} = 0.5, 1, and 1.5°) and two angular target distances (3_{TD} = 5 and 20°), which yields 6 unique ID between 2.12 and 5.36. Each subject performed ($2_{GS} \times 2_{DD} \times 3_{RJ} \times 3_{TS} \times 2_{TD} \times 11$ repetitions) + ($2_{GS} \times 2_{DD} \times 3_{PJ} \times 3_{TS} \times 2_{TD} \times 11$ repetitions) = 1584 trials.

5   Data Analysis

To assess the user performance, we used Repeated Measures (RM) ANOVA in SPSS 24.0. We used Skewness (S) and Kurtosis (K) to analyze the normality. As in previous work, (Batmaz et al. 2020b; Mallery and George 2003; Mayer et al. 2018), we considered the data to be normally distributed if S and K were between ± 1.

For *brevity*, we only report and focus on significant results. We used the Bonferroni method for post-hoc analyses. Results are illustrated as means and standard error of means in figures. We applied Huynh-Feldt correction when $\epsilon < 0.75$ and used the Bonferroni method for post-hoc analyses.

Since participants experienced two different types of jitter, we first share the rotational jitter results, then the positional jitter results.

Table 2 Main factor results for rotational jitter

	Rotational jitter	Grip style	Depth distance	ID
Time	$F(1.08, 7.5) = 0.78$ n.s., $\eta^2 = 0.100$	$F(1, 7) = 3.88$ n.s., $\eta^2 = 0.357$	$F(1, 7) = 67.39$ $p < 0.001, \eta^2 = 0.906$	$F(1.74, 12.28) = 101.837$ $p < 0.001, \eta^2 = 0.936$
Error rate	$F(2, 14) = 241.524$ $p < 0.001, \eta^2 = 0.972$	$F(1, 7) = 0.99$ n.s., $\eta^2 = 0.115$	$F(1, 7) = 18.06$ $p < 0.01, \eta^2 = 0.721$	$F(3.74, 26.12) = 259.85$ $p < 0.001, \eta^2 = 0.974$
Throughput	$F(2, 14) = 141$ $p < 0.001, \eta^2 = 0.953$	$F(1, 7) = 1.37$ n.s., $\eta^2 = 0.164$	$F(1, 7) = 1.25$ n.s., $\eta^2 = 0.152$	$F(3.96, 27.77) = 1827.5$ $p < 0.001, \eta^2 = 0.996$

5.1 Results for Rotational Jitter

In this part of the results section, we first present the main factor results in Table 2 for rotational jitter, followed by the corresponding interaction results from the two four-way RM ANOVAs. For rotational jitter data, time ($S = 0.94$, $K = 0.52$), error rate ($S = 0.056$, $K = -0.68$) and throughput ($S = 0.04$ $K = -0.99$) were normally distributed.

5.1.1 Rotational Jitter Main Factor Results

Time: For rotational jitter and ID, Mauchly's sphericity test was violated for time ($\chi^2(14) = 69.29$, p < 0.001 and $\chi^2(2) = 13.39$, $p < 0.001$, respectively). According to the results in Table 2, subjects were slower with targets at farther distances (Fig. 4a).

Error rate: For the ID, Mauchly's sphericity test was violated for error rate ($\chi^2(14) = 61.21$, p < 0.001). According to the results in Table 2, subjects made more errors when the rotational jitter increased (Fig. 4b) and when the targets were closer (Fig. 4c).

Throughput: For the ID, Mauchly's sphericity test was violated for throughput ($\chi^2(14) = 50.72$, p < 0.001). The results in Table 2 illustrate that the effective throughput performance of the participants decreased with increased rotational jitter (Fig. 4d).

5.1.2 Rotational Jitter Interaction Results

We found significant interactions between grip style and rotational jitter for error rate ($F(2, 14) = 3.778$, $p < 0.05$, $\eta^2 = 0.49$) and throughput ($F(2, 14) = 14.45$, $p < 0.05$, $\eta^2 = 0.674$). According to these results, participants made more errors (Fig. 5a) and their throughput performance decreased (Fig. 5b) with the precision grip while interacting with distant targets.

We also found a significant interaction between the depth distance and grip style ($F(1, 7) = 6.34$, $p < 0.05$, $\eta^2 = 0.475$). Results showed that user's throughput decreases with the precision grip and $\pm 0.5°$ rotational jitter (Fig. 5c).

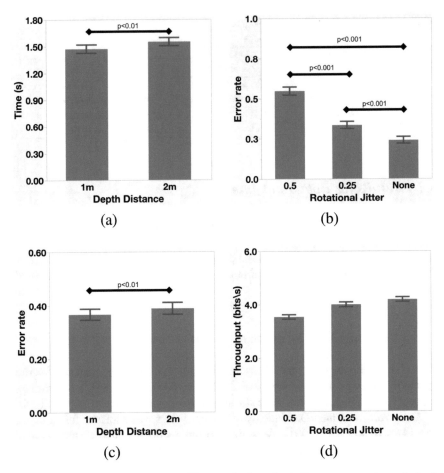

Fig. 4 Analysis of rotational jitter data. Time results for **a** depth distance, error rate results for **b** rotational jitter and **c** depth distance, and effective throughput results for **d** rotational jitter

5.2 Positional Jitter Results

In this subsection, we first present the main factor results in Table 3 for positional jitter, followed by the corresponding interaction results from the two four-way RM ANOVAs. For positional jitter data, error rate ($S = 0.057$, $K = -0.75$) and throughput ($S = 0.5$, $K = -0.9$) were normally distributed. The dependent variable time was log-normal ($S = 0.07$, $K = -0.31$).

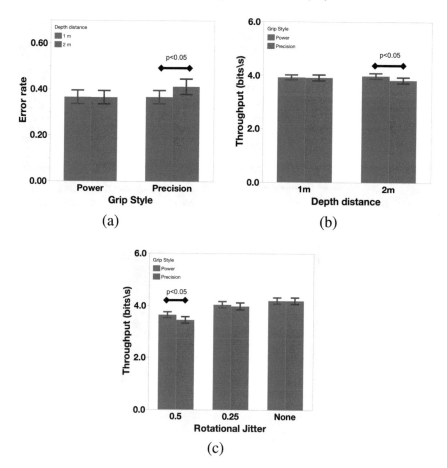

Fig. 5 Analysis of rotational jitter interaction. Error rate results for **a** grip style and depth distance and throughput results for **b** grip style and depth distance, and **c** rotational jitter and grip style

5.2.1 Positional Jitter Main Factor Results

Time: For the ID, Mauchly's sphericity test was violated for time ($\chi^2(14) = 34.51$, $p < 0.01$). According to the results in Table 3, subjects were slower with a higher level of positional jitter (Fig. 6a) and with targets at farther distances (Fig. 6b).

Error rate: For the ID, Mauchly's sphericity test was violated for error rate ($\chi^2(14) = 40.06$, $p < 0.001$). According to the results in Table 3, subjects made more errors when the positional jitter increased (Fig. 6c).

Throughput: Results in Table 3 showed that the effective throughput performance of the participants decreased with an increased depth distance (Fig. 6d).

Table 3 Main factor results for positional jitter

	Positional jitter	Grip style	Depth distance	ID
Time	$F(2, 14) = 4.602$ $p < 0.5, \eta^2 = 0.367$	$F(1, 7) = 0.416$ n.s., $\eta^2 = 0.56$	$F(1, 7) = 55.426$ $p < 0.001, \eta^2 = 0.888$	$F(2.16, 15.12) = 215.68$ $p < 0.001, \eta^2 = 0.969$
Error rate	$F(2, 14) = 124.537$ $p < 0.001, \eta^2 = 0.975$	$F(1, 7) = 0.8$ n.s., $\eta^2 = 0.401$	$F(1, 7) = 3.38$ n.s., $\eta^2 = 0.326$	$F(1.77, 12.43) = 275.07$ $p < 0.001, \eta^2 = 0.975$
Throughput	$F(2, 14) = 0.176$ n.s., $\eta^2 = 0.026$	$F(1, 7) = 0.306$ n.s., $\eta^2 = 0.042$	$F(1, 7) = 45.45$ $p < 0.001, \eta^2 = 0.867$	$F(5, 35) = 814.826$ $p < 0.001, \eta^2 = 0.991$

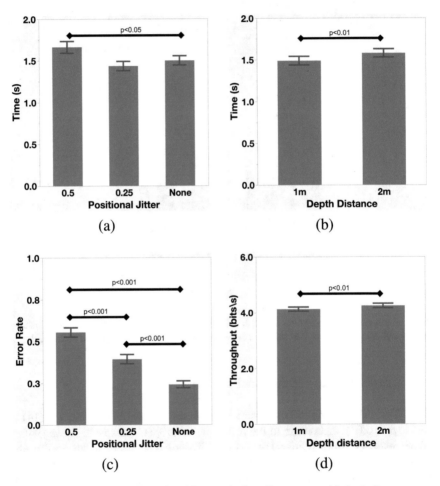

Fig. 6 Analysis of positional jitter data. Time results for **a** jitter range and **b** depth distance, error rate results for **c** positional jitter, and effective throughput results for **d** depth distance

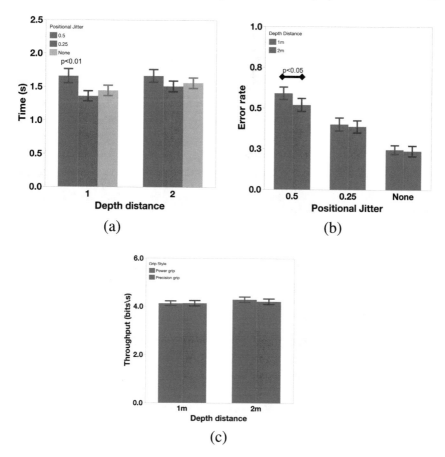

Fig. 7 Analysis of positional jitter interaction. Time results for **a** positional jitter and depth distance, error rate results for **b** positional jitter and depth distance, and throughput results for **c** grip style and grip depth distance interaction

5.2.2 Positional Jitter Interaction Results

For positional jitter, we found significant interactions between depth distance and positional jitter for time ($F(2, 14) = 7.27$, $p < 0.05$, $\eta^2 = 0.510$) and error rate ($F(2, 14) = 11.544$, $p < 0.01$, $\eta^2 = 0.623$). According to the results in Fig. 7a, participants were slower with $\pm0.5°$ jitter at 1 m depth distance compared to the $\pm0.25°$ and no jitter conditions. Similarly, participants made more errors at 1 m compared to the 2 m condition when there was $\pm0.5°$ positional jitter (Fig. 7b). We also found a marginally significant interaction between depth distance and grip style for throughput ($F(1, 7) = 5.31$, $p = 0.55$, $\eta^2 = 0.431$), where participants' throughput was slightly higher with the power grip at 2 m (Fig. 7c).

Table 4 Fitts' law analysis results for positional and rotational jitter

		Movement time					
		Rotational jitter			Positional jitter		
		a	b (*ID)	R^2	a	b (*ID)	R^2
Jitter range	None	0.1740327	0.3705272	0.93	0.1615238	0.3757853	0.94
	0.25	0.1692218	0.3666509	0.96	0.1112581	0.3655716	0.96
	0.5	0.2729441	0.3556668	0.97	0.4294787	0.3406824	0.97
Grip style	Precision grip	0.1894118	0.3500515	0.98	0.2803358	0.3496736	0.96
	Power grip	0.2135234	0.3813734	0.95	0.193603	0.3707219	0.97
Depth distance	1m	0.0842535	0.3851425	0.94	0.2536366	0.3420209	0.97
	2m	0.3274077	0.3438672	0.97	0.2162922	0.3794306	0.96

5.3   Fitts' Law Analysis

The results for a Fitts' law analysis for both positional and rotational jitter are given in Table 4 and Fig. 8 for jitter range, grip style, and depth distance. The regression analyses results show that all the determination coefficients (R^2) were above 0.9.

5.4   Subjective Results

According to the subjective results, only one out of eight participants preferred the VRInk pen. Most participants commented that "*(The HTC Vive Pro Controller was) more comfortable and [required] smaller movements,*" "*My hand was shaking with the Pen device [VRInk]. The [HTC Vive Pro] controller was a lot [more] comfortable and therefore easier to point,*" "*[HTC Vive Pro Controller was] less tiring, flexible,*" "*[HTC Vive Pro Controller] was easier and more familiar to control compared to the ink pen,*" and "*It was easier for me to grab the [HTC] vive controller since it's heavier and easier to control compared to the pen. The pen was light and controlling it in the air to select the objects made my hand to shake more.*" The participant who preferred the VRInk with the precision grip commented "*It's more precise and easy to work with.*"

According to the 7-point Likert scale questions, all the participants thought that jitter reduced their performance (1-Very likely, 7-Very Unlikely, Mean(M) = 1, Standard Deviation (SD) = 0). Participants also thought that while they could see themselves "somewhat likely" using an HTC Vive Pro with jitter (1-Very likely, 7-Very Unlikely, $M = 3$, SD = 0.53), it is unlikely that they will use a VRInk pen with jitter (1-Very likely, 7-Very Unlikely, $M = 4.625$, SD = 1.18).

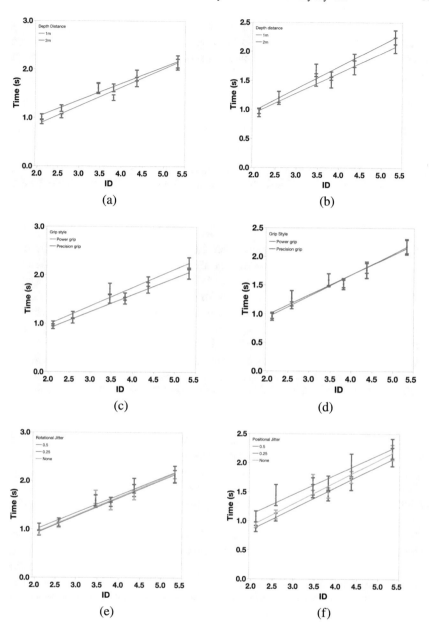

Fig. 8 Fitts' law results. Top row: depth distance Fitt's law results for **a** rotational jitter and : positional jitter. Middle row: grip style Fitt's law results for (**c** rotational jitter and **d** positional jitter. Bottom row: jitter range Fitt's law results for **e** rotational jitter and **f** positional jitter)

After the user study, the participants did not report any significant physical fatigue (1-I feel extremely rested, 7-I feel extremely fatigue $M = 4.625, SD = 0.51$) nor mental fatigue (1-I feel extremely rested, 7-I feel extremely fatigued, $M = 4.25$, SD $= 1.16$).

6 Discussion

In this study, we examined how positional and rotational jitter impact user performance with targets at in different depth distances and with different controller grip styles.

Our results support the findings of previous work on both positional and rotational jitter: user performance significantly decreases when there is jitter in the system (Batmaz et al. 2020b; Batmaz and Stuerzlinger 2019a, b). Extending previous findings, the results in this work revealed that user throughput performance decreases and error rate increases with a higher level of rotational jitter. Similarly, the participants' execution time and error rate increased with $\pm 0.5°$ of jitter. Overall, when a new VR input device is designed for interaction with virtual environment in Everyday VR/AR applications, the designed system should exhibit less than $\pm 0.5°$ jitter, to increase the user performance in terms of time, error rate, and throughput.

Previous work had showed that user performance can decrease with $\pm 1°$ rotational jitter. Our current study indicates that participants' error rate already decreases with (only) $\pm 0.25°$ added rotational and positional jitter. We believe that this result is an outcome of conducting a study with angular measures in VR. Since we converted Euclidean distances to angular measures and applied WGN jitter to these angular measurements, we were able to correlate the amount of jitter to the target sizes and distances. This also confirms our hypothesis $H1$, i.e., that angular size plays a critical role for user performance when jitter is present. Thus, we suggest practitioners and developers evaluate the performance of their selection hardware and software methods in terms of angular measures, (and not simply in Euclidean distances) for everyday VR/AR applications.

Since we used angular sizes, we also increased the Euclidean target sizes and distances at farther distances. This allowed us to present the same size target as seen by a perspective camera. In this case, one could expect a similar user performance for targets at different distances. However, previous work had hypothesized that VR headsets suffer from various stereo deficiencies, such as the vergence and accommodation conflict, which has detrimental effects on the user performance (Barrera Machuca and Stuerzlinger 2018, 2019; Batmaz et al. 2019, 2022). Based on this previous work, we also hypothesized that user performance at increasing depth distances might decrease. And our result indeed confirmed that the participants' error rate and throughput performance decrease with farther targets, which also supports our hypothesis $H2$, i.e., that user performance depends on the depth distance in the virtual environment. Even though we increased the size of the targets for farther targets, the user performance was negatively affected, likely due to the stereo deficiencies of the VR headsets. This negative impact was also observed in the interaction between depth distance and positional jitter: the participants were faster with lower jitter levels at 1 m. However, they got slower with lower jitter levels at targets at a farther distance. We speculate that stereo deficiencies increased the execution time of the participants with the targets at 2 m, even with smaller jitter ranges.

In this study, we examined the effects of two different input devices with different grip styles. The first one was the precision grip, i.e., the grip that a VRInk is designed to be held in. The second one was the power grip, which is how a HTC Vive Pro controller is typically held. Both input systems were commercially available when this manuscript was written. Further, they were used in everyday VR/AR applications. Based on the previous literature, we hypothesized that we observe better user performance in terms of time, error rate and throughput, for the precision grip with higher levels of jitter. Since previous work had indicated that the precision grip increases user performance, we also expected to see a positive impact of the precision grip in the presence of jitter. However, the results of our study showed that user throughput decreases with the precision grip with $\pm 0.5°$ rotational jitter. Therefore, this result does not support our hypothesis *H3*, i.e., that the precision grip improves user performance when jitter is present in the system.

Since the previous work highlighted technical issues with the VRInk (Batmaz et al. 2020a), we used a current version of the device, and confirmed that there are no obvious technical tracking issues with the hardware. However, the subjective results of our study were similar to previous work that compared the precision and power grip (Batmaz et al. 2020a). Our participants commented that the Vive Pro controller was heavier and easier to control compared to the VRInk and that the interaction with the VRInk pen was not as precise. Thus, even though the device we used is technically capable enough for a pointing experiment, we believe that the current hardware design had an negative impact on the participants' user performance and experience.

As in previous work, in this experiment, we used an HTC Vive Pro HMD, one of its controllers and a Logitech VRInk pen with three V2 Lighthouses. We deliberately chose this VR setup because it has a relatively low level of noise. Previous work had used only two V2 Lighthouses (Batmaz et al. 2020b; Batmaz and Stuerzlinger 2019b), which might explain why we could observe differences at lower jitter levels: it seems that our inclusion of a third Lighthouse for tracking, pointed directly at where the controllers were held in space, improved tracking performance. The HTC Vive Pro system includes one of the best tracking systems currently available on the market. Even though the system is precise and accurate enough to collect data for VR pointing experiments (Batmaz and Stuerzlinger 2020; Pham and Stuerzlinger 2019), the data still contains some level of jitter, caused by a combination of measurement errors, human errors, signal processing artifacts, and other noise sources.

Another potential limitation of this work is the relatively low number of participants. In this study, we had eight participants. Still, according to statistical effect size calculations, the minimum effect size we observed in this work is $\eta^2 = 0.36$, i.e., a large effect, commonly defined through a criterion of $\eta^2 > 0.14$. These large effect sizes are evidence that our research findings are robust and have practical significance. Furthermore, the results we found in this work confirm the findings of previous work on jitter in virtual environments.

In this work, we deliberately did not conduct a user study with a full-factorial design and did not compare rotational and positional jitter. First, previous work identified that participants report a higher level of fatigue when they perform jitter experiments (Batmaz et al. 2020b). Hence, we thought that a more complex experiment might negatively impact the performance of the participants, which can hinder and affect the outcomes. Second, previous work did not identify a significant interaction between positional and rotational jitter (Batmaz et al. 2020b). Thus, we decided to focus on both jitter types separately.

The questionnaire we used in this work is in line with previous work on VR jitter. This allows us to compare the user experience across different studies. As a general finding, we can conclude that an increased level of jitter decreases the user performance and participants do not prefer to interact with targets in virtual environment where the jitter levels are high.

Another result of this work concerns the angular ID. In this study, we used Kopper et al.'s angular ID formula (Kopper et al. 2010), and set $k = 1$ for simplicity. With this, the minimum R^2 value we observed in this work was 0.93, which is a very respectable fit. Our work did not aim to compare different angular ID formulations, but based on the R^2 results found in this paper, Kopper et al.'s angular ID formula can be used to analyze angular 3D pointing studies for VR systems.

The importance of this work for everyday VR/AR research is evident when one considers that both positional and rotational jitter is present in current 3D tracking systems. Thus, while the researcher and developers design a new input device, they have to consider the impact of jitter on user performance and their experience. Furthermore, jitter is a part of electronic tracking systems of VR/AR headsets that are used every day and we know that 3D pointing performance does not differ between VR and AR headsets (Batmaz et al. 2019)—which means that the results reported here naturally apply to AR systems. Still, it is essential to investigate the effects of jitter further to improve the quality of user interaction during everyday usage of VR/AR systems.

7 Conclusion

In this work, we studied the effects of positional and rotational jitter for targets at different depth distances while participants used two different input systems with two different grip styles. Our results indicate that user performance significantly declines already with $\pm 0.25°$ added jitter in terms of error rate and throughput. Based on our outcomes, we also suggest practitioners evaluate their VR systems and report user performance based on angular measures, as this methodology can have an impact on research on everyday VR/AR applications. We also saw some indications that stereo display deficiencies can aggravates the negative impacts of jitter for farther targets. Moreover, our results indicate that the power grip can better compensate the detrimental effects of jitter compared to the precision grip. We believe that our outcomes are useful for increasing the user performance and improving the user experience for everyday VR and AR applications and also to inform the development of future, improved 3D tracking systems.

Acknowledgements The raw data of the this study can be found in https://osf.io/kyz7f/.

References

Ang WT (2004) Active tremor compensation in handheld instrument for microsurgery. Ph.D. thesis, Carnegie Mellon University, Pittsburgh, PA, USA (2004). AAI3126920

Argelaguet F, Andujar C (2013) A survey of 3D object selection techniques for virtual environments. Comput Graph 37(3):121–136

Barber SR, Jain S, Son YJ, Chang EH (2018) Virtual functional endoscopic sinus surgery simulation with 3d-printed models for mixed-reality nasal endoscopy. Otolaryngol-Head Neck Surg 159(5):933–937

Barrera Machuca MD, Stuerzlinger W (2018) Do stereo display deficiencies affect 3D pointing? In: Extended abstracts of the 2018 CHI conference on human factors in computing systems. ACM, p LBW126

Barrera Machuca MD, Stuerzlinger W (2019) The effect of stereo display deficiencies on virtual hand pointing,. In: 2019 CHI conference on human factors in computing systems. Pages. ACM, p 14

Batmaz AU, Barrera Machuca MD, Pham DM, Stuerzlinger W (2019) Do head-mounted display stereo deficiencies affect 3D pointing tasks in AR and VR? In: 2019 IEEE conference on virtual reality and 3D user interfaces (VR)

Batmaz AU, Barrera Machuca MD, Sun J, Stuerzlinger W (2022) The effect of the vergence-accommodation conflict on virtual hand pointing in immersive displays. In: Conference on human factors in computing systems, CHI '22. https://doi.org/10.1145/3491102.3502067. To appear

Batmaz AU, Mutasim A, Stuerzlinger W (2020a) Precision vs. power grip: a comparison of pen grip styles for selection in virtual reality. In: Workshop on novel input devices and interaction techniques (NIDIT) at IEEE VR 2020

Batmaz AU, Seraji MR, Kneifel J, Stuerzlinger W (2020b) No jitter please: effects of rotational and positional jitter on 3d mid-air interaction. In: Proceedings of the future technologies conference. Springer, pp 792–808

Batmaz AU, Stuerzlinger W (2019a) The effect of rotational jitter on 3D pointing tasks. In: Extended abstracts of the 2019 CHI conference on human factors in computing systems, CHI EA '19, vol 6. ACM, New York, NY, USA, pp LBW2112:1–LBW2112. https://doi.org/10.1145/3290607. 3312752

Batmaz AU, Stuerzlinger W (2019b) Effects of 3D rotational jitter and selection methods on 3D pointing tasks. In: Workshop on novel input devices and interaction techniques (NIDIT) at (IEEE) (VR) 2019)

Batmaz AU, Stuerzlinger W (2020) Effect of fixed and infinite ray length on distal 3D pointing in virtual reality. In: Extended abstracts of the 2020 CHI conference on human factors in computing systems. Association for Computing Machinery, New York, NY, USA

Bowman D, Wingrave C, Campbell J, Ly VQ (2001) Using pinch gloves (tm) for both natural and abstract interaction techniques in virtual environments

Casiez G, Roussel N, Vogel D (2012) 1 € filter: A simple speed-based low-pass filter for noisy input in interactive systems. In: Proceedings of the SIGCHI Conference on Human Factors in

Computing Systems, CHI '12, p. 2527-2530. Association for Computing Machinery, New York, NY, USA. https://doi.org/10.1145/2207676.2208639

Cha Y, Myung R (2013) Extended fitts' law for 3D pointing tasks using 3D target arrangements. Int J Ind Ergonom 43(4):350–355

Clark LD, Bhagat AB, Riggs SL (2020) Extending fitts' law in three-dimensional virtual environments with current low-cost virtual reality technology. Int J Human-Comput Stud 139:102413

Cutkosky M, Wright P (1986) Modeling manufacturing grips and correlations with the design of robotic hands. In: Proceedings. 1986 IEEE international conference on robotics and automation, vol 3. IEEE, pp 1533–1539

De Haan G, Koutek M, Post FH (2005) Intenselect: using dynamic object rating for assisting 3d object selection. In: Ipt/egve. Citeseer, pp 201–209

Elble RJ, Sinha R, Higgins C (1990) Quantification of tremor with a digitizing tablet. J Neurosc Methods 32(3):193–198

Fang W, Zheng L, Deng H, Zhang H (2017) Real-time motion tracking for mobile augmented/virtual reality using adaptive visual-inertial fusion. Sensors 17(5):1037

Fitts PM (1954) The information capacity of the human motor system in controlling the amplitude of movement. J Exper Psychol 47(6):381

Gloumeau PC, Stuerzlinger W, Han J (2020) Pinnpivot: object manipulation using pins in immersive virtual environments. Trans Visual Comput Graph 27(4):2488–2494. https://doi.org/10.1109/TVCG.2020.2987834

Guna J, Jakus G, Pogačnik M, Tomažič S, Sodnik J (2014) An analysis of the precision and reliability of the leap motion sensor and its suitability for static and dynamic tracking. Sensors 14(2):3702–3720

Hefter H, Hömberg V, Reiners K, Freund HJ (1987) Stability of frequency during long-term recordings of hand tremor. Electroencephalogr Clin Neurophysiol 67(5):439–446

ISO 9241-411:2012: Ergonomics of human-system interaction—part 411: evaluation methods for the design of physical input devices. ISO (2012). https://www.iso.org/standard/54106.html

Kartick P, Quevedo AJU, Gualdron DR (2020) Design of virtual reality reach and grasp modes factoring upper limb ergonomics. In: 2020 IEEE conference on virtual reality and 3D user interfaces abstracts and workshops (VRW). IEEE, pp 798–799

Kern F, Kullmann P, Ganal E, Korwisi K, Stingl R, Niebling F, Latoschik ME (2021) Off-the-shelf stylus: using xr devices for handwriting and sketching on physically aligned virtual surfaces. Front Virt Real p 69

Kopper R, Bowman DA, Silva MG, McMahan RP (2010) A human motor behavior model for distal pointing tasks. Int J Human-Comput Stud 68(10):603–615

LaViola Jr, JJ, Kruijff E, McMahan RP, Bowman D, Poupyrev IP (2017) 3D user interfaces: theory and practice. Addison-Wesley Professional (2017)

Liang, J, Green M (1994) JDCAD: a highly interactive 3D modeling system. In: Computers and graphics: proceedings of the conference on computer. Aided Design and Comparer Graphic, pp 499–506

Liao KH (2014) The effect of wrist posture and forearm position on the control capability of hand-grip strength. Int J Ind Eng 21(6):295–303

MacKenzie IS (1992) Fitts' law as a research and design tool in human-computer interaction. Human-Comput Interact 7(1):91–139

MacKenzie IS, Isokoski P (2008) Fitts' throughput and the speed-accuracy tradeoff. In: Proceedings of the SIGCHI conference on human factors in computing systems, CHI '08. Association for Computing Machinery, New York, NY, USA, pp 1633-1636. https://doi.org/10.1145/1357054.1357308

MacKenzie IS, Oniszczak A (1998) A comparison of three selection techniques for touchpads. In: Proceedings of the SIGCHI conference on Human factors in computing systems. ACM Press/Addison-Wesley Publishing Co, pp 336–343

Mallery P, George D (2003) Spss for windows step by step: a simple guide and reference. Allyn, Bacon, Boston

Marsaglia G, Bray TA (1964) A convenient method for generating normal variables. SIAM Rev 6(3):260–264

Mayer S, Schwind V, Schweigert R, Henze N (2018) The effect of offset correction and cursor on mid-air pointing in real and virtual environments. In: Proceedings of the 2018 CHI conference on human factors in computing systems. ACM, p 653

Mendes D, Relvas F, Ferreira A, Jorge J (2016) The benefits of dof separation in mid-air 3d object manipulation. In: Proceedings of the 22nd ACM conference on virtual reality software and technology. ACM, pp 261–268

Murata A, Iwase H (2001) Extending fitts' law to a three-dimensional pointing task. Human Movement Sci 20(6):791–805

Nguyen TTH, Duval T, Pontonnier C (2014) A new direct manipulation technique for immersive 3D virtual environments. In: ICAT-EGVE, pp 67–74

Oh JH, Lee SH, Lee BH, Park JI (2016) Probability analysis of position errors using uncooled IR stereo camera. Infrared Phys Technol 76:346–352

Pavlovych A, Stuerzlinger W (2009) The tradeoff between spatial jitter and latency in pointing tasks. In: Proceedings of the 1st ACM SIGCHI symposium on engineering interactive computing systems. ACM, pp 187–196

Pham DM, Stuerzlinger W (2019) Is the pen mightier than the controller? a comparison of input devices for selection in virtual and augmented reality. In: 25th ACM symposium on virtual reality software and technology, VRST '19. Association for Computing Machinery, New York, NY, USA. https://doi.org/10.1145/3359996.3364264

Romat H, Fender A, Meier M, Holz C (2021) Flashpen: A high-fidelity and high-precision multi-surface pen for virtual reality. In: 2021 IEEE virtual reality and 3D user interfaces (VR), pp 306–315. IEEE

Schwarz RJ, Taylor C (1955) The anatomy and mechanics of the human hand. Artificial limbs 2(2):22–35

Shih YC (2005) Effect of a splint on measures of sustained grip exertion under different forearm and wrist postures. Applied ergonomics 36(3):293–299

Song P, Goh WB, Hutama W, Fu CW, Liu X (2012) A handle bar metaphor for virtual object manipulation with mid-air interaction. In: Proceedings of the SIGCHI conference on human factors in computing systems, pp 1297–1306

Stiles RN (1980) Mechanical and neural feedback factors in postural hand tremor of normal subjects. J Neurophys 44(1):40–59 https://doi.org/10.1152/jn.1980.44.1.40 PMID: 7420138

Stoelen MF, Akin DL (2010) Assessment of fitts' law for quantifying combined rotational and translational movements. Human Factors 52(1):63–77

Stuerzlinger W, Wingrave CA (2011) The value of constraints for 3d user interfaces. In: Virtual realities. Springer, pp 203–223

Teather RJ, Pavlovych A, Stuerzlinger W, MacKenzie IS (2009) Effects of tracking technology, latency, and spatial jitter on object movement. In: IEEE symposium on 3D user interfaces, 2009. 3DUI 2009. IEEE, pp 43–50

Vanacken L, Grossman T, Coninx K (2007) Exploring the effects of environment density and target visibility on object selection in 3d virtual environments. In: 2007 IEEE symposium on 3D user interfaces. IEEE

Vanacken L, Grossman T, Coninx K (2009) Multimodal selection techniques for dense and occluded 3d virtual environments. Int J Human-Comput Stud 67(3):237–255

Vetter S, Bützler J, Jochems N, Schlick CM (2011) Fitts' law in bivariate pointing on large touch screens: Age-differentiated analysis of motion angle effects on movement times and error rates. In: International conference on universal access in human-computer interaction. Springer, pp 620–628

Welch GF (2009) History: the use of the kalman filter for human motion tracking in virtual reality. presence: teleoperators and virtual environments 18(1):72–91

Wolf D, Gugenheimer J, Combosch M, Rukzio E (2020) Understanding the heisenberg effect of spatial interaction: a selection induced error for spatially tracked input devices. In: Proceedings of the 2020 CHI conference on human factors in computing systems, pp 1–10

Xi C, Chen J, Zhao C, Pei Q, Liu L (2018) Real-time hand tracking using kinect. In: Proceedings of the 2nd international conference on digital signal processing, pp 37–42

Yan JH, Downing JH (2001) Effects of aging, grip span, and grip style on hand strength. Res Quart Exerc Sport 72(1):71–77

Development and Validation of a Mixed Reality Exergaming Platform for Fitness Training of Older Adults

Sergi Bermúdez i Badia, João Avelino, Alexandre Bernardino,
Mónica S. Cameirão, John Edison Muñoz, Heitor Cardoso,
Afonso Gonçalves, Teresa Paulino, Ricardo Ribeiro, Hugo Simão,
and Honorato Sousa

Abstract Populations are becoming older in developed countries because of low birth rates and increased life expectancy. At the same time, sedentary lifestyles are the 4th mortality factor worldwide. Exergames have been shown to motivate players to get physically active by promoting fun and enjoyment while exercising. However,

S. Bermúdez i Badia (✉) · M. S. Cameirão · A. Gonçalves · T. Paulino
Faculdade de Ciências Exatas e da Engenharia, Universidade da Madeira, Funchal, Portugal
e-mail: sergi.bermudez@staff.uma.pt

M. S. Cameirão
e-mail: monica.cameirao@staff.uma.pt

T. Paulino
e-mail: teresa.paulino@arditi.pt

S. Bermúdez i Badia · M. S. Cameirão · T. Paulino
NOVA Laboratory for Computer Science and Informatics (NOVA LINCS), Lisbon, Portugal

J. Avelino · A. Bernardino · H. Cardoso · R. Ribeiro · H. Simão
Instituto Superior Técnico, Universidade de Lisboa, Lisbon, Portugal
e-mail: joao.manuel.avelino@gmail.com

A. Bernardino
e-mail: alex@isr.tecnico.ulisboa.pt

H. Cardoso
e-mail: cheitor.cardoso@tecnico.ulisboa.pt

R. Ribeiro
e-mail: ribeiro@isr.ist.utl.pt

H. Simão
e-mail: hugalexsimon@gmail.com

J. E. Muñoz
System Design Engineering Department, University of Waterloo, Waterloo, ON, Canada
e-mail: john.munoz.hci@uwaterloo.ca

H. Sousa
Departament of Physical Education and Sport, University of Madeira, Funchal, Portugal
e-mail: honorato.sousa@staff.uma.pt

most exergames are not designed to produce recommended levels of exercise that elicit adequate physical responses in the aged population. Designing meaningful and enjoyable exergames for fitness training in older adults pose critical challenges in matching user's needs and motivators with game elements and typically do not consider the usability and cost-effectiveness constraints of target end-users and institutions. Here, we present the conception and field validation of PEPE—a gaming platform with mixed reality components whose purpose is to fight a sedentary lifestyle by promoting active aging in elderly-care centers. We show that PEPE's custom-made exergames can be successfully used by trainers for delivering sustained long-term training, with benefits in terms of efficiency, elicited physical activity, and perceived effort. Also, PEPE improved the overall perception of the quality of life and social relations in institutionalized older adults.

1 Introduction

The world population is aging at a fast pace. According to the United Nations, by 2050, 17% of the population will be 65 years old and over (United Nations, Department of Economic and Social Affairs, and Population Division 2020). This is a projected increase of 84% in Australia and New Zealand and 48% in Europe and Northern America. In Portugal, predictions indicate that the aging ratio will almost double by 2080, to 300 elderly people for every 100 young people, and the most aged region will be the Região Autónoma da Madeira, with 429 elderly people for every 100 young people ("Resident Population Projections 2018–2080" n.d.). These demographic changes parallel an increase in the life span that challenges our societies and the sustainability of health systems as we know them today. In addition, globally, more than 1.4 billion adults are at risk of disease from not doing enough physical activity (Guthold et al. 2018). In contrast, physically active elderly (≥ 60 years old) are at a decreased risk of cardiovascular mortality, breast and prostate cancer, falls, cognitive decline, and dementia and have a better quality of life and cognitive working (Cunningham et al. 2020). Dealing with the social and economic burden resulting from the increasing number of age-related disabilities represents a significant challenge for modern societies, particularly during the subsequent decades when an important aging of the world population is expected. Therefore, there is the need to develop solutions to promote active aging and prevent sedentarism, as well as to find new tools to support the large populations of patients that suffer chronic conditions because of aging.

In this context, the advances in information and communication technologies (ICT) and assistive technologies have the potential to increase quality of life (Chaumon et al. 2014) and change healthcare delivery models, reducing costs, and improving monitorization (Andreassen, Kjekshus, and Tjora 2015). These technological advances have a strong potential toward novel and low-cost treatments, health promotion, and disease monitoring and prevention. At a community level, such eHealth applications support the development of personalized and person-centric care methods and services that easily transfer from clinic-based training to at-home applications for telerehabilitation, creating a continuum of diagnostics and training possibilities, making real the new healthcare paradigm of 'home as care environment' (Datta et al. 2015; Korzun et al. 2017).

One possibility is the use of gaming technologies for physical exercising, known as exergames. Exergames have been shown to motivate players to get physically active by promoting fun and enjoyment while exercising. However, most exergames are not designed to produce recommended levels of exercise that elicit adequate physical responses for optimal training in the aged population. The design of meaningful and enjoyable exergames for fitness training in older adults poses critical challenges in matching user's needs and motivators with game elements. These challenges are often due to the lack of knowledge of game preferences of older adults, their little, or no technology literacy and reduced involvement of the target population in the design process. Furthermore, exergame platforms design typically does not take into consideration the usability and cost-effectiveness constraints of target end-users and institutions. Aspects like the simplicity of use for healthcare professionals, easy configuration for users with different motor abilities, easy maintenance, and setup are often disregarded and compromise the frequent and long-term use of the resources.

In the last 20 years, many mixed reality gaming platforms have been proposed engaging users through physical activity and some gained popularity in commercial devices. Two main components characterize the different solutions: the display type and the command interface. Most current solutions use portable display types carried by the player, such as headsets, mobile consoles, smartphones, and tablets. The games are commanded by moving the device around in the surrounding space and through interaction with tactile displays, buttons, or motion capture sensors on the device. A successful case is Pokémon Go, where players carry their mobile phones outdoors to collect items, with reported benefits in the reduction of psychological distress in workers (Watanabe et al. 2017). Although mixed reality games are mainly targeted at young adults, the aging population can also benefit from such an approach as it is prone to have a sedentary lifestyle and lack of motivation for exercise. However, decaying physical, perceptual, and cognitive capabilities in this population set specific constraints in the games and gaming platforms. Smartphone or tablet screens are often too small for older adults' visual acuity, and headsets are hard to set up and uncomfortable. There are, however, some intergenerational approaches such as the Age Invaders game (Khoo et al. 2008) to put together in play children, their parents, and grandparents in a mixed reality environment (Khoo et al. 2009).

Another approach is to use human body signals to interface games and interactive applications. This has been widely promoted among the game user research community (Hughes and Jorda 2021). Measuring players' responses when interacting with games by using physiological sensors provides the possibility of knowing seamlessly players' inner states that can be beneficial to adapt the experience. The most popular body signals used to create physiologically adaptive games are (i) electrocardiography (ECG) and other cardiovascular sensing (e.g., photoplethysmography), (ii) electroencephalography (EEG), (iii) electrodermal activity (EDA), (iv) electromyography (EMG), and (v) eye-tracking (Hughes and Jorda 2021). Physiological signatures of human states such as stress, cognitive load, cardiorespiratory performance, mood, and even emotions are constantly used to create adaptive experiences in interactive systems (Cowley et al. 2016). The concept of feeding back the measured body signals in real-time has also been popularized when using games for training self-regulation skills, known as biofeedback, and it is considered the grandparent of the more modern physiological computing approaches (Pope et al. 2014). A more sophisticated way of using body signals is to empower the system with algorithms capable of inferring human states (e.g., stress, engagement) by using physiological signals and react accordingly. This concept, known as the biocybernetics loop, uses knowledge from control theory to close the loop, allowing real-time automatic modulations to take place during the interaction for enhancing user experience (Pope et al. 2014). Biocybernetic loops to create physiologically adaptive applications can enhance the experience by assisting players in adjusting the game challenge via modifying the difficulty (e.g., dynamic difficulty adaptation). Although it is a fascinating and promising area in the field of affective and adaptive gaming, a recent review pointed out the lack of studies documenting and evaluating physiologically adaptive systems that can work outside research laboratories (Loewe and Nadj 2020). This aspect could be due to many variables associated with (i) the difficulties when interfacing physiological sensors to game engines, (ii) the challenges in deploying physiologically adaptive games in non-controlled environments (e.g., connectivity, data transmission), and (iii) the lack of integrated solutions (both hardware and software) that are user-friendly and do not require technologists for operation. Most of the applications that have used automatic adaptation driven by body signals are in the aviation and military applications, where the conditions are strictly monitored (e.g., body movements), and the activities are reduced to highly controlled working tasks (Loewe and Nadj 2020). In exergames, the automatic adaptation using fitness variables (e.g., heart rate) that can maximize the benefits of gaming while exercising has been previously implemented (Robinson et al. 2020). This concept, called the dual flow model, uses the conventional flow model (human state of full involvement) proposed by Csikszentmihalyi and adds an extra dimension of physiological correctness (Sinclair et al. 2009). The design of exergames considering elements of the dual flow model has been proposed as a way to create experiences that can be enjoyable and effective in eliciting the desired physiological effects (Martin-Niedecken and Götz 2017; Muñoz et al. 2018). Interfacing custom-made exergames with commercially available wearable devices have been proposed as one of the most feasible solutions with the potential to be adopted by players outside research laboratories (Pope et al. 2014; John Edison Muñoz et al. 2016a, b, c). However, commercially available solutions that combine body signals and exergaming are scarce, and they can be mainly found as experimental prototypes in research laboratories.[1]

Here, we present the conceptualization and field validation of PEPE—a gaming platform with mixed reality components whose purpose is to fight a sedentary lifestyle

---

[1] https://www.fitness-gaming.com/.

by promoting active aging in retirement homes. Its conceptualization followed several user-centered design cycles with end-users, therapists, gerontologists, physicians, sports scientists, and elderly institution managers, to provide easy to use, enjoyable, and effective experiences for both the exercise practitioners and trainers. The end result—PEPE—is a mixed reality platform that can be easily transported, configured, and deployed in elderly institutions to promote exercise. PEPE incorporates feedback from seniors from its physical implementation to its games, allowing the informed design and gamification of fitness training routines. The system uses floor-projected games and depth sensing, where the users can interact through body movements, either standing or sitting. By playing exergames, older adults can work on their physical fitness while training cognitive function through a rich diversification of stimuli. PEPE allows users to engage in personalized task-oriented activities, engaging motivational factors, a key aspect for successful training (Rizzo et al. 2011). Additionally, PEPE integrates physiological computing for online adaptation of exercise regimes. Further, the inclusion of multi-user gameplay to enable social interactions among users makes the approach unique. Bringing in social aspects into exercising can increase adherence as well as resistance to age-related cognitive decline (Dause and Kirby 2019). PEPE has been shown to be effective in stimulating elderly to practice physical exercise with the addition of fun and social interaction in multiple settings. Finally, the proposed approach has a high generalization potential as it can be applied to many other domains where goal-oriented repetition is needed to learn a skill (e.g., professional sports, dance, martial arts, etc.).

2 Developing PEPE: Portable Exergames Platform for the Elderly

PEPE is a novel, integrative, and cross-disciplinary approach that combines innovation and fundamental research in the areas of human–computer interaction, serious games, and physiological computing. Our goal was to develop a new generation of ICT-based solutions that can transform healthcare by optimizing resource allocation, reducing costs, improving, and enabling novel therapies, thus increasing quality of life. To that end, we developed an adaptive mixed reality physical training tool that can deliver online feedback on performance to prevent sedentarism, support active aging, and provide personalized tools for function (re-)training in the elderly population, which can be achieved thanks to its monitoring capacity by employing biosensors, computer vision systems, and exercise performance data (Fig. 1).

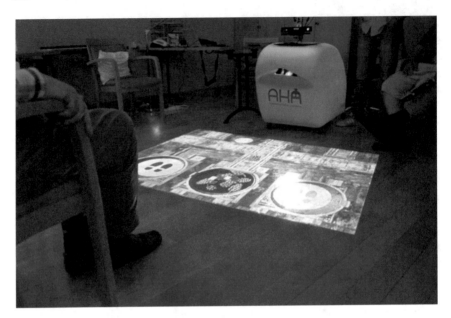

Fig. 1 PEPE consists of a wheeled mobile platform with a depth sensing camera and floor projection capabilities. It delivers a customizable exercise program through gamified activities and physiological adaptation that can be used through full-body interaction

2.1 User-Centered Design Targeting End-Users and Institutions

As our work targets institutionalized older adults, the perspectives of the caretakers and institution managers must be considered. In group activities, occupational therapists have the challenge of preparing sessions of physical or cognitive stimulation exercises. The preparation should be simple to prevent the drop of motivation in both the participants and the therapists. Games based on devices like headsets or smartphones often require a significant overhead in preparing the devices and the gaming space. Furthermore, maintenance and economic aspects are involved in the decisions of the institution managers to acquire those devices. In this section, we describe a study on the design of a mixed reality platform considering the expectations and needs of the users, therapists, and directors of elderly-care services. This study is based on user-centered design techniques to generate a customized solution that attempts to satisfy the desires and constraints of all interested parts. We departed from a technological basis and logistic requirement imposed by the nature of our research project augmented human assistance (AHA)[2] (Gouveia et al. 2018) associated with this work: The infrastructure required for the mixed reality platform should

---

[2] http://aha.isr.tecnico.ulisboa.pt/.

be easily transported and installed in multiple end-user sites to test and deploy the proposed solution in several contexts.

From that initial requirement, we performed an exploratory study in three elderly-care institutions: one private institution more focused on daily occupations, and two senior residences (one public and one private) with occupational and care services. The users and professionals of the institutions were consulted on the desirable characteristics of a platform for mixed reality games. Three sessions of about 60 min each were run in each institution, orchestrated by an investigator who watched, took notes, and recorded audio, supported by a professional of the visited institution. Participants were from multidisciplinary areas of the geriatric sector: 2 psychologists, one gerontologist, one occupational therapist, one psychotherapist, and one technical director. A total of 24 older adults, ranging in age from 66 to 94 years, were consulted during the three sessions. Seven participants were male, and 17 were female. Eleven participants had some type of motor disability. During the first session, we presented very basic concepts of possible instantiations of portable mixed reality platforms. In the second session, some drawings and sketches based on the outcomes of the first session were presented. Finally, participants could interact directly with a prototype developed following the user-centered design process in the last session. More details on the study can be found elsewhere (Simão and Bernardino 2017).

The results of the study pointed out in three main directions. The first issue pointed out by professionals related to the cognitive and motor limitations of some older adults, for example, dementia or reduced mobility. This implies that solutions requiring non-natural interfaces to control the games, like smartphones or joysticks, should be excluded, and games should be controlled by simple body gestures. This suggested non-intrusive motion captures devices, like the Kinect, to be the most adequate. Also, due to the motor limitations, participants should be able to play while standing, or sitting by people using wheelchairs or crutches, and controlled by any body part that is functional. So, game control should be easily customized for each particular player. As limitations in perceptual acuity demand for large displays of information, this also excludes smartphones, tablets, or mobile console platforms, instead suggesting projection-based mixed reality solutions.

The second issue pointed out by the professionals was related to the quick and easy setup of the exercise sessions. Due to the shortage of staff, time is an essential resource. It should be dedicated to effective exercise and not spent on complex setup procedures like installing wearable devices or external motion capture systems. Space management is also an issue since some rooms in institutions may be used for multiple purposes. Thus, the installation and uninstallation of the setup should be optimized. Also, the exercise sessions may have to be run in different spaces and sometimes in individual rooms. These constraints led to the concept of a compact platform that could integrate all the necessary components and be easily transportable between rooms.

The third issue was related to ergonomics and esthetics aspects. Professionals stated that the platform design should have an empathic design to increase the levels of acceptance and participation. Several forms, colors, decorations, and materials were proposed and iterated during the study. Esthetic lines from the robot Vizzy (Moreno et al. 2016), also used in the research project AHA, were exploited to reinforce a technology "brand" associated with this research. Combining the different user constraints with the initial requirements of the research team (easy transport, deploy, and test in different institutions), this resulted in a wheeled and compact system containing all necessary system components (motion sensor, projector, computer, configuration interfaces), able to fit in a normal car boot. Figure 2 presents the three main concepts developed during the user-centered design sessions. Both professionals and older users voted on the first design at the end of the sessions due to more empathic colors and rounded forms.

Fig. 2 Different design concepts worked out in the user-centered design sessions that illustrate the shape and color of the PEPE mobile platform when parked. The size is approximately of 80 × 60 × 60 cm. All designs consist of a wheeled platform that contains all hardware components, with openings for the floor projection and depth sensor, and a lid on top to uncover the access to the monitor and computer system

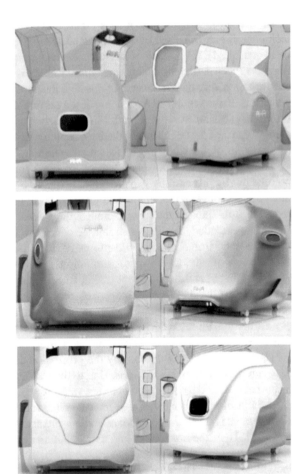

2.2 The Mobile Platform

During the user-centered co-design sessions, the concept of a compact and standalone prototype of the mixed reality platform for exergames was developed, integrating all the necessary components for the interactions and easy and quick transport and setup. The main components of the platform are the game interfaces for the users (display, command) and configuration interfaces for the professionals (touch screen). All components are managed by a PC computer.

The design of PEPE is presented in Fig. 3. Figure 3a shows the front view. Inside an enclosure of approximately 77 × 62 × 68 cm (length × 6 width × 6 height) are a computer and a projector. The projector beam passes through an opening in the enclosure to project the game elements on the floor. On the outside, fixed to an articulated arm, there is a Kinect sensor to sense the body pose and movement of players. The monitor in the front displays additional information of interest to the player but, in some cases, can be distracting to the player; thus, it can be removed. The monitor in the back displays information to the health professional and has a touch screen to facilitate the input of configuration commands. The articulated arm can be folded to store the external elements inside the enclosure (see Fig. 3b). Figure 3c shows the rear part with the detail of the opening on the back to fold the articulated arm, the rear touch screen panel for configuration, a folder with a wireless keyboard/mouse for advanced configuration and maintenance, and the mains plug. A mobile base with four freewheels supports the platform. To transport the platform in non-flat surfaces or over obstacles, there are two handles on the sides.

A critical decision had to be made regarding the projection surface. From the point of view of ease of configuration, two alternatives were considered: projection on the floor or a wall. Both technical and practical issues favored the decision for floor projection. First, image focus and sharpness exclusively depend on the distance between the projector and the projection's surface; therefore, a floor projection requires calibration once. Instead, a wall projection requires a re-calibration every time it is moved. Second, a wall projection configuration is hard to prevent occluding the projection (if the player is between the projector and the wall) or occluding the player's view (if the platform is between the player and the wall). Third, a projection on the floor ensures that the game area is free of obstacles and that the user actively observes the floor, reducing the chances of locomotion hazards.

However, there are two main issues in floor projections requiring attention. First, textured, very reflective, or dark floor surfaces can significantly change the graphical aspect of the game projections. In these cases, a white, non-reflective mat, or carpet can be used in front of the platform. If external illumination is kept at controlled levels, even dark and textured pavements like wood can be used comfortably (see Fig. 1). Second, the angle of players looking to the floor should not be too steep. This can be prevented by letting players play in a sitting position or at a larger distance from the projection.

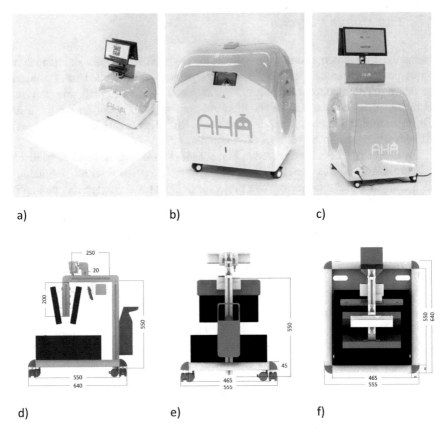

Fig. 3 PEPE prototype. Top row—with cover: **a** front view, **b** folded for car transportation, **c** rear view. Bottom row—folded views without cover: **d** lateral view, **e** front view, **f** top view. Dimensions are indicated in cm

2.2.1 Biocybernetic Loop Engine

The creation of software tools that streamline the integration of physiological signals in interactive games has been investigated, and multiple systems have been proposed. Neuromore[3] and NeuroPype[4] are two of the most interesting software tools that have included visual language programming and compatibility with popular physiological sensors (both research-grade and wearables) and communication protocols (e.g., lab streaming layer—LSL). A behavioral and affective rule-based tool was also created using one of the most popular game engines, Unity (Unity Technologies, San Francisco, USA) (Benlamine et al. 2021). Nevertheless, these software tools are mainly focused on algorithms and applications using neurophysiological signals (e.g., EEG), and their use to create physiologically adaptive exergames has not been

---

[3] https://www.neuromore.com/.

[4] https://www.neuropype.io/.

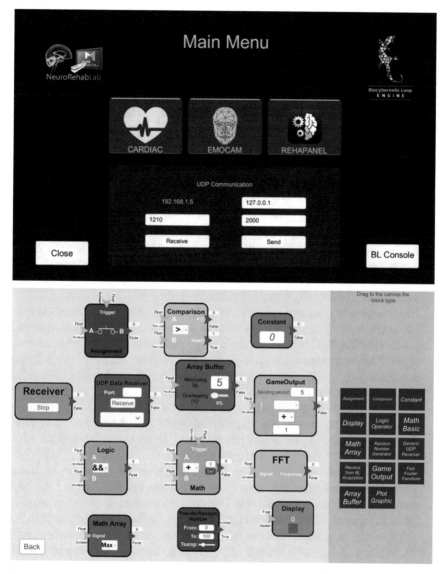

Fig. 4 Biocybernetic loop engine is a physiological computing tool created to facilitate integrating body signals into games and interactive applications. Top: acquisition panel. Bottom: adaptive rule console

reported. To tackle the previously reported limitations when integrating physiological signals into adaptive games, we have created a freely available integrative software tool that can be used to create and validate physiologically responsive exergames, the biocybernetic loop engine (BL engine)[5] (Muñoz et al. 2017).

The BL engine utilizes the closed-loop construct to create rule-based adaptations using physiological signals as inputs to modify game variables in real-time. It integrates multiple sensing technologies and a rule-creator environment that allows physiological computing designers to architect the logic behind the intended physiological adaptation to be integrated into the exergames. The BL engine is divided into three modules:

1. **Signal Acquisition (Fig. 4, top panel)**: The BL engine uses external software clients that access services (e.g., raw data, processed features) and allows streaming them through user datagram protocol (UDP), a popular message-oriented layer that facilitates data structuring and transmission. The BL engine uses a graphical user interface to allow capturing information from cardiovascular sensing devices (e.g., Polar Chest Strap Sensor, BioPlux, Bitalino), facial expression through the EmoCam (Freitas et al. 2017), which uses the Affectiva SDK,[6] EEG data using the Muse EEG wearable sensor and others using the Reh@Panel (Vourvopoulos et al. 2013). The BL engine is able to capture information from multiple devices simultaneously.

2. **Physiologically adaptive rule creator (Fig. 4, bottom panel)**: To create rule-based adaptations, the BL engine includes a console that runs in real-time and allows creating IF/THEN rules using both physiological features and game variables. The environment has multiple blocks to receive features from multiple protocols (e.g., UDP, open sound control—OSC, LSL) and create rules using comparisons, mathematical, and/or logical operations, as well as game output blocks to modulate game variables in real-time. Visual scripting allows the creation of adaptive rules via dragging/dropping those boxes and connecting them to create the physiological pipeline (e.g., IF heart rate is more than 100 BPMs, THEN increase game difficulty).

3. **Communication with exergames**: Games developed in Unity can be transformed into physiologically adaptive games using the BL engine.[7] A game connector (prefabricated package in Unity) facilitates the integration of custom-made exergames with the adaptive rule creator; therefore, the modulation in the game can be programmed in the BL engine. The communication between the BL engine and a game is bidirectional, meaning that, the game informs the BL engine which variables are susceptible to be adapted, and in turn, the BL engine streams back the value changes that should be applied.

The BL engine has been validated as an integrative and agile tool for integrating physiological adaptation in exergames (Muñoz et al. 2017) and virtual reality simulators (Muñoz et al. 2016a, b, c).

---

[5] http://neurorehabilitation.m-iti.org/tools/en/ble.

[6] http://developer.affectiva.com/.

[7] https://sites.google.com/view/physio2games/material.

2.2.2 Exergames

A set of 5 different exergames were developed to address the main dimensions of fitness training according to the recommendations of the ACSM (American College of Sports Medicine and Bushman 2017). These games were created in a user-centered design process involving researchers, sports professionals, and older adults as described in (Muñoz et al. 2019) and reproduce a cultural journey of Portuguese traditions. These are described in the following:

1. **Grape Stomping (Fig. 5a)**: It replicates the traditional methods of wine production, where people step on grapes to extract the juice to produce wine. The game aims to produce as much grape juice as possible, which elicits a stepping-in-place exercise, typically used in aerobic training. This is combined with arm pulling motion for extra variety. This game presents three barrels, and grapes are brought into the play area with a conveyor belt. The grape bunches can come in three kinds, green, red, and rotten (distractors). The players stand on the projected barrels and, by flexion–extension of the arms, catch the grapes from the conveyor. Once in the barrels, the player can tread the grapes, which are converted into a rising level of juice contained on the barrel. Each grape bunch needs some steps to be successfully processed. As soon as the grape juice hits the top that barrel starts emptying its contents through a channel and becomes unavailable to play, forcing players to move laterally into another barrel. The game can be configured to have an extra cognitive difficulty layer by having each barrel requiring specific amounts of red and green grape bunches. Pulling rotten grapes into any barrel freezes the barrel for some time. The height that the feet must be raised from the ground to stomp a grape successfully can be configured at startup, together with the percentage of rotten grapes (distractors), the grape type requirements per barrel, and the time between new grape bunches on the belt. This allows an adjustment of the exercise difficulty.

2. **Rabelos (Fig. 5b)**: For centuries, the Douro river valley has been a wine-producing region of Portugal, famous for the port wine. In the past, to transport the wine barrels downstream, from the vineyards to the city's cellars, wooden cargo boats, named Rabelos, were used. This game replicates those voyages. The goal of the game is to collect as many barrels as possible while avoiding the river rocks. The player is in charge of navigating a Rabelo boat downriver, avoiding obstacles, and docking on the margins to collect barrels. The game aims at exercising upper limbs and takes a third-person perspective from behind the boat, where the riverbanks are aligned with the projection's lateral edges. The boat position on the river is controlled through the player's waist position, directly mapped to the projection or by leaning the trunk sideways. To move the boat forward, an arm rotation gesture that replicates the rowing activity is required. As the players row the boat downriver, they encounter rocks they have to avoid through lateral movement and barrel-filled docks at the river's margins. These docks must be approached, and their barrels collected via an elbow extension-flexion motion. The difficulty is set by adjusting the rowing mode (light or hard),

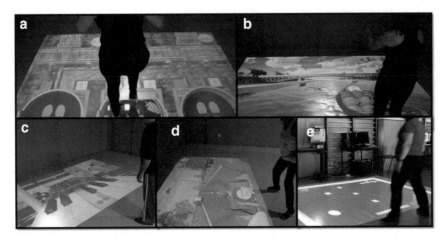

Fig. 5 Set of exergames developed. Grape stomping (**a**) and Exerpong (**e**) train aerobic fitness. Rabelos (**b**) trains upper and lower limb strength while the Exerfado (**c**) and Toboggan Ride (**d**) train motor ability

the distance between docks, rocks, and their probability of appearing during gameplay.

3. **Exerfado (Fig. 5c)**: This game reproduces the environment of a typical Fado house from Lisbon, Portugal, where people go at night to eat, drink, and listen to live music. Inspired by the Guitar Hero video game, Exerfado resorts to music's potential as a physical activity stimulator. The projection renders a keyboard on the floor with seven keys aligned with the projection's bottom. The player stands at the bottom of the projection, and both feet control which key they want to activate as musical notes travel downwards. The goal is to have the correct key activated when a musical note hits it. Therefore, the player must play the piano with their feet in synchrony with the visual cues. Over which track each note appears depends on the pitch of the music being played, with low pitch-making notes spawn at the keyboard's left keys and high pitch at the right. Some special notes can be activated by an arm "swiping" movement. This activity is intended to train agility in both upper and lower limbs. This swiping gesture can be set to short or wide arm extension, enabling it to be personalized to users with different capabilities. Missed musical notes lead to distortion of the song being played, producing negative audio feedback. The music to be played can be chosen from an extensive list of midi files, each with different durations. By setting, at startup, the falling notes' speed, the percentage of bonuses, and the time between consecutive notes, the difficulty is controlled.

4. **Toboggan (Fig. 5d)**: In Madeira, Portugal, a unique way of transportation was used in the past. Wicker toboggans, driven by two people, would carry passengers downhill, from the hills to the city center. In the game, this activity is recreated virtually. The toboggan and player are presented in the center of the screen from a third-person perspective. Lateral movement is controlled just like Rabelos,

by moving sideways along the bottom edge of the projection. Alternatively, the lateral movement can be also controlled by trunk rotation. The speed is adjusted through trunk inclination; leaning the trunk forward accelerates the toboggan while leaning backward deaccelerates it. The trunk inclination angles can be adjusted to each user for both acceleration and deacceleration options. Over the path, there are pedestrian crossings and car intersections to force the player to slow down. While the game's goal is to drive as far as possible in the allotted time, there are also obstacles to avoid, bonuses to collect, and speed limits to keep. Difficulty is set by changing the distance between bonuses, and the percentage of bonuses and obstacles during game play.

5. **Exerpong (Fig. 5e)**: This is an exergame adaptation of the classic games of Pong or Breakout, used to provide a fast-paced game experience aimed at training aerobic endurance (Muñoz et al. 2016a). In this game, the player controls a virtual paddle through lateral movements while a ball bounces around the walls. The player, who stands along the bottom of the projection, has his or her waist tracked, and the game matches the paddle location on the screen with it so that both player and paddle are always aligned. The ball bounces around the other three edges of the screen covered by walls; the player must then use the paddle by moving laterally along the bottom of the projection to prevent the ball from going through the lowest edge. A pattern of colorful bricks is represented at the center of the screen; these bricks get destroyed whenever the ball passes over them twice. The game's goal is to clear these bricks without letting balls pass through the bottom of the screen. The game difficulty can be adjusted by varying the paddle's width and the ball's size and velocity. Alternatively, the game can adjust its difficulty according to the player's physiological responses when controlled by the BL engine.

All exergames implement the same rewarding system which consists of offering a medal whenever one of the three ranks is reached, which can be bronze, silver, or gold. Those ranks are set proportionally to the difficulty setting and gameplay duration. Moreover, all games are able to store user data and display the score evolution over time.

3   Field Studies

This section reports on three different studies performed with PEPE, to validate (1) its effectiveness as a tool for physical activity training in a longitudinal randomized controlled study, (2) assess the feasibility of the biocybernetic adaptation, and (3) to assess its acceptance by end-users in elderly-care institutions.

3.1   Impact of Exergames in Physical Activity in the Senior Gym

To evaluate the effectiveness of the five exergames presented previously (Gonçalves et al. 2017) in eliciting moderate–to-vigorous physical activity (MVPA) levels in the elderly, we conducted a three-month-long randomized controlled trial (Gonçalves et al. 2021). Two conditions were tested, each with its corresponding participants' group: a combined exercise (exergames and conventional) training group and a conventional exercise training group, acting as a control. Both groups underwent two weekly physical training sessions, equivalent in frequency, intensity, time, and type (FITT) (Heyward and Gibson 2014). The ACSM recommendations for multi-dimensional training for older adults (American College of Sports Medicine and Bushman 2017) were followed to structure the training, while the difference between the groups was in the exercise modality practiced at the sessions.

- *Exergames group*—Combination of exergames and conventional training. Engaging once a week in an individual exergames session and also on a conventional group exercise session.
- *Control group*—Conventional training. Engaging in conventional exercise group sessions two times per week.

All sessions were performed in an exercise room of a local senior gymnasium. Conventional training sessions were based on the gym's exercise patterns. Odd-numbered sessions (1–23) of both groups were always conventional exercise, while the even sessions (2–24) were conventional for the *control* group and exergames for the *exergames* group.

We relied on both objective (measured) and subjective [rate of perceived exertion (RPE)] data to quantify physical activity (PA) levels. The ActiGraph WGT3X-BT (Actigraph, Florida, USA) accelerometer was used to quantify PA: time people spent in MVPA (in minutes), the EE (metabolic equivalent—METs). This sensor has been widely used and is considered a gold-standard tool to quantify PA in different populations (Chu et al. 2017). Subjective data on the levels of physical exertion after each exercise routine was collected using a pictorial version of the 0–10 rating of RPE scale OMNI (Chodzko-Zajko et al. 2009).

A total of 31 active community-dwelling older adults were recruited where the study took place, with inclusion criteria of: 50–75 years old, able to read and write, members of the gymnasium for more than three months, able to understand the procedure, game rules and goals, no severe visual impairments, no impediment to exercise practice, no severe or unstable heart diseases, and no falls over the past six months. 16 were allocated to the *control* group (12 females, age avg. 69.1 SD 4.4) and 15 to the *exergames* group (10 females, age avg. 67.6 SD 5). All the participants gave their informed written consent.

Data was divided into two, the odd sessions consisting of the conventional sessions of both conditions and the even sessions of both conventional and exergames. This allowed us to analyze: (1) the differences between conventional exercise and exergames' sessions and (2) the users' response to the exercise training program. For analysis of these data, a two-way mixed MANOVA was used. The between-subjects factor was the training program, each participant was allocated to (2 levels), and the within-subjects factor was program progression (session number). The dependent variables were RPE on the OMNI scale, METs spent, and minutes of MVPA in a session. Separate ANOVAs were run for each dependent variable to ascertain which ones were genuinely affected by the training program, where the degrees of freedom were corrected using the Huynh–Feldt estimate of sphericity. There was incomplete data from accelerometry on the 1st, 2nd, 6th, 7th, 9th, and 11th weeks of the study. Thus, as the two-way mixed MANOVA requires complete data, we removed those weeks from the analysis. Additionally, data from the 5th and 8th weeks was also excluded for failing Levene's test of equal variance. The remaining weeks, 3rd, 4th, 10th, and 12th were analyzed using the MANOVA with four levels of within-subjects factor. The significance level used was $\alpha = 0.05$, and Bonferroni's correction was used to correct for multiple comparisons. All analysis was done using IBM SPSS Statistics 22 (IBM, New York, USA).

Comparing the conventional exercise sessions of the *control* group with the corresponding weekly exergame sessions of the *exergames* program group revealed a statistically significant effect of the type of training program, Wilks' $\Lambda = 0.244$, $F(3, 27) = 27.958$, $p < 0.05$. Univariate ANOVAs exposed significant differences on all three outcomes, with more METs spent on *control* sessions ($M = 2.976$, SD $= 0.106$) than *exergames* ($M = 2.046$, SD $= 0.110$), $F(1, 29) = 37.138$, $p < 0.05$ (Fig. 6); but, on the other hand, MVPA, $F(1, 29) = 11.044$, $p < 0.05$, and OMNI, $F(1, 29) = 7.977$, $p < 0.05$, had higher marginal means for the *exergames* program ($M = 36.183$, SF $= 0.545$; $M = 3.767$, SD $= 0.271$) than *control* ($M = 33.664$, SD $= 0.527$; $M = 2.703$, SD $= 0.262$) (Fig. 6).

The interaction effect between the type of training program and time, Wilks' $\Lambda = 0.526$, $F(9, 21) = 2.106$, $p = 0.077$, was not statistically significant. The univariate ANOVAs of the outcome variables presented no significant differences for OMNI, $F(2.517) = 1.253$, $p = 0.296$, METs, $F(3.000) = 1.733$, $p = 0.166$, and MVPA, $F(2.911) = 1.198$, $p = 0.315$.

Comparing conventional exercise sessions of participants in the *exergames* exercise program with the equivalent (conventional) session by the *control* group revealed a statistically significant effect of the type of training program on the dependent variables, Wilks' $\Lambda = 0.723$, $F(3, 27) = 3.444$, $p < 0.05$. Separate univariate ANOVAs on the outcomes did not show significant differences in both spent METs, $F(1, 29) = 2.280$, $p = 0.142$, and MVPA, $F(1, 29) = 0.041$, $p = 0.841$. However, significant differences were observed in the OMNI scale, $F(1, 29) = 6.119$, $p < 0.05$, with higher score of RPE ($M = 4.117$, SD $= 0.302$) for the *exergames* exercise program than *control* group ($M = 3.078$ SD $= 0.292$) (Fig. 6). There was not a statistically significant interaction effect between the type of training program and time, Wilks' $\Lambda = 0.563$, $F(9, 21) = 1.810$, $p = 0.126$. Univariate analysis of the outcomes also failed to find significant difference in METs, $F(2.220) = 2.905$, $p = 0.057$, MVPA, $F(2.260) = 0.805$, $p = 0.465$, and OMNI, $F(2.596) = 0.830$, $p = 0.467$.

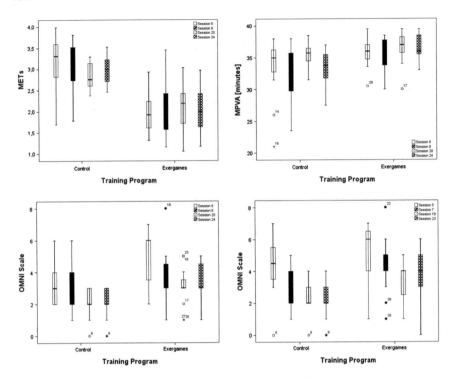

Fig. 6 Total METs spent (top left) and minutes of MVPA (top right) during conventional sessions by participants in the control program and exergame sessions by the subjects in the exergames exercise program, at weeks 3, 4, 10, and 12. Self-reported exertion, on the OMNI scale, weeks 3, 4, 10, and 12 at the end of the conventional exercise sessions by subjects in the control program and the end of the exergames sessions by the subjects in the exergames program (bottom left) and at the end of the conventional exercise sessions by participants of both the conventional and combined exercise program (bottom right)

Our results show that exergaming sessions performed by older adults can meet the international recommendations of MVPA. Exergame sessions were able to meet the MVPA goals and surpassed the minutes of MVPA spent during conventional exercise, which is a benefit for the growth and preservation of functional aptitude. Having more time spent in MVPA and lower METs during exergaming might be interpreted as participants in the conventional workout having exercised with higher intensities but spending less time within the recommended levels when compared with exergaming. Therefore, participants during exergaming were able to exercise with lower intensity levels but, at the same time exercising within the recommended levels for longer, being more efficient in their training as more energy expenditure does not necessarily mean greater health benefits in the older population (Heyward and Gibson 2014). One possible explanation of why the participants spent more time in MVPA during exergames sessions than traditional exercise is that the games can keep players engaged with the activity, as the participants get absorbed by the individual stimulation of a game that reacts to them, which in conventional training would equate to personal training. This might have meaningful impacts on the long-term adoption of exergaming technology in the older population, producing a firm notion of a safe environment for exercising (Skjæret et al. 2016). Subjective data from the OMNI never exceeded the hard intensity (score = 8), which successfully meets the ACSM guidelines (Jones and Rose 2005).

3.2 Assessing the Effect of Physiological Adaptation

A cardio-adaptive, floor-projected version of the classic game pong, Exerpong, was used to investigate the effectiveness of using the BL engine to create physiological adaptation in real-time. A Motorola 360 smartwatch was used to stream to the BL engine heart rate (HR) data from the photoplethysmography (PPG) sensor at a frequency of 1 Hz. The goal of the physiological adaptation was to drive players to their target HR zone, for which we used 55% of the HR reserve, which is within the ACSM guidelines (40–70%) for older adults (Heyward and Gibson 2014). An experiment was conducted to explore how physiological adaptation could modulate the cardiorespiratory responses of older adults to Exerpong, in two different versions of the game, with and without physiological adaptation. This stage is called psychophysiological modeling (Muñoz et al. 2016a). Results from this stage revealed that the ball speed was a good candidate to modulate older adults' HR in real-time. Hence, Exerpong was interfaced with the BL engine, and the ball speed was used as a variable to close the loop using HR data. That is, based on the average difference every 30 s between the current and the target HR, the ball speed was altered through a proportional controller with the following equation being $Kp = 0.06$:

$$\Delta Speed_{Ball} = K_p \Delta \left(HR_{target} - HR_{30s\_average} \right)$$

Subsequently, an experiment involving 15 community-dwelling older adults (11 females, ages 66 ± 7 years, height 1.60 ± 0.08 m, weight 73.7 ± 14.8 kg) was conducted in a local senior gymnasium, comparing the cardio-adaptive version of the Exerpong (adaptive Exerpong) versus conventional cardiorespiratory training (control) sessions for seniors. Results demonstrated that participants spent around 40% more time in their individual target HR zone (state of desired cardiorespiratory performance) when using the adaptive Exerpong compared to conventional exercise (Fig. 7). In addition, participants showed lower RMSE values in the adaptive Exerpong ($M = 15.2$, $SD = 8.3$) when compared with the control condition ($M = 24.3$, $SD = 6.4$). Statistical analysis revealed that the difference was significant, $F(1.0, 14.0) = 12.3$, $p < 0.05$, $r = 0.44$. (Muñoz et al. 2018). Finally, we can conclude that the biocybernetic adaptation delivered a more controlled, safe, and effective cardiovascular training avoiding risky situations while maintaining good levels of enjoyment.

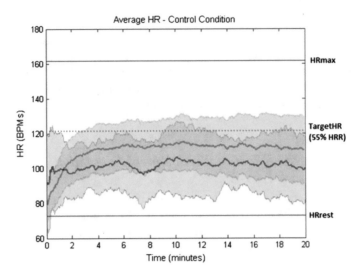

Fig. 7 HR responses during the control (blue) and the adaptive Exerpong (black) conditions over the 20 min of exercise. The solid line indicates the mean participant response ± standard deviation (solid area). The resting and maximum HR and target HR values used for the physiological adaptation are also indicated. Adapted from (Muñoz et al. 2018)

3.3 Group Sessions in Senior Facilities

The benefits of mixed reality games in physical, cognitive, and psychological dimensions have been demonstrated before, but not many works have addressed the social dimensions, which are quite important for the overall quality of life (QoL). To bridge this gap, we have studied how our mixed reality exergaming approach contributes to the social dimensions of QoL of institutionalized older adults. We have run a series of groups sessions with residents of a nursing home in Lisbon, Portugal, where participants played exergames with cultural motifs to trigger memories and promote relatedness and engagement.

A sample of $n = 18$ participants (85.28 ± 6.02 year-old, gender $F = 12$, $M = 6$) was selected among the resident of a nursing home and divided in 3 groups, suggested by the therapist of the residence and based on Barthel index score. Group 1 (G1: $n = 6$, $F = 5$, $M = 1$) includes participants with high levels of autonomy and functionality that perform the exergames while standing. Group 2 (G2: $n = 5$, $F = 0$, $M = 5$) and Group 3 (G3: $n = 7$, $F = 7$, $M = 0$) have lower levels of autonomy and perform the exergames while seated. For a detailed description of the selection and exclusion criteria, please refer to (Cardoso et al. 2019).

The study ran for three months with weekly sessions. It started with one assessment session to assess the baseline condition of the users. Then, there were 11 group training sessions and a final assessment session at the end of the study. Each group training session lasted for about 90–120 min. The group sessions were run in two different settings. G1 performed activities in a large room with enough space for

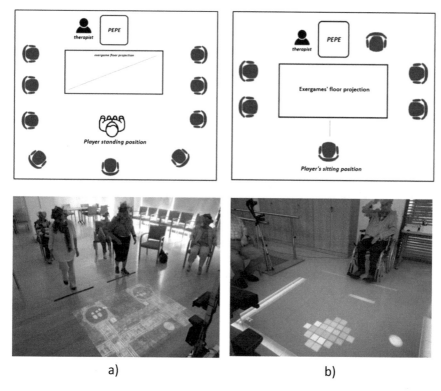

a)   b)

Fig. 8 Schematics of the experimental settings (top) and illustrative picture during the trials (bottom). **a** Main activities room, where Group 1 participants play in standing mode. **b** Physiotherapy gym where Groups 2 and 3 play in sitting mode

the playing area and chairs set in a semicircle around the playing area where the participants (or other residents not participating in the study) could observe the player executing its exercise. Groups 2 and 3, which had reduced mobility and need of careful supervision, performed the exercises in a private room where only the participants and therapists were present.

During the sessions, participants played each game for three minutes. After a player finished the game, there was a period to visualize and communicate the score to stimulate the competitiveness among players. Then, the player returned to his/her seat, and the next player in the round started the exergame. Overall, G1 participants play 5 of the exergames in our library during a session. G2 and G3, due to limited mobility, played only 4 of the 5 exergames, which were adapted to the sitting position. Other exergames configurations (speed, difficulty, distracting elements) were also carefully configured and adapted considering the disabilities of the participants of each group (Cardoso et al. 2019).

For assessment, besides demographic data such as age, gender, schooling, and number of attended sessions, were used the *satisfaction with social support scale*

(SSSS) (Wethington and Kessler 1986), which analyzes the person's perceived satisfaction with friends, family, and social activities they do together. SSSS has 15 items evaluated in a 1–5-point Likert scale, where a higher score corresponds to better social support. The 15 items are organized into 4 sub-dimensions: "satisfaction with friends", to measure the satisfaction with friends; "intimacy", which measures the perception of the existence of intimate social support; "family satisfaction", which measures satisfaction with existing family social support; and "social activities", which measures the satisfaction with the performed social activities.

We also used the WHOQOL-BREF scale (Skevington et al. 2004), a 5 Likert points scale composed of 26 items, with four assessment domains, physical health domain (sleep, energy, mobility, medical treatment to function in daily life, level of satisfaction with their capacity for work), psychological domain (concentrate, self-esteem, body image, spirituality, frequency of positive or negative feelings), social relationships (satisfaction with personal relationships, social support systems, and sexual satisfaction), and environment domain (safety and security, home and physical environment satisfaction, finance, information, leisure activity, accessibility, and transportation satisfaction). This scale is often used under the elderly population with good accuracy in quality of life perception evaluation.

Statistical analysis was performed with SPSS v.25 software. Despite the reduced sample size ($n = 18$), the Shapiro–Wilk test showed that data was normally distributed. Two-tailed paired samples T-tests were executed to determine the significance of differences between the study's beginning and end. ANOVA was used to find statistical differences between groups, and Pearson correlation test analyzed the correlation between the number of attendances to the group training sessions with any other variable. In G3, 3 participants attended less than 50% of the group sessions and were removed from the post-intervention analysis. However, they were still considered for the correlation analysis.

From the statistical analysis, we observed some interesting results such as score improvements between pre (1) and post (2) intervention regarding the perception of social relations quality domain (from WHOQOL-BREF scale) and in the satisfaction with friends domain (from SSSS) at the end of the study (Table 1).

Regarding differences between groups, the ANOVA analysis revealed that G1 had a higher and significantly different mean score in the satisfaction with social activities domain (from SSSS) when compared to the others groups (see Table 2).

Table 1 Paired sample tests

Variable	Paired sample test			
	N	Mean	p	df
Soc. relation quality (1)	15	3.64	0.003	14
Soc. relation quality (2)	15	4.06		
Satisf. w/friends (1)	15	18.40	0.044	14
Satisf. w/friends (2)	15	9.66		

Table 2 Significant differences between groups in ANOVA test

Social activities satisfaction	ANOVA		
	Mean diff	P	95% confidence interval
Group 1–Group 2	4.000*	0.001	1.6826–6.3174
Group 2–Group 3	2.750*	0.035	0.1827–5.3173

* p < 0.05

Concerning correlations, the attendance of group sessions (number of attended sessions by the participants) showed a positive and significant moderate correlation with the social relations domain ($r = 0.491, p = 0.038$), indicating that attendance to the group sessions was an important element to establish social relations and improve their quality over the time.

4 Conclusions

Here, we presented the portable exergames platform for the elderly (PEPE). This is an integrated mixed reality platform including custom-designed hardware and software to address the needs of the older adult population and healthcare institutions. Our main goal was to develop a system capable of promoting physical activity following validated guidelines and a user-centered approach involving all stakeholders. The participatory approach informed us on the challenges of cognitive and motor constrains in institutionalized populations and strategies to overcome them through customizable natural user interfaces. Also, it informed us about the deployment requirements and setup limitations in shared spaces in healthcare institutions, and of esthetic preferences. From a hardware point of view, a quick and easy to set up mobile platform was developed, which addresses cognitive and motor limitations of our target population with the integration of depth sensing cameras. A short-through floor projection system combined with the on-board depth sensing makes this system calibration free and deployable in a couple of minutes, while allowing standing and seated interaction with its content. Also the ergonomics and esthetics were chosen to facilitate its acceptance. The final system, PEPE, consists of a mobile mixed reality platform that delivers floor-projected exergames controlled through markerless full-body tracking. PEPE includes five highly customizable mixed reality games developed in Unity that address the main dimensions of fitness training according to the recommendations of the ACSM. Additionally, PEPE utilizes a closed-loop construct that exploits rule-based adaptations through physiological signals to intelligently modify game requirements in real-time. This is achieved through the biocybernetic loop engine, which enables the easy creation of adaptation rules through a visual language that communicates in real-time with both physiological measurement devices and the exergames, using standard and open protocols.

The system has been deployed in multiple sites aiming to address and validate its multiple facets in the context of different studies and has been shown to be effective in stimulating elderly to practice physical exercise with the addition of fun and social interaction. First as a feasible social platform to engage elderly in physical activity in elderly-care institutions. Then, addressed its efficacy in a randomized controlled trial compared to training sessions delivered by certified personal trainers. Finally, its adaptation capabilities compared to a non-adaptive approach. When applied regularly in group sessions at nursing homes, PEPE improved the overall perception of the quality of life and social relations in institutionalized older adults. We also show that the developed set of custom-made exergames can be successfully used by trainers to set up personalized training sessions and can be used in combination with regular exercise for sustained long-term training, exposing differences between traditional physical training and exergaming in terms of efficiency, elicited physical activity, and perceived effort. Data revealed that while participants spent more time in moderate-to-vigorous physical activity during exergaming, they also spent less energy, thus working out at lower intensities but for a more sustained amount of time. We also showed that physiologically augmented exergames with PEPE lead players to exert around 40% more time in the recommended effort levels than conventional training, avoiding over-exercising, and maintaining good enjoyment levels. Hence, the use of the combination of the multiple facets of PEPE—gaming, physiological adaptation, and its deployment in elderly institutions—has a high potential for the higher efficacy of computer mediated training and additional extrinsic motivational factors of gaming. However, it is very difficult to disentangle the actual contribution of each of those components and the particular software and hardware design decisions of PEPE in the presented studies. Thus, it is possible that other means of VR other than floor projection or set of games could deliver different results. Factors such as, for instance, the size of the area of the play as well and the details on the full-body interaction modalities used during gaming have a decisive effect on exertion.

There are, however, some limitations in the work here presented. First, the PEPE design has been developed through a participatory design with day care institutions and end-users that may not necessarily capture the specific needs of all potential end-user populations as well as healthcare institutions. The technology available at this time limited the size of the floor projection, being it now possible to have short-throw projectors with larger aperture and more contrast. In addition, none of the presented studies were performed exploiting all the features of PEPE. That is, the 3-month longitudinal study did not include the biocybernetic loop construct. Hence, the efficacy of a PEPE exploiting all its features is likely to differ from the one reported here. Similarly, the population tested on our randomized controlled trial and biocybernetic loop construct is a healthy sample and does not represent the average institutionalized end-user. Hence, further studies are needed to quantify PEPE's efficacy on different patient populations.

Overall, the work presented here shows the potential of using entertainment technologies to develop new training paradigms that are easy to use, engaging, effective, and well-received by end-users and institutions. The results show that exergames can be used by older adults to perform exercise sessions that meet the international recommendations of MVPA and that are a feasible complement to current practices in senior gymnasiums and elderly-care institutions.

Acknowledgements The authors thank Funchal's Santo António municipal gymnasium and all the participants for their cooperation. This work was supported by the Fundação para a Ciência e Tecnologia through the AHA project (CMUPERI/HCI/0046/2013), NOVA-LINCS [PEest/UID/CEC/04516/2019] and LARSyS—[PEest/UID/50009/2020], and ARDITI (Agência Regional para o Desenvolvimento da Investigação, Tecnologia e Inovação).

References

American College of Sports Medicine, Bushman BA (2017) ACSM's Complete Guide to Fitness and Health. Human Kinetics

Andreassen HK, Kjekshus LE, Tjora A (2015) Survival of the project: a case study of ICT innovation in health care. Soc Sci Med 132:62–69. https://doi.org/10.1016/j.socscimed.2015.03.016

Benlamine MS, Dufresne A, Beauchamp MH, Frasson C (2021) BARGAIN: behavioral affective rule-based games adaptation interface–towards emotionally intelligent games: application on a virtual reality environment for socio-moral development. User Model User-Adap Inter 31(2):287–321

Cardoso H, Bernardino A, Sanches M, Loureiro L (2019) Exergames and their benefits in the perception of the quality of life and socialization on institutionalized older adults. In: 2019 5th experiment international conference (Exp.at'19), pp 298–304. https://doi.org/10.1109/EXPAT.2019.8876469

Chaumon M-E, Michel C, Bernard FT, Croisile B (2014) Can ICT improve the quality of life of elderly adults living in residential home care units? from actual impacts to hidden artefacts. Behav Inf Technol 33(6):574–590. https://doi.org/10.1080/0144929X.2013.832382

Chodzko-Zajko WJ, Proctor DN, Fiatarone Singh MA, Minson CT, Nigg CR, Salem GJ, Skinner JS (2009) Exercise and physical activity for older adults. Med Sci Sports Exerc 41(7):1510–30

Chu AHY, Ng SHX, Paknezhad M, Gauterin A, Koh D, Brown MS, Müller-Riemenschneider F (2017) Comparison of wrist-worn fitbit flex and waist-worn actigraph for measuring steps in free-living adults. PLoS ONE 12(2):e0172535

Cowley B, Filetti M, Lukander K, Torniainen J, Henelius A, Ahonen L, Barral O et al (2016) The psychophysiology primer: a guide to methods and a broad review with a focus on human–computer interaction. Found Trends® Human–Comput Interact 9(3–4):151–308

Cunningham C, Sullivan RO, Caserotti P, Tully MA (2020) Consequences of physical inactivity in older adults: a systematic review of reviews and meta-analyses. Scand J Med Sci Sports 30(5):816–827.https://doi.org/10.1111/sms.13616

Datta SK, Bonnet C, Gyrard A, Ferreira da Costa RP, Boudaoud K (2015) Applying internet of things for personalized healthcare in smart homes. In: 2015 24th wireless and optical communication conference (WOCC), pp 164–169. https://doi.org/10.1109/WOCC.2015.7346198

Dause TJ, Kirby ED (2019) Aging gracefully: social engagement joins exercise and enrichment as a key lifestyle factor in resistance to age-related cognitive decline. Neural Regen Res 14(1):39–42. https://doi.org/10.4103/1673-5374.243698

Freitas D, Muñoz JE, Badia SBi (2017) EmoCam: capturing emotions using non-invasive technologies. https://neurorehabilitation.m-iti.org/lab/wp-content/uploads/2017/07/Diogo_Freitas_-_Projecto__Esta%C3%ACgio_-_Sergi_Bermu%C3%ACdez_i_Badia.pdf

Gonçalves A, Muñoz J, Cameirão MS, Gouveia ÉR, Sousa H, Bermudez i Badia S (2021) The benefits of custom exergames for fitness, balance, and health-related quality of life: a randomized controlled trial with community-dwelling older adults. Games Health J 10(4):245–253.https:// doi.org/10.1089/g4h.2020.0092

Gonçalves A, Muñoz J, Gouveia É, Cameirão M, Badia SBi (2017) Portuguese tradition inspired exergames for older people. In: IcSPORTS 2017 - Extended Abstracts - AHA. Funchal, Portugal. https://www.researchgate.net/profile/Sergi_Bermudez_i_Badia/publication/320852961_Portug uese_Tradition_Inspired_Exergames_for_Older_People_Strategic_Tools_to_Promote_Functio nal_Fitness/links/59fdff68458515d0706ac05a/Portuguese-Tradition-Inspired-Exergames-for-Older-People-Strategic-Tools-to-Promote-Functional-Fitness.pdf

Gouveia ÉR, Bernardino A, Cameirão MS, Cardona JM, Gonçalves A, Paulino T, Sousa H et al (2018) Augmented human assistance (AHA)—active aging · serious games · assistive robotics · augmented reality · virtual coach: in *Opportunities And Challenges for European projects*, 20–41. SCITEPRESS - Science and Technology Publications, Portugal. https://doi.org/10.5220/000886 1800200041

Guthold R, Stevens GA, Riley LM, Bull FC (2018) Worldwide trends in insufficient physical activity from 2001 to 2016: a pooled analysis of 358 population-based surveys with 1·9 million partic- ipants. Lancet Glob Health 6(10):e1077–e1086. https://doi.org/10.1016/S2214-109X(18)303 57-7

Heyward VH, Gibson A (2014) Advanced fitness assessment and exercise prescription 7th Edition. Human Kinetics

Hughes AA, Jorda S (2021) Applications of biological and physiological signals in commercial video gaming and game research: a review. Front Comput Sci 3:37

Jessie JC, Rose DJ (2005) Physical activity instruction of older adults. human kinetics. https:// www.google.com/books?hl=es&lr=&id=ohfWKmzGDuIC&oi=fnd&pg=PR17&dq=Physical+ Activity+Instruction+of+Older+Adults&ots=XWn0h_r6Vn&sig=dN3GJD7KSoiWceUtqhcmN MP4mAg

Khoo ET, Cheok AD, Nguyen THD, Pan Z (2008) Age invaders: social and physical inter- generational mixed reality family entertainment. Virtual Real 12(1):3–16. https://doi.org/10.1007/ s10055-008-0083-0

Khoo ET, Merritt T, Cheok AD (2009) Designing physical and social intergenerational family entertainment. Interact Comput 21(1–2):76–87. https://doi.org/10.1016/j.intcom.2008.10.009

Korzun DG, Meigal AY, Borodin AV, Gerasimova-Meigal LI (2017) On mobile personalized health- care services for human involvement into prevention, therapy, mutual support, and social reha- bilitation. In: 2017 international multi-conference on engineering, computer and information sciences (SIBIRCON), pp 276–281. https://doi.org/10.1109/SIBIRCON.2017.8109888

Loewe N, Nadj M (2020) Physio-adaptive systems-a state-of-the-art review and future research directions. In: ECIS

Martin-Niedecken AL, Götz U (2017) Go with the dual flow: evaluating the psychophysiological adaptive fitness game environment 'Plunder Planet.' In: Joint international conference on serious games. Springer, pp 32–43

Moreno P, Nunes R, Figueiredo R, Ferreira R, Bernardino A, Santos-Victor J, Beira R, Vargas L, Aragão D, Aragão M (2016) Vizzy: a humanoid on wheels for assistive robotics. In: Reis L P, Moreira AP, Lima PU, Montano L, Muñoz-Martinez V (eds) Robot 2015: second iberian robotics conference, advances in intelligent systems and computing. Springer International Publishing, Cham, pp 17–28. https://doi.org/10.1007/978-3-319-27146-0_2.

Muñoz JE, Bermudez S, Rubio E, Cameirao M (2016a) Modulation of physiological responses and activity levels during exergame experiences. In: 2016a 18th international conference on virtual worlds and games for serious applications, In press. IEEE

Muñoz JE, Pope AT, Velez LE. (2016b) Integrating biocybernetic adaptation in virtual reality training concentration and calmness in target shooting. Physiological Computing Systems. Springer, pp 218–237

Muñoz JE, Paulino T, Vasanth H, Baras K (2016c) PhysioVR: a novel mobile virtual reality frame- work for physiological computing. In: 2016c IEEE 18th international conference on E-health networking, applications and services (Healthcom), pp 1–6. IEEE. http://ieeexplore.ieee.org/abs tract/document/7749512/

Muñoz JE, Gonçalves A, Gouveia ÉR, Cameirão MS, Badia ISB (2019) Lessons learned from gamifying functional fitness training through human-centered design methods in older adults Games. Health J 8(6):387–406https://doi.org/10.1089/g4h.2018.0028

Muñoz J, Gouveia ER, Cameirão MS, Bermudez i Badia S (2018) Closing the loop in exergaming— health benefits of biocybernetic adaptation in senior adults. In . Melbourne, Australia.

Muñoz JE, Rubio E, Cameirao M, Bermúdez S (2017) The biocybernetic loop engine: an integrated tool for creating physiologically adaptive videogames. In: 4th international conference in physiological computing systems. Madrid, España. https://www.researchgate.net/publication/ 317823153_The_Biocybernetic_Loop_Engine_an_Integrated_Tool_for_Creating_Physiologica lly_Adaptive_Videogames

Pope AT, Stephens CL, Gilleade K (2014. Biocybernetic adaptation as biofeedback training method. In Advances in physiological computing. Springer, pp 91–115

"Resident population projections 2018–2080 (n.d.) Instituto nacional de estadística. Accessed 9 June 2021. https://www.ine.pt/xportal/xmain?xpid=INE&xpgid=ine_destaques&DESTAQUES dest_boui=406534255&DESTAQUESmodo=2&xlang=en

Rizzo AS, Requejob P, Winsteinc CJ, Langea B, Merianse A, Pattonf J, Banerjeeg P, Aisenb M (2011) Virtual Reality Applications for Addressing the Needs of Those Aging with Disability. In: Westwood JD et al (eds) Medicine meets virtual reality ,vol 18. IOS Press

Robinson R, Wiley K, Rezaeivahdati A, Klarkowski M, Mandryk RL (2020) Let's get physiological, physiological!' a systematic review of affective gaming. In: Proceedings of the annual symposium on computer-human interaction in play, pp 132–147

Simão H, Bernardino A (2017) User centered design of an augmented reality gaming platform for active aging in elderly institutions:" In: Proceedings of the 5th international congress on sport sciences research and technology support. Funchal, Madeira, Portugal: SCITEPRESS - Science and Technology Publications, pp 151–62. https://doi.org/10.5220/0006606601510162

Sinclair, J, Hingston P, Masek M (2009) Exergame development using the dual flow model. In: Proceedings of the sixth australasian conference on interactive entertainment, vol 11. ACM. http://dl.acm.org/citation.cfm?id=1746061

Skevington SM, Lotfy M, O'Connell KA (2004) The world health organization's WHOQOL-BREF quality of life assessment: psychometric properties and results of the international field trial. a report from the WHOQOL group. Qual Life Res 13(2):299–310. https://doi.org/10.1023/B: QURE.0000018486.91360.00

Skjæret N, Nawaz A, Morat T, Schoene D, Helbostad JL, Vereijken B (2016) Exercise and rehabil- itation delivered through exergames in older adults: an integrative review of technologies, safety and efficacy. Int J Med Inf 85(1):1–16. https://doi.org/10.1016/j.ijmedinf.2015.10.008

United Nations (2020) Department of economic and social affairs, and population division. World Population Ageing, 2019 Highlights

Vourvopoulos A, Faria AL, Cameirão MS, Badia SBi (2013) RehabNet: a distributed architecture for motor and cognitive neuro-rehabilitation. In: 2013 IEEE 15th international conference on e-health networking, applications services (Healthcom), pp 454–459. http://www.m-iti.org/upl oads/RehabNet%20-%20A%20Distributed%20Architecture%20for%20Motor%20and%20C ognitive%20Neuro-Rehabilitation.pdf

Watanabe K, Kawakami N, Imamura K, Inoue A, Shimazu A, Yoshikawa T, Hiro H et al (2017) Pokémon GO and psychological distress, physical complaints, and work performance among adult workers: a retrospective cohort study. Sci Rep 7(1):10758. https://doi.org/10.1038/s41598- 017-11176-2

Wethington E, Kessler RC (1986) Perceived support, received support, and adjustment to stressful life events. J Health Soc Behav 27(1):78–89. https://doi.org/10.2307/2136504

Networked Virtual Reality and Enhanced Sensing for Remote Classes and Presentations

Christoph W. Borst and Arun K. Kulshreshth

Abstract Networked virtual reality is gaining recognition as a way to conduct remote classes or meetings when in-person meetings are difficult or risky. This chapter summarizes our ongoing work to develop and assess VR techniques for remote education. We first present two case studies of remote teaching in VR: a classroom-embedded virtual field trip of an energy center guided by a remote teacher, and a remote university class conducted for several weeks in a social VR tool. We then summarize our ongoing research to enhance remote educational VR interfaces using enhanced sensing, for example, to visualize or detect student attention based on eye-tracked gaze. Finally, we identify several practical considerations that will need to be addressed for the long-term success of educational deployments of virtual reality. This can help educators, researchers, and VR developers make informed decisions about how to best use VR technology for designing and deploying educational VR in everyday contexts such as schools and homes.

1 Introduction

Remote networked presentation or instruction tools can help broaden access to expert teachers, overcome barriers of travel or timing, and reduce carbon use of travel (Le et al. 2020). For example, the remotely conducted IEEE VR 2020 conference had a high number of registrations and increased attendee diversity enabled by reduced travel costs and reduced demand on family caregivers (Ahn et al. 2021).

Traditional remote instruction tools have become associated with high dissatisfaction and learning loss for home-based students, for example, during the spread of the SARS-CoV-2 virus (Engzell et al. 2021). This may be due in part to fatigue from video-based meeting tools (Bailenson 2021; Peper et al. 2021). Speculated factors include limited mobility and differences from a natural in-person view: increased

C. W. Borst (✉) · A. K. Kulshreshth
University of Louisiana at Lafayette, Lafayette, USA
e-mail: cwborst@gmail.com

A. K. Kulshreshth
e-mail: arunkul@louisiana.edu

eye gaze at a close distance, constant viewing of self-video, and associated increased cognitive load.

VR meetings might be valuable for remote classrooms by supporting co-presence, a more naturalistic view of a class, or other aspects lacking in video-only tools, (Yoshimura and Borst 2020b; Steinicke et al. 2020). Students seem to appreciate being seen as avatars rather than on camera (Yoshimura and Borst 2020a). More general benefits of VR for education may include increased engagement and motivation of students, better communication of size and spatial relationships of modeled objects, and stronger memories of the experience. Virtual reality (VR) has long been suggested as a way to enhance education (Youngblut 1998).

This chapter overviews our work to improve educational VR interfaces and to evaluate the strengths and weaknesses of approaches in everyday contexts. We summarize two studies on networked educational VR, our ongoing work on enhanced sensing (especially eye tracking) to enhance teacher/student VR, and practical considerations for the success of everyday VR in educational applications.

2 Two Studies of Networked Educational VR in Everyday Contexts

Studies of educational VR in real-world home or classroom environments can provide a level of ecological validity lacking from lab-based studies. In this section, we review two of our studies of networked VR for education. In the first study, VR equipment in high school classrooms allowed students to experience virtual field trips of a solar energy plant, led by a live remote guide (Borst et al. 2018). In the second study, students attended a university class remotely from home using a combination of headset-based VR and desktop-based viewing of a 3D social VR environment (Yoshimura and Borst 2021).

2.1 Kvasir-VR: Remotely-Guided VR Field Trips

Real field trips have promising effects such as long-term information recall (Falk and Dierking 1997) and a first-person view that communicates size and spatial relationships of objects. VR field trips may provide such benefits without requiring students to leave the home or classroom. VR also allows environments to be augmented with additional educational content, such as embedded educational animations and simulations of rare events.

The Kvasir-VR project (Borst et al. 2018) investigated two educational VR approaches for a virtual field trip given at high schools. In one approach, networked student groups were guided by a live teacher captured as live-streamed depth camera imagery. In the second approach, a standalone (non-networked) version allowed students to individually experience the field trip based on depth camera recordings of the same teacher. Both approaches were tested at two high schools using a VR environment that teaches students about solar energy production via tours of a solar plant. The networked approach was also deployed across a transpacific network connecting Lafayette, Louisiana to Adelaide, Australia, and in an interstate deployment that allowed a teacher in Lafayette to remotely guide students and visitors at the Chattanooga Public Library in Tennessee.

2.1.1 Kvasir-VR Student Interface

Students were immersed in the environment using standard consumer hardware including an Oculus CV1 headset and a tracked hand-held controller (see Fig. 1). For safety and practical reasons related to classroom use, students were seated. Students visited various educational stations and used ray-based pointing to trigger embedded educational elements such as animations. To provide a simple interface requiring minimal explanation and practice, only one button was used for all interactions (all programmable buttons performed the same function). Students moved between stations by selecting teleportation targets (viewing platforms at educational stations) with the ray. A multi-step teleport motion was chosen to minimize motion sickness risks for seated students while still providing some sense of the path and of the environment's spatial layout. The teleport motion first stepped the student to the target position through several intermediate positions with short fades between them, and then rotated the student through several steps about their vertical axis, to keep seated students facing a consistent real direction while they were virtually oriented to face educational content. During teleportation, the system also displayed a leading indicator (an arrow) that moved smoothly just ahead of the student as both an in-progress indicator and to help users anticipate and understand motion.

2.1.2 Kvasir-VR Teacher Interface

Kvasir-VR placed teachers in VR with a novel combination of depth camera imagery, heterogeneous displays, and a virtual mirror view. A teacher guided immersed students from a TV-based teacher interface (Fig. 2) with a depth camera (Kinect) mounted at the bottom to capture a live-streamed teacher mesh (Ekong et al. 2016). This provided a less immersive and less natural view for the teacher, but it had advantages of allowing capture of the teacher's face for the mesh model and avoiding headset-related fatigue for a teacher conducting many sessions. Depth camera imagery can provide higher social presence and better convey behavior than current conventional avatars (Yu et al. 2021).

The teacher gave verbal descriptions of the environment and of educational concepts, asked questions to check understanding and attention, directed students to click on interactable objects or teleport targets, and monitored students overall. Besides verbal descriptions, pointing was the main aspect of communication and is generally

Fig. 1 A student wearing a VR headset stands at a virtual tower overviewing a virtual solar plant (the background duplicates the student's view for illustration). A teacher (seen to the left) provides an introduction to the plant and is represented by a mesh captured by a Kinect depth camera

a key mechanism for guiding others in collaborative VR (Nguyen and Duval 2014). Due to the television's narrow field of view (FOV), the teacher had a "virtual mirror" view with an exaggerated field of view. Thus, the teacher saw themself as mirrored in this view. This view supported the teacher pointing at objects behind the teacher (virtually) while facing the students.

The teacher was aided by additional visuals (see Fig. 2). Students' views of the environment were reproduced as inset images and could be checked by the teacher to ensure a student saw what was intended or to resolve communication problems. Pointing cues, visible only to the teacher, allowed the teacher to point to correct depths with a mirror view. Different cues were considered, as described by Woodworth and Borst (2017). Live webcam videos of students were overlayed in semi-transparent ovals. The ovals were positioned for correct teacher gaze toward a student, using perspective projection that considers teacher head tracking and TV geometry (Ekong et al. 2016). The teacher's view also included minimal representations of student interaction rays.

2.1.3   Kvasir-VR Study and Results

We used a virtual solar power plant modeled after a real pilot-scale energy plant (Chambers et al. 2014) for a virtual field trip that initially resembled real field trips at the facility. This provided schools who could not visit the real facility with an alternative way of experiencing the tour and meeting a remote expert. The VR tour

Fig. 2 The teacher guided students from a TV interface with a Kinect mounted at its bottom. This interface leaves the teacher's face clear of obstructions. The TV visuals include: (1) a mirror view of the environment, (2) duplicated student views at the TV's lower left, (3) webcam views of students, in ovals hovering at positions for teacher eye gaze toward the students, and (4) pointing cues to help the teacher point correctly in 3D

was additionally extended with educational content beyond that visible in real tours, and interaction was added to increase student involvement.

In the networked approach, a live teacher guided small groups of students from the teacher interface. The students were each locally placed at the same virtual viewing location as each other (on a teleport platform), with other student avatars appearing offset to the left or right according to seating order in a real classroom. Students saw minimal avatars of other students, consisting of generic heads, which were typically not in view, and minimal pointing rays when relevant. Students and the teacher all heard each other through a networked voice server using TeamSpeak. Environment responses to student actions (teleport, animation) were reflected at all networked computers.

A standalone (non-networked) version was developed to provide a similar experience (to the extent possible) using a pre-recorded teacher to allow students to learn the material independently, at reduced deployment cost and complexity, and with each student experiencing all interactions.

The main study of Kvasir-VR assessed and compared the two teacher-guided VR approaches (networked vs. standalone) with 88 students in high school classrooms. The study showed an educational benefit of the live networked approach over the standalone approach, especially in terms of test score gains. We believe this resulted from a live teacher being more interesting to students and better being able to correct misunderstandings and respond to questions. This echoes studies wherein conventional live lectures produced higher gains than videos, e.g., Ramlogan et al. (2014).

The study, along with a related pilot study (Ritter 2016), suggested that distractions encountered in classrooms are a likely problem for VR deployments, so a dedicated or quiet space could be important.

Further research is needed to identify which specific aspects of the live teacher presence or guidance (or the presence of other students in the environment) contributed to learning. For example, results could be related to student beliefs about the extent to which a real person observes them. Deeper consideration of these aspects can help guide other approaches and address some of the trade-offs between live and pre-recorded teachers.

Improving standalone approaches also remains relevant for research, considering practical advantages: deployment is relatively simple as it does not require a live expert instructor, the associated extra equipment, coordination, or extra setup time. Our standalone field trip took less student time due to reduced communication, and the saved time could be used to present more content. Standalone approaches scale up readily to large numbers of students and to more general audiences. A balance may be achieved using a mix of live and standalone activities, with a live teacher being available for key discussions or to address difficulties.

2.2   Study of a Remote Class Using Mozilla Hubs

Educational VR may be best-suited to environments that emphasize spatial learning. But, it is studied less often for lecture-style classes. Although there is substantial prior work considering VR for education (Radianti et al. 2020), there is minimal published work on students attending class using headset-based VR in homes, or on such students presenting class assignments with VR headsets.

We studied student experiences of a VR-based class using Mozilla Hubs for remote instruction, with students attending class remotely for 7 weeks (Yoshimura and Borst 2021). Mozilla Hubs is a lightweight web-based social VR platform that supports many devices. Students were at home, using various consumer devices, and the study did not change course content or delivery methods (which resulted from a VR class using remote instruction during the spread of SARS-CoV-2). The study evaluated student experiences viewing lectures in both VR headsets and on desktop monitors. We additionally evaluated student experiences presenting project updates in VR headsets. Presenters, both the teacher and students, used VR headsets and tracked controllers.

2.2.1   Mozilla Hubs Interface

Hubs features are rudimentary but support key aspects of remote VR classes and Hubs is deployable on a broad range of devices. Features that we used include: upload/download of lecture slides and videos, per-user selectable avatars with tracked head and hands, livestream video of the teacher, viewing capabilities like maximiz-

Fig. 3 Lecture in Mozilla Hubs as viewed by an audience member at the back of the room, showing the full field of view for desktop viewing

ing content with a button, walk/fly/teleport navigation, voice/text chat, and emo-jis emitted from avatars. Other social VR platforms such as AltspaceVR (https://altvr.com/), Engage (https://engagevr.io/), Virbela (https://www.virbela.com/), and VRChat (https://hello.vrchat.com/) have varying levels of accessibility in terms of cost and portability.

Figure 3 shows a Hubs lecture with a mix of students using desktop VR and headset VR. The image shows a lecture screen (uploaded PDF content) near its center, uploaded video objects to the right of the screen, a teacher avatar near the bottom left of the lecture screen, a live-streamed webcam view of the teacher to the left of the screen, and student avatars in the virtual room. Some students were floating (fly mode) for a better view. Figure 4 shows a student presenting their project update in a VR headset. Four lecture periods were reserved as presentation days on which students presented project updates. Main presentation content consisted of slides and these were accompanied by supplementary materials such as VR-embedded videos, a timeline to show project progress, and sometimes 3D objects in the virtual environment.

2.2.2 Mozilla Hubs Study Results Summary

Thirteen students alternated between attending with headsets and conventional desktop monitors. They rated factors such as presence, social presence, usability, and sickness. Additional questionnaire topics investigated communication methods, avatar features, Hubs features, etc. (Yoshimura and Borst 2021).

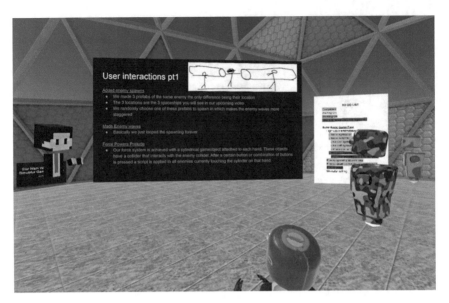

Fig. 4 A student presenting a project update in Mozilla Hubs, as viewed by an audience member. The presenter is seen at the left. The field of view has been cropped for clarity

Results suggested that social VR platforms can be effective for remote classes, but that this is limited by discomfort with headsets and technical difficulties for some users. Headset use provided increased presence over desktop use, overall. Ratings for headset use varied widely, appearing less consistent than for desktop use. Even students with negative headset experiences tended to report high expectations for VR as a remote class platform for the future. Students reported a high sense of belonging and motivation for headset VR in comparison with remote technologies being used in other classes that they were taking. Students liked the reduced visibility or reduced anxiety of using avatars instead of being seen via cameras.

Discomfort appeared related to ergonomic factors like heat or facial pressure in combination with substantial duration of use. Some students removed headsets due to discomfort or for external tasks. Most students reported some audio or video glitches, and about half encountered some external distraction. Based on strong demonstrated correlations between reported discomfort and other ratings in the headset conditions, we expect that future VR technologies with improved comfort will extend advantages of headsets to a wider range of users. In the meantime, desktop viewing is a good alternative for those students who experience sickness or technical problems with headsets. Most students indicated that they would like to attend using some mix of headset and desktop viewing, rather than a single type.

The results resemble those recently reported by others (Ahn et al. 2021) for a remote conference with Hubs, illustrating both the promise and problems with current VR technology in home environments. In contrast, problems were minimal in the Kvasir-VR study for which we controlled the computers, headsets, and networks, although some distractions were noted for classrooms. For remote attendees of the IEEE VR 2020 conference, Ahn et al. (2021) reported headset removal for keyboard use or fatigue. Audio and network problems were reported. Hubs is most successful for social activities, and less so for viewing talks. Some attendees suggested that joining conversations was easier than at real physical venues.

3 Enhanced Sensing in Educational VR

This section presents our recent and in-progress research to enhance the educational VR interfaces and use additional sensor information such as tracked eye gaze. Eye tracking has started to appear in consumer headsets, along with other added sensing (e.g., Vive Pro Eye, Vive Facial Tracker, emteqPro, OpenBCI Galea, LooxidVR, HP Reverb G2 Omnicept). Sensors in emerging VR headsets may be useful for detecting visual attention, detecting physiological responses, or even for inferring psychological states.

We first present three simple ways to use eye gaze: (1) to provide attention guidance or attention restoration cues to students who look away from relevant objects (Yoshimura et al. 2019a), (2) to visualize eye gaze to a networked teacher or other users for enhanced communication (Woodworth et al. 2020), and (3) to make the environment respond to student gaze and, in particular, to modify the playback of teacher clips based on visual attention (Khokhar et al. 2019).

We then consider how sensor data such as eye gaze and physiological readings might be used to automatically detect student state such as distraction or frustration to provide an improved overview to a teacher or to support a responsive environment (Asish et al. 2021; Woodworth and Borst 2021). Next, we summarize a VR-embedded teacher interface that can integrate such information about student state (along with student actions) to help a networked teacher oversee a VR class (Broussard et al. 2021a). Finally, we incorporate elements of this interface, along with desktop-based eye and hand tracking, into an interface that allows a networked teacher to better control a VR avatar from a desktop presentation environment (Woodworth et al. 2022).

3.1 Attention Restoration Cues

Loss of student attention is a common problem for educational presentations. In VR, there may be distracting objects or scenery for students to look at besides the objects relevant to the current presentation. We demonstrated several visual cue styles (Yoshimura et al. 2019a, b) to encourage students to return visual focus to the correct object when their visual focus shifts elsewhere. The cues are conceptually like some of those found in prior work on guiding attention to objects in AR, for example, for indicating the next target object in an AR training sequence (Biocca et al. 2006;

Renner and Pfeiffer 2017), although the prior work does not specifically focus on restoring attention after it has been lost.

Cue styles are described below and shown in Fig. 5. Cues appear with increased intensity as eye gaze moves away from relevant instructional objects. Multiple parameters (e.g., transparency, fade angle, size, placement, etc.) were tuned in a pilot study to control the appearance or fading of cues. The cues were integrated into Kvasir-VR (Sect. 2.1) and were demonstrated in an offshore training system.

- **Standard Arrow**: a single 3D arrow oriented to point toward a target.
- **Trail of Arrows**: multiple arrows along an arc or curve between the student's gaze and the target object.
- **Field of arrows**: (formerly named Navigation Sphere) a field of arrows at vertices of an (invisible) head-centered icosphere, each oriented to point along an arc toward the target.
- **DynSWAVE**: concentric circles move along a head-centered sphere toward the target object, and the circles move faster as the student looks away from the target (based on Renner and Pfeiffer 2017).
- **Border**: displays a circle on a head-centered sphere, where the circle's position on the sphere is centered around the target object. The circle's edge follows the student's gaze until it reaches a boundary.
- **Vignette**: (formerly named Tunnel Vision) a vignette-type cue that progressively darkens portions of the scene far from the target as the student attention drifts.
- **Line Strip**: A thick line strip (appearing like a curved banner) is displayed along the arc or cubic curve, showing a full path from the student's current gaze to the target.
- **Attention Funnel**: multiple rings or other markers are placed along a cubic curve between the student and the target (based on Biocca et al. 2006).
- **Highlight**: the target object changes to a highlight color as the eye gaze moves away from it.

A networked teacher or an automated agent can give descriptions of devices or objects during field trips, and cues can appear or fade in when student gaze drifts away from relevant objects. Based on the level of student inattention, a different cue style may be used depending on its markedness (Dillman et al. 2018). For example, if the student is looking very far away, we can use a tunnel vision effect because it is overlained on the screen rather than just a background effect.

Preliminary observations from an ongoing study of the tuned cues (see the Appendix) suggest a different pattern of relative cue performance than seen in prior studies, which focus on guidance instead of restoration. Additionally, based on inspection of ratings, we expect that users like the visual appearance of the trail of arrows, linestrip, and highlight, and they believe that the trail, linestrip, and attention funnel have a strong influence on their attention. However, the attention funnel does not appear promising based on speed of restoring attention, and highlight is the most promising cue provided it appears clearly in view.

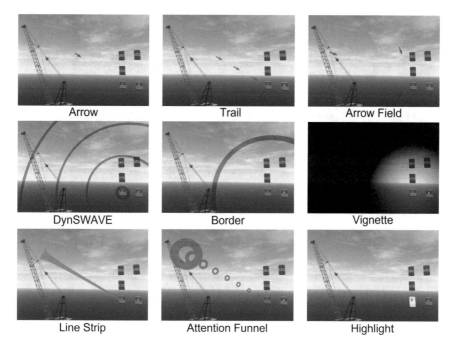

Fig. 5 Attention restoration cues

3.2 Visualizing Gaze Data in Collaborative or Multi User Environments

Visualizing gaze may help communication in collaborative environments by giving an indication of where others are looking. This subsection discusses our work on gaze visualization for collaborative geosciences visualization and for a teacher to monitor student gaze in VR.

3.2.1 Gaze Trail and Location Tether in Collaborative Geosciences VR

In large collaborative VR environments, like those for geological exploration, users need tools for communicating with each other and for maintaining awareness of other users when they are not in view.

We developed geological dataset interpretation systems, wherein a teacher can guide students through discussions that include interactive annotation and interpretation of surfaces (Woodworth et al. 2020; Borst and Kinsland 2005). The application visualizes terrain-like surfaces above which users navigate and change scale, view, and visualization options to study topography, gravity, and magnetic data. Interactive annotation tools allow placing markers and drawing on a surface to help users point

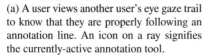

(a) A user views another user's eye gaze trail to know that they are properly following an annotation line. An icon on a ray signifies the currently-active annotation tool.

(b) The tether connects the remote user's avatar to a nearby nametag that displays a remote-view indicator.

Fig. 6 Gaze and location visualizations for geosciences exploration in VR

out features to each other. During these interactions, the users are often looking at a feature of a surface or an annotation that is being placed, instead of looking toward user avatars.

Among others, two desired capabilities are: (1) the ability to quickly determine where other users are and (2) the ability to understand what other users are looking at. Sharing eye gaze has been shown to be effective at enhancing communication in collaborative applications (Zhang et al. 2017). We developed a gaze trail by placing a moving particle emitter at the intersection of a remote user's gaze direction ray and the viewed geological surface. The emitter moves with gaze and the particles fade between colors. As seen in Fig. 6a, this immediately shows if a remote student is following an annotation as it is being drawn by a teacher's ray.

Additionally, a tether along a cubic curve from a nearby dashboard to a remote user helps point out the location of the remote user (see Fig. 6b). Nametags both in the dashboard and above the remote user can display a copy of the remote user's view, and clicking the nametag allows direct teleporting to the remote user.

Based on a small evaluation with a geology professor guiding 4 students (Woodworth et al. 2020), our main impression from observation and feedback was that the gaze trail is promising for aiding in communicating attention. The professor appreciated its inclusion as it helped him know when students were paying attention to the feature he was describing. Students appreciated the feature for letting them know what feature the professor was describing when it was not immediately clear based on verbal description. The avatar, its tether, and a remote view image (to improve awareness of location and view) were described as less important by users than we expected.

(a) Gaze Ring: a ring appears at the gaze location.

(b) Gaze Disc: a disc appears at the gaze location.

(c) Gaze Arrow: an arrow indicates the current gaze point.

(d) Gaze Trail: a trail of particles is shown for each user based on his/her gaze points over the last three seconds.

(e) Gaze Trail with Arrows: line segments with arrows represent gaze point movement.

(f) Gaze Heatmaps: change the color of the object being gazed at.

Fig. 7 Eye gaze visualization techniques shown from a teacher's point of view

3.2.2 Gaze Data Visualizations for a Teacher

Eye gaze visualizations could help a teacher identify confused/distracted students to help the teacher adjust explanations or better guide those students toward the objects of interest. We evaluated six real-time gaze visualizations (visual cues) for a teacher who guides or monitors students from within VR (Rahman et al. 2020). The visualizations are shown in Fig. 7.

In a within-subjects study of the visual cues, 26 participants played the role of a teacher's assistant and pressed a button when they detected any student as distracted. They tried both single-student and multi-student environments (conditions with 1 or 5 pre-recorded students). The gaze trail (GT), a short particle trail as in the geosciences work, was the technique most frequently given the top rank by participants. In contrast, the study revealed problems of applying a quickly fading heat map color directly on 3D object surfaces for real-time gaze visualization. The heat map was not rendered in mid-air, so the cue movement could appear to jump discontinuously as the eye moved between objects. Our results did not show significant differences in terms of accuracy or response time between cues. However, they appear to show better accuracy in case of multiple students for all the techniques. This could be because there were more total distractions in the 5-student group, and fewer button presses counted as false positives (fewer presses corresponded to a time period without any distraction).

We considered only gaze-based distraction for this experiment. However, attention cannot be determined solely based on eye gaze data because distraction or attention could sometimes be dominated by internal (mental) factors. A student looking at the important object could still be distracted mentally, or a student may still be listening carefully even if looking off to the side intermittently. Thus, for future work, other sensors such as EEG may be helpful in detecting distraction or other problems.

3.3 Gaze-Responsive Presentation

The Kvasir-VR project (2.1) presented virtual field trips with either a live teacher or pre-recorded clips of the same teacher. The live teacher could better respond to students, but a standalone version could be deployed more broadly and easily. We consider that eye tracking could be used to make a virtual teacher or educational objects more responsive to a student's visual attention or distraction. Pedagogical agents provide an educational benefit (Wang et al. 2006) over a fixed presentation sequence by being more interesting and could respond to misunderstandings or attentional shifts by using animated clips. Eye gaze can provide a basis for a system to monitor and respond to focus shifts (D'Mello et al. 2012).

We demonstrated a framework for segmenting and sequencing the teacher recordings to consider student distraction by pausing or responding and rewinding based on student eye gaze (Khokhar et al. 2019, 2020). More generally, the framework contains mechanisms for sensing distraction (generalized hotspots), defining critical periods in which certain sensed conditions are evaluated, and selecting from possible behaviors for a pedagogical agent or other responsive objects. Using teacher recordings from the Kvasir-VR project for a virtual oil rig tour environment, three possible automated teacher behaviors were demonstrated for playing back recordings:

- **Normal**: The teacher recording plays normally. For example, the teacher points at the iron roughneck and explains what the iron roughneck does regardless of where the student looks.
- **Pause**: The teacher pauses (see Fig. 8). For example, when pointing to the iron roughneck, the teacher waits for the student to look there (if the student has not already looked there).

Fig. 8 Left: The teacher agent points at a deck crane and a student looks (indicated here by a yellow gaze trail that is not seen by the student). If the student does not look, the teacher can pause until the student looks. Right: The student receives a notification and the teacher pauses due to the distraction

- **Respond**: The teacher pauses for a second, then responds to the student if needed. For example, the teacher explains the drill string and points at it. If the student does not look at the drill string, the teacher will ask the student to look a little bit to the left (for example). Continued distraction will cause the teacher to rewind and repeat instructions; however, if attention is regained, then the teacher will continue to the next topic if appropriate.

The Timeline feature of the Unity 3D development tool is used to coordinate audio, animation, and object activations. We extended this to support annotations (metadata) for teacher recordings. These specify the timing of responses, critical periods, requirements to progress the sequence, and distractions. Critical periods specify what a student needs to do in order for the teacher to continue default behavior and progress the sequence. Our generalized hotspot is a conceptual high-level sensor that sets up candidate behaviors for further consideration by a response selection mechanism (a Utility AI such as that described by Dill et al. 2012). Some hotspots can be automatically created based on analyzed teacher pointing (e.g., to estimate where students should look). Combiners, within hotspots, are elements that receive low-level sensor data and perform calculations that modify or compose low-level data into higher-level information such as minimum eye gaze angle away from any relevant objects (e.g., teacher and described devices).

Preliminary results from an ongoing study (see the Appendix) show subject preferences for the Respond behavior. Based on observations and discussion with subjects, merely pausing the clip (Pause behavior) could appear strange or unnatural because the teacher appears frozen. More sophisticated combinations of teacher clips and hotspots, or mapping to other types of avatars, could appear more natural or seamless.

3.4   Detecting Mental State or Problems with Enhanced Sensing

This section summarizes two works related to detecting mental state. In the first, we use eye tracking data to detect overall distraction level of a student during a VR field trip (Asish et al. 2021). In the second, we propose VR-oriented tasks to elicit states such as frustration, confusion, boredom, and pleasure (Woodworth and Borst 2021).

In a physical classroom, a teacher may be able to read student emotions through behavioral or facial cues, but this ability is reduced when using VR avatars as some cues are tracked or reconstructed coarsely (especially in everyday VR) and the displays have limited resolution and field of view. Techniques that infer student states using enhanced sensing could make it possible to signal a teacher when there is a notable problem, or to provide feedback or guidance to the teacher about effectiveness of their techniques in keeping students engaged.

A student's cognitive or emotional state can affect their ability to process and understand information (Bower et al. 1983). Emotions are experienced across three response systems (Mauss et al. 2005): experiential (psychological), behavioral (e.g., posture or movement), and physiological (e.g., rising heart rate). Various researchers are attempting to use physiological sensors and machine learning techniques to detect a person's emotional state, e.g., Marín-Morales et al. (2018); Liao et al. (2019). Useful information for class management might include emotional engagement based on electrodermal readings (Lascio et al. 2018; Villanueva et al. 2018) or facial muscle activation (Cacioppo et al. 1986; Gnacek et al. 2022), cognitive load and attention based on blinking rate and fixation time (Fowler et al. 2019; Nourbakhsh et al. 2013), or stress based on cardiovascular readings (McDuff et al. 2016, 2014; Bousefsaf et al. 2013).

3.4.1   Detecting Distraction Level

Gaze visualizations such as those in Sect. 3.2.2 can help a teacher understand students' visual attention. However, continual visualization of gaze from many students is not practical because a teacher would monitor many cues in a VR classroom while teaching. One solution is to automatically filter students based on attention level and visualize details only for students who may need extra consideration, allowing a teacher to more easily monitor a class.

We proposed a deep learning approach to identify the distraction level of a student based on gaze data in VR (Asish et al. 2021), without using the simple gaze angle test of the gaze-responsive presentation (Sect. 3.3). This would help handle cases for which the gaze direction does not reflect distraction level of the student.

The approach was studied with the virtual solar energy center from the Kvasir-VR project (Borst et al. 2016), with various components to assist learning (Fig. 9). A conventional avatar explained the functionality of center components using pre-

(a) An avatar describing a solar panel.　　　　(b) An avatar explaining the cooling process.

Fig. 9 Educational VR environment to explain how a solar field generates power. An avatar explains different components using audio, animations and text slides

Table 1 Precision, recall, and F1-score of the CNN, LSTM, and CNN-LSTM models for the classification of distraction level

Name	Class	Precision %	Recall %	F1-score %
CNN	Low	0.88	0.85	0.86
	Mid	0.87	0.88	0.87
	High	0.85	0.89	0.87
LSTM	Low	0.91	0.85	0.88
	Mid	0.88	0.90	0.89
	High	0.85	0.91	0.88
CNN-LSTM	Low	0.90	0.89	0.90
	Mid	0.91	0.89	0.90
	High	0.88	0.91	0.90

recorded audio instructions, slides, and animations. Relevant solar field components were highlighted to help students focus on the component being discussed.

Distractions can be internal (e.g., psychological) or external (e.g., auditory). We focused on external audio distractions, simulating three audio distractions (social media notifications, mobile ringtones, and external conversations/sounds) because these are the three major student distractions in classes (David et al. 2015; Agrawal et al. 2017). The experiment presented short educational sessions both with and without the audio distractions. Raw gaze data included timestamps, eye diameter, eye openness, eye wideness, gaze position, and gaze direction. For training a classifier, the data was first labeled as low-, mid-, or high-distraction based on self-reported distraction level (low, mid or high), drowsiness level (yes or no), and quiz answers about the content presented.

Three deep learning models were trained and evaluated with the gaze data: CNN, LSTM, and CNN-LSTM. The CNN-LSTM model was proposed to combine the best features of the other two models. The precision, recall, and F1-scores for the three models are reported in Table 1. With an F1-score of 90%, the CNN-LSTM model performed best of the three models. We also measured the AUC and ROC values of the three classifiers to evaluate how good they were in distinguishing between the three distraction classes. The results suggested that the proposed CNN-LSTM model was able to distinguish between the three distraction classes more effectively than the other two models.

This work is a step toward an automatic detector of distraction level for educational VR. However, it was demonstrated for per-session detection only and requires retraining when the educational session varies. A main goal for future work is to extend it to real-time detection and explore other data features to consider additional and more generalizable features. We would also like to consider more distraction types and more sensor types (EEG, heart rate, skin conductance, etc.) to improve detection or to detect other internal states.

3.4.2 Affective Tasks for Emotion Elicitation

To build or evaluate an affect detection model, typically a dataset is collected under controlled conditions that elicit relevant affective states and obtain ratings. Lab-based emotion elicitation has often been done using passive activities such as viewing films (Coan and Allen 2007), images (Lang et al. 1997), or sounds (Bradley and Lang 1999). The user is typically given no task other than to absorb the stimulus and report aspects of their emotions. However, there is evidence to suggest that affective models can be better when they are built on stimuli closer to the context in which they are eventually applied (Bevilacqua et al. 2019). Virtual reality is becoming more widely known as an immersive medium able to emotionally engage the user through the user's ability to interact more directly with the virtual world (Rivu et al. 2021). So, we designed interactive tasks for eliciting emotion in VR with a goal to understand and later recognize states relevant for students using training or educational VR, such as frustration, confusion, boredom, and pleasure (Woodworth and Borst 2021). These states correspond to different positions in valence-arousal or circumplex models of emotion (Russell 1980). The two key dimensions of emotion terms as described by Russell are valence (the positive/negative continuum), and arousal (the calm/excited continuum) (Russell 1978).

We describe four tasks in terms of the emotion they are intended to elicit. The tasks can be varied with the intent to produce different levels of an emotion, or to apply concepts from other tasks to produce other responses. Tasks are pictured in Fig. 10:

- **Buzzer Box**: aims to elicit frustration by presenting a deceptively simple task with a difficult goal and high amounts of negative feedback. Frustration is considered to have high arousal with moderately low valence. Buzzer Box asks the user to keep the green ball in the blue dome center, while an invisible force pushes it away. When the ball hits a peg or side of the box, a loud buzzer is played.
- **Box Sorting**: aims to elicit confusion by presenting a simple task and occasionally breaking its rules unfairly (without informing the user). Box Sorting asks the user to sort the box into the correctly colored bin while occasionally giving incorrect feedback for correct sorts. Confusion is generally considered to have moderately

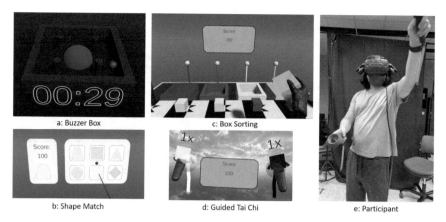

Fig. 10 Affective tasks (**a–d**), **e** shows a participant performing Guided Tai Chi

high arousal and low valence, thus placing it in a different position on the same low-valence / high-arousal quadrant as frustration.

- **Shape Match**: asks the user to select the shape shown on the left from the selection on the right. This task aims to elicit boredom by presenting a simple task for a long period of time. Boredom is considered to have low arousal and valence. We consider a boring but relevant task to be one that is easy but requires frequent interaction (Bevilacqua et al. 2019).
- **Guided Tai Chi**: asks the user to follow the colored spheres with their tracked hands while providing positive feedback. This task aims to elicit pleasure by mimicking a low-intensity analog activity (basic tai chi movements) typically done for relaxation and pleasure (Huston and McFarlane 2016). Pleasure is typically considered to have a high valence and neutral arousal.

Additionally, a neutral room was designed to be placed in between tasks so that users could recover from the emotion elicited from the previous task, as is commonly recommended for films (Coan and Allen 2007). The room contains a sky-blue skybox with basic rain sounds and a timer showing time remaining until the next task.

We conducted an initial assessment with 5 participants as an initial validation of the elicitation tasks (Woodworth and Borst 2021). We used an HTC Vive Pro Eye headset and Empatica E4 wristband to collect eye and physiological data (heart rate, electrodermal activity (EDA), eye openness, and pupil diameter). Results involved end-of-task self-assessments (Fig. 11) and discussion questionnaires given after all tasks were completed. Our study suggested that three of the four tasks, except for Box Sorting, primarily elicited the targeted emotion, with ratings in the expected quadrants of the valence-arousal model. Box Sorting did not elicit confusion for all the participants. Only one participant reported confusion and others reported either frustration (due to rule breaks) or excitement (as they enjoyed the activity). A difference between tasks was detected for eye-related features (such as blink rate) indicating a potential for its use as a feature for differentiating emotional states.

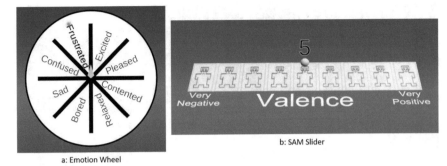

a: Emotion Wheel

b: SAM Slider

Fig. 11 Example of response mechanisms that allowed subjects to rate emotion, valence, and arousal

3.5 Teacher Interface for Awareness of Student Actions and Attention

For a VR-immersed teacher to better understand students and respond to problems or actions, we developed a teacher interface that summarizes key information about student actions, attention, and temperament (Broussard et al. 2021a, b). It presents either floating indicators or centrally arranged face icons with gaze information, location tethers or other location indicators, estimated attention or mental state, and filtering options to reduce the amount of presented information.

VR tools so far do not provide as many cues about audience actions and attention as in-person meetings, for example, subtle face and body motion cues are missing. In the Mozilla Hubs class study, we noticed that student positions were relatively unrestricted, making it harder to keep the class in view (for example, student avatars may space out very widely or hover in the air as noted by Yoshimura and Borst 2020b). The students sometimes had difficulty asking questions and getting the teacher's attention, even though Hubs has an audible beep and question text in the environment (Yoshimura and Borst 2020b, a). Additionally, some students encountered discomfort, technical problems, and distractions different from in-person classes (Yoshimura and Borst 2020a).

To help the teacher in such environments, we extended a Hubs-like environment with indicators such as those seen in Fig. 12. Three main components work together for the extended interface: a scoring component to classify student behavior, an indicator placement component that mitigates clutter, and a display component.

The importance scoring component first estimates whether or not a student has a problem (such as a distraction) or is performing an action that the teacher needs to be aware of. This can use angle-based metrics as in Sect. 3.1 along with emerging approaches for detecting student state from other sensors (Sect. 3.4). The top-level per-student importance score indicates whether or not the teacher needs to be especially aware of (and therefore see an indicator for) a student.

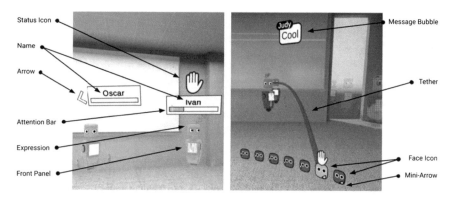

Fig. 12 Indicator elements: Floating (left), Class-wide (right)

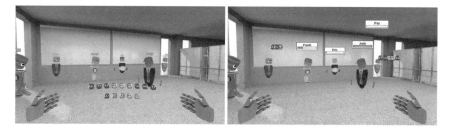

Fig. 13 Indicator placement: Class-wide (left), Floating (right)

An indicator is a visual element in the teacher's view that summarizes student status. To mitigate overlapping of indicators at the same view angle, a group of nearby indicators can be combined or collapsed to reduce space required to display information. We considered two indicator placement styles:

Class-wide: A single class-wide collapsed group that moves to remain in the teacher's field of attention (Fig. 13, left). To visually represent student statuses with an indicator, various visual elements are used (Fig. 12).

Floating: A more common indicator position above a student's head to make the relationship between the indicator and the student clear (Fig. 13, right). If this position is outside the field of attention, the indicator will be displayed at the closest point inside the field of attention.

Three multi-student indicator styles were considered (Fig. 14):

1. Face Icons: Icons colored according to importance (green to red) with a status icon above to depict current student action such as typing. The eyes of the icons move to indicate student gaze direction relative to the teacher, giving some sense of student attention or distracted students.

2. Single Bar: A bar emphasizing only the most critical students in a group indicator, reducing the summary complexity.

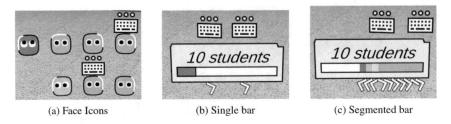

| (a) Face Icons | (b) Single bar | (c) Segmented bar |

Fig. 14 Collapsed indicator types

3. Segmented Bar: A bar containing multiple importance scores as segments, with critical scores on the left and good scores on the right, allowing the teacher to further overview the distribution of importance scores.

For the class-wide indicator style with face icons, additional cues were added to help a teacher locate a student avatar associated with a face icon. Tethers could appear from icons to students and 3 styles of on-icon directional cues were also considered: *Edge Highlights* color a portion of the icon edge according to student direction, as in Fig. 14a. *Blips* are small arrows on the icon edges, pointing toward the student. *Arrows* are larger and appear underneath icons. An example of *tethers* is seen in Fig. 12: a red 3D cubic curves connects a face icon to the avatar of a student who has raised a hand.

Some elements in the interface are responsive and expose additional information when the teacher hovers on them with ray pointing or eye gaze. One is the front panel on the avatar's chest—it flips out to display supplementary information. Additionally, we had on-avatar temperament visualizations, where temperament is loosely related to student emotion and mental state such as distress, frustration, and confusion.

Our study gathered input and preference ratings from 11 subjects (Broussard et al. 2021a). Subjects preferred to see all student indicators in one place (class-wide) and suggested minimizing the information displayed. They felt these modifications would help a teacher focus more effectively on the most urgent students while reducing clutter. From the results, we can design a tuned interface, wherein students would be represented by indicators displayed in a class-wide group with indicators and tethers shown only for critical students (particularly when the class is large). Integration with other cues, such as audio or haptic alerts, can also be considered. We expect these are useful for occasional critical alerts, but less useful for providing a continuous overview.

3.6 Desktop Interface with Input Redirection to a VR Presenter Avatar

We developed methods to increase the liveliness and expressiveness of a teacher or presenter avatar when the teacher is using a desktop platform rather than a headset

Fig. 15 A user sitting at the teacher interface waving to students. A Leap Motion Controller is positioned on the desk directly in front of them. A Tobii Eye Tracker 5 is attached to the bottom of the monitor. The interface shows a presentation board, a row of student icons above, and the teacher's avatar at a podium

(Woodworth et al. 2022). The Hubs study (Sect. 2.2) found that students rate the teacher avatar and actions like its pointing to be among the most helpful items during VR presentations. Although the immersive nature of headset-based VR can have positive effects for education (Youngblut 1998), results from the Hubs study and from others, e.g., Ahn et al. (2021), suggest that some users will prefer or need desktop interfaces. Our desktop approach enables desktop and immersed users to better share virtual worlds, by allowing desktop-based users to have more engaging "cross-reality" avatars.

In our desktop interface, input redirection methods from desktop input to a 3D avatar consider mouse pointing and drawing for a presentation, eye-tracked gaze toward audience members, hand tracking for gesturing, and associated avatar motions such as head and torso movement. These are enabled in part by commodity desktop sensors including a Leap Motion controller on a desk and a Tobbi Eye Tracker 5 on a monitor. Future developments may bring such sensing capabilities to commodity cameras at desktops, as a result of their increasing image quality and emerging machine learning techniques for user tracking from camera imagery.

The interface, seen in Fig. 15, shows a presentation board in the context of the virtual environment viewed from a central classroom position. The teacher's avatar is visible at a podium so that the teacher has feedback about its behavior in relation to desktop inputs. Students are represented by a row of indicators above the board, using visual representations from the class-wide indicators of Sect. 3.5, so the teacher does not need to manipulate view controls to look at regular avatars to understand students. When a teacher looks at one of the student indicators, the teacher avatar's

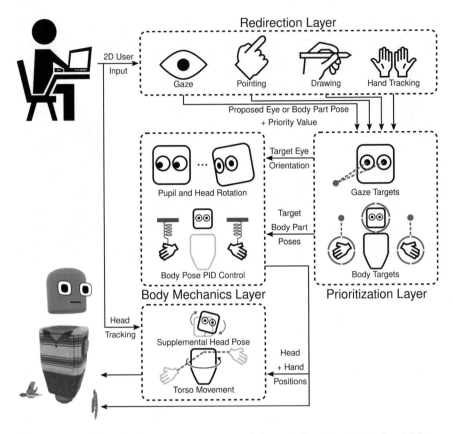

Fig. 16 An overview of major components to control the avatar based on desktop input. Mouse, eye, and hand tracking inputs produce corresponding avatar motion

gaze is directed toward the corresponding student in the 3D VR environment. This involves an interpolation of gaze targets between student indicators and other key interface positions using a triangulation and barycentric coordinates of the desktop gaze within a triangle. When the teacher uses the mouse to point at or draw on the presentation board, the avatar is directed to point or draw on the board in 3D using a ray-like pointing tool. Multiple specific methods were implemented, including interpolating pointing poses recorded from a fully tracked VR user and a simple kinematic pointing approach. In addition to these redirection techniques, the avatar includes an oscilloscope-like mouth that animates based on teacher audio input, subtle idle hand motions to add liveliness when hands are otherwise idle, and blinks based on sensed blinks of the desktop teacher.

Figure 16 overviews the layers of the redirection system. User input from the desktop devices is used by individual redirection methods in the *Redirection Layer*. Each redirection method produces a target position and rotation for the avatar's various body parts. These target poses are provided to the *Prioritization Layer* along with priority levels. This allows certain redirection methods to interrupt others. For example, a gaze redirection method may ask to make the teacher avatar look at a certain student avatar, but it could be interrupted by a higher-priority board-pointing action that makes the avatar look at a board. The priority-based target poses are sent to the *Body Mechanics Layer*, where each body part is animated toward a target pose. Body parts are driven toward targets by a PID controller, which gives more human-like ballistic movements than sudden changes (Woodworth 1899). Head and pupil rotations are controlled by a model of human motion allowing the pupils to rotate without triggering head rotation unless certain thresholds are met. The torso is moved in a way that balances between head and hand motions. Additional motions are layered on top. For example, our implementation reads head position and orientation from the Tobii Eye Tracker, subtracts that from a calibrated position in the center of the user work space, and moves the avatar's head by the corresponding amount. As a result, the teacher can nod or shake their head to respond to a student and have their natural animated character be reflected by the avatar.

A study with 36 viewers in headsets gathered their impressions of the teacher avatar for short presentations (Woodworth et al. 2022), in comparison to avatars animated by a tracked VR headset user, to a more conventional first-person desktop controller, and to our desktop interface without the use of the Tobii eye tracker or Leap Motion hand tracker. The study conclusions can be summarized as: (1) conventional desktop interfaces provide reduced avatar quality (e.g., humanity) compared to headset interfaces, (2) our redirected interface provides different quality from at least one of these conventional approaches, and most likely differs more from the conventional desktop, (3) viewers gazed at the headset and redirected desktop avatars more than at conventional desktop avatars, and (4) some redirected motion (e.g., pointing) was ranked higher with one of the redirected interfaces (and with headset) compared to a conventional desktop.

4 Conclusion and Practical Considerations for Everyday Use

We summarized two of our networked educational VR studies and presented several techniques that could work in combination to improve the interfaces. Finally, based on our observations during these studies and on more general considerations, we suggest the following items are main items that must be addressed for the long-term success of educational VR in everyday contexts:

- *Technical glitches*: substantial visual, audio, and network glitches were encountered in the Hubs study with students attending VR-based classes remotely from home. Technical and setup problems are also common in non-VR remote meetings, e.g., Jennings and Bronack (2001); Grant and Cheon (2007). Such problems were minimal in the Kvasir-VR study when we could control the network and computing devices in a classroom, but substantial effort was involved in setup. Technological improvements for stability and ease of use, along with user pre-training (Meyer et al. Oct 2019), can help.

- *Headset comfort*: The Hubs study results suggest that recent headset designs lack sufficient comfort, for class-duration use, for a substantial number of users. Comments mentioned pressure or heat on the face, fatigue, or difficulty focusing. Headset designs have improved over decades, in terms of weight and performance, so improvements are likely to continue.

- *Support users who can't use headsets*: non-headset viewing methods should be supported as an alternative for accessibility and due to the discomfort noted above. Desktop interfaces may be enhanced by techniques such as those in Sect. 3.6. Another possibility is to reconsider stationary displays that were more common in VR work before the resurgence of headsets, such as large 3D monitors or TVs. Some users may not be able to benefit from any common VR methods, so detailed descriptions or other educational presentation methods will still be required.

- *Ease of startup*: Broad adoption requires getting started with VR to be easy for teachers and students. They may not have much time to configure or learn new technology or interfaces. The Kvasir-VR project involved substantial network configuration and device setup in classrooms. In the Hubs study, some students did not succeed at getting headsets set up on their first attempted class day, so they used desktop viewing. New standalone headsets simplify deployment substantially, with a tradeoff of reduced computing power. Still, devices must be networked, with accounts set up, and applications installed or configured.

- *Writing or note taking*: In a traditional classroom, teachers can generate content extemporaneously and interactively by writing and sketching on a board, and students can readily take notes on paper or on portable devices. Reproducing such features in VR has often led to awkward results. The missing capability was noted for the Hubs study (Yoshimura and Borst 2021), and headset-based attendees of the IEEE VR 2020 conference sometimes removed headsets to access their keyboards (Ahn et al. 2021). There is increasing research on note taking (Chen et al. 2019), sketching (Kern et al. 2021), and typing (Grubert et al. 2018; Pham and Stuerzlinger 2019) interfaces for VR, along with commercial efforts such as the Logitech Ink stylus. Common problems for writing or sketching interfaces include the high precision and haptic sensations that would be needed to match real-world sketching. In some VR environments, it will be beneficial if writing or annotations can be placed more generally in 3D, such as on 3D objects.

- *3D content requirements*: The Kvasir-VR project involved the creation of 3D models by a dedicated artist, and the Hubs class uploaded PDF slides and separate video files. Good 3D models can make better use of VR's capabilities than flat presentations, especially when spatial aspects of objects or surroundings are important for class topics. Teachers may not have time or experience to develop such models, and would benefit from simple 3D content generation methods or libraries of relevant models. In some cases, real objects may be captured for VR using photogrammetry tools. Easy-to-use presentation authoring tools are needed to coordinate such objects in cohesive educational presentations. Teachers may also want to add annotations or modifications extemporaneously in response to class questions or discussions. Overall, a VR content generation and presentation system is desirable that is as easy to use as writing on a board or preparing presentation slides.

- *Large-scale delivery and portability*: A motivation for choosing Hubs for a remote class was that, because it was web-browser-based, it was readily available and widely deployable. It also supported various headsets, desktop, and mobile devices. Such deployability across platforms will be important for long-term success of VR as more consumer options become available. Also, for broad deployability and longevity, standards such as file formats for sharing VR-based educational content or recorded sessions, viewable in multiple tools, could be useful.

- *Privacy/Security*: The increased use, streaming, or storage of sensor data in some of our proposed techniques raises concerns about privacy and security. These have already been raised more broadly for everyday VR, for example, as Facebook (now Meta) can track and mine motions of its headset users (Robertson 2018). Expectations vary by organization and task. For example, gathering data internally during military training may be well-tolerated or justified, but concerns are different for gathering data about school children. Gatekeeping modules, downsampling, or the addition of noise could help prevent detection of user properties beyond those needed for an instructional activity (David-John et al. 2021). Intuitive interfaces for providing users with information and control of data streaming and collection are important, e.g., (Yao et al. 2021). Algorithms for detecting user state should be modular, using only signals that the user opts to share, to give the best estimate possible with a given configuration. Users would be able to toggle which signals are sent, opt out entirely, or simply turn off or omit certain sensors. Users should be given a clear understanding of what information reveals and how it will be used. Special care has to be taken for any long-term storage to provide security, address legal requirements, and avoid misuse of data. In our Hubs study (Yoshimura and Borst 2021), 10 of 13 students indicated having no concerns about others seeing their avatar movements, and the other 3 had slight to moderate concern. All 13 found some value in avoiding showing their real face or surroundings (8 very significantly). So, at least for basic movement tracking, it appears such students favor VR sensing to conventional video capture.

- *Long-term effects on students or children*: The long-term effects of regular use of educational VR are not known, as the currently available educational VR experiences only cover a small or brief part of educational activities. Effects of long VR sessions (several hours) are surveyed by Chap. 2 in this book by Biener, Ofek, Pahud, Kristensson and Grubert. Our Hubs study (Yoshimura and Borst 2021) raises substantial concerns about discomfort with current VR headsets for class-length sessions, with results varying widely across the students. There are some concerns about the general use of VR by young children. They are more susceptible to the arousing impact of the stimuli and less able to regulate the experience of presence (Baumgartner et al. 2008). VR could lead to false memories in young children (Segovia and Bailenson 2009). Additionally, VR use should be limited for young children because their postural control is not yet mature and they strongly rely on visual feedback for motor functions (Miehlbradt et al. 2021). More generally,

VR experiences could effect a person's mental well-being and real-life behavior (Madary and Metzinger 2016). The effects on individuals and society should be considered, and VR users should be informed about known and speculated risks.

Acknowledgements We would like to thank the co-authors of cited work presented in this chapter, who have also provided pictures, tables, and other information: David Broussard, Jason Woodworth, Andrew Yoshimura, Adil Khokhar, Yitoshee Rahman, Ekram Hossain, Sarker Asish, and Ethan Bruce. We are also grateful to collaborators of our earlier related work, and to school and community personnel who supported deployment of Kvasir-VR to Lafayette classrooms and to the Chattanooga Public Library. This material is based upon work supported by the National Science Foundation under Grants No. 1451833 and 1815976, grants from the Mozilla Gigabit Community Fund, US Ignite Application Development Awards, and by the Louisiana Board of Regents under contracts No. LEQSF(2015–16)-ENH-TR-30 and LEQSF(2019-20)-ENH-DE-22.

Appendix

Preliminary results from two ongoing studies are presented here, in support of Sects. 3.1 (Attention Restoration Cues) and 3.3 (Gaze-responsive Presentation).

Figure 17 summarizes performance of 9 attention restoration cues and a no-cue baseline. 65 subjects in a virtual oil rig looked at numbered barrels in sequential order. Distraction spheres appeared in a randomized manner, requiring the subject to glance at the spheres and then return to the barrel task. Visual restoration cues appeared during the distraction. Two conditions, wide and narrow, had the barrels spaced out by different distances. The figure shows the time taken for subjects to look back at the barrel from which they were distracted. A notable result, besides showing the relative performance of cues, is that it differs substantially from prior studies, which focused on guidance to new targets rather than attention restoration. A likely cause is the subjects' memory of the prior attention target. Statistical analysis, and analysis of other metrics, is ongoing.

Figure 18 summarizes ratings given by 37 subjects who viewed the three possible pedagogical agent behaviors during pre-recorded student distractions (Khokhar and Borst 2022). The subjects used a VR headset to watch the student and agent, with an "over-the-shoulder" view behind the student. Three different distraction events were viewed, each with three possible agent behaviors. For each of the resulting 9 combinations, subjects ranked behavior appropriateness, naturalness, and strangeness. Per subject, ratings were averaged across the three events, giving one score per behavior per subject. Preliminary analysis results were that ratings of behavior appropriateness were significantly different between all three behavior pairs. Also, the respond behavior differed significantly from continue and pause in ratings of naturalness and strangeness. Other experiment phases considered reviews of longer presentation sequences and of first-person experiences with the subjects as students. There was some evidence of a respond behavior benefit in each phase.

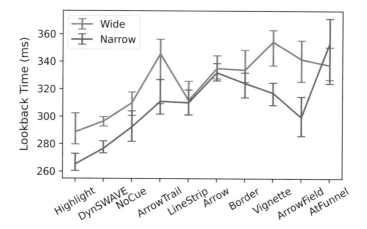

Fig. 17 Time taken for attention restoration with various cues, for wide and narrow target layouts. The median is plotted for 65 subjects. The error bars are computed by bootstrapping and show the range containing 68 percent of 5000 median estimates

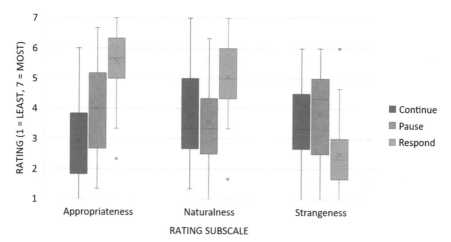

Fig. 18 Ratings of three pedagogical agent behaviors during distraction

References

Agrawal P, Sahana H, De' R (2017) Digital distraction. In: Proceedings of the 10th international conference on theory and practice of electronic governance, pp 191–194

Ahn SJG, Levy L, Eden A, Won AS, MacIntyre B, Johnsen K (2021) IEEEVR2020: exploring the first steps toward standalone virtual conferences. Front Virtual Reality 2:28

Asish SM, Hossain E, Kulshreshth AK, Borst CW (2021) Deep learning on eye gaze data to classify student distraction level in an educational vr environment. In: ICAT-EGVE 2021— international conference on artificial reality and telexistence and Eurographics symposium on virtual environments

Bailenson JN (2021) Nonverbal overload: a theoretical argument for the causes of zoom fatigue. Technol Mind Behav 2(1)

Baumgartner T, Speck D, Wettstein D, Masnari O, Beeli G, Jäncke L (2008) Feeling present in arousing virtual reality worlds: prefrontal brain regions differentially orchestrate presence experience in adults and children. Front Human Neurosci 2:8

Bevilacqua F, Engström H, Backlund P (2019) Game-calibrated and user-tailored remote detection of stress and boredom in games. Sensors 19(13):2877

Biocca F, Tang A, Owen C, Xiao F (2006) Attention funnel: omnidirectional 3d cursor for mobile augmented reality platforms. In: Proceedings of the SIGCHI conference on human factors in computing systems, pp 1115–1122

Borst CW, Kinsland L, Gary (2005) Examples from the chicxulub impact crater. Visualization and interpretation of 3-d geological and geophysical data in heterogeneous virtual reality displays. Trans Gulf Coast Assoc Geol Societies 55:284–293

Borst CW, Lipari NG, Woodworth JW (2018) Teacher-guided educational VR: assessment of live and prerecorded teachers guiding virtual field trips. In: Proceedings of the 2018 IEEE conference on Virtual Reality and 3D user interfaces (VR)

Borst CW, Ritter KA, Chambers TL (2016) Virtual energy center for teaching alternative energy technologies. In: 2016 IEEE Virtual Reality (VR)

Bousefsaf F, Maaoui C, Pruski A (2013) Remote assessment of the heart rate variability to detect mental stress. In: 7th international conference on pervasive computing technologies for healthcare and workshops, pp 348–351

Bower GH, Sahgal A, Routh DA (1983) Affect and cognition. Philos Trans R Soc; Ser B 302(1110):387–402

Bradley MM, Lang PJ (1999) International affective digitized sounds (iads): stimuli, instruction manual and affective ratings (tech. rep. no. b-2). The Center for Research in Psychophysiology, University of Florida, Gainesville, FL

Broussard DM, Rahman Y, Kulshreshth AK, Borst CW (2021a) An interface for enhanced teacher awareness of student actions and attention in a VR classroom. In: 2021 IEEE conference on Virtual Reality and 3D User Interfaces Abstracts and Workshops (VRW), pp 284–290

Broussard DM, Rahman Y, Kulshreshth AK, Borst CW (2021b) Visual indicators for monitoring students in a VR class. In: 2021 IEEE conference on Virtual Reality and 3D User Interfaces Abstracts and Workshops (VRW), pp 502–503

Cacioppo J, Petty R, Losch M, Kim H (1986) Electromyographic activity over facial muscle regions can differentiate the valence and intensity of affective reactions. J Personality Soc Psychol 50:260–268

Chambers T, Raush J, Russo B (2014) Installation and operation of parabolic trough organic Rankine cycle solar thermal power plant in South Louisiana. Energy Proc 49:1107–1116

Chen Y-T, Hsu C-H, Chung C-H, Wang Y-S, BabuSV (2019) ivrnote: design, creation and evaluation of an interactive note-taking interface for study and reflection in VR learning environments. In: 2019 IEEE conference on Virtual Reality and 3D User Interfaces (VR). IEEE, pp 172–180

Coan JA, Allen JJ (2007) Handbook of emotion elicitation and assessment. Oxford University Press

David P, Kim J-H, Brickman JS, Ran W, Curtis CM (2015) Mobile phone distraction while studying. New Media Soc 17(10):1661–1679

David-John B, Hosfelt D, Butler K, Jain E (2021) A privacy-preserving approach to streaming eye-tracking data. IEEE Trans Visualization Comput Graph 27(5):2555–2565

Dill K, Pursel ER, Garrity P, Fragomeni G, Quantico V (2012) Design patterns for the configuration of utility-based AI. In: Interservice/Industry Training, Simulation, and Education Conference (I/ITSEC), number 12146 in I/ITSEC, pp 1–12

Dillman KR, Mok TTH, Tang A, Oehlberg L, Mitchell A (2018) A visual interaction cue framework from video game environments for augmented reality. In: Proceedings of the 2018 CHI conference on human factors in computing systems, pp 1–12

D'Mello S, Olney A, Williams C, Hays P (2012) Gaze tutor: a gaze-reactive intelligent tutoring system. Int J Human-Comput Stud 70(5):377–398

Ekong S, Borst CW, Woodworth J, Chambers TL (2016) Teacher-student VR telepresence with networked depth camera mesh and heterogeneous displays. International symposium on visual computing. Springer, Heidelberg, pp 246–258

Engzell P, Frey A, Verhagen MD (2021) Learning loss due to school closures during the covid-19 pandemic. Proc Natl Acad Sci 118(17)

Falk JH, Dierking LD (1997) School field trips: assessing their long-term impact. Curator: Museum J 40(3):211–218

Fowler A, Nesbitt K, Canossa A (2019) Identifying cognitive load in a computer game: an exploratory study of young children. In: 2019 IEEE Conference on Games (CoG), pp 1–6

Gnacek M, Broulidakis J, Mavridou I, Fatoorechi M, Seiss E, Kostoulas T, Balaguer-Ballester E, Kiprijanovska I, Rosten C, Nduka C (2022) emteqpro—fully integrated biometric sensing array for non-invasive biomedical research in virtual reality. Front Virtual Reality 3

Grant MM, Cheon J (2007) The value of using synchronous conferencing for instruction and students. Journal of Interactive Online Learning 6(3):211–226

Grubert J, Witzani L, Ofek E, Pahud M, Kranz M, Kristensson PO (2018) Text entry in immersive head-mounted display-based virtual reality using standard keyboards. In: 2018 IEEE conference on Virtual Reality and 3D User Interfaces (VR). IEEE, pp 159–166

Huston P, McFarlane B (2016) Health benefits of tai chi: What is the evidence? Can Family Physician 62(11):881–890

Robertson A (2018) How much vr user data is oculus giving to facebook? https://www.theverge.com/2018/4/9/17206650/oculus-facebook-vr-user-data-mining-privacy-policy-advertising

Jennings M, Bronack SC (2001) The use of desktop video conferencing as a medium for collaboration between beginning instructional designers and intern teachers. Int J Educ Telecommun 7(2):91–107

Kern F, Kullmann P, Ganal E, Korwisi K, Stingl R, Niebling F, Latoschik ME (2021) Off-the-shelf stylus: using xr devices for handwriting and sketching on physically aligned virtual surfaces. Front Virtual Reality 2:69

Khokhar A, Borst CW (2022) Modifying pedagogical agent spatial guidance sequences to respond to eye-tracked student gaze in VR. In: ACM Symposium on Spatial User Interaction (SUI 2022), Article No. 15

Khokhar A, Yoshimura A, Borst CW (2019) Pedagogical agent responsive to eye tracking in educational VR. In: 2019 IEEE conference on Virtual Reality and 3D User Interfaces (VR). IEEE, pp 1018–1019

Khokhar A, Yoshimura A, Borst CW (2020) Modified playback of avatar clip sequences based on student attention in educational VR. In: 2020 IEEE conference on Virtual Reality and 3D User Interfaces Abstracts and Workshops (VRW). IEEE, pp 850–851

Lang PJ, Bradley MM, Cuthbert BN et al (1997) International affective picture system (IAPS): technical manual and affective ratings. NIMH Center Stud Emotion Attention 1(39–58):3

Lascio ED, Gashi S, Santini S (2018) Unobtrusive assessment of students' emotional engagement during lectures using electrodermal activity sensors. In: Proceedings of the ACM on interactive, mobile, wearable and ubiquitous technologies, vol 2. issue 3, pp 1–21

Le DA, MacIntyre B, Outlaw J (2020) Enhancing the experience of virtual conferences in social virtual environments. In: 2020 IEEE conference on Virtual Reality and 3D User Interfaces Abstracts and Workshops (VRW). IEEE, pp 485–494

Liao D, Shu L, Liang G, Li Y, Zhang Y, Zhang W, Xu X (2019) Design and evaluation of affective virtual reality system based on multimodal physiological signals and self-assessment manikin. IEEE J Electromagnetics RF Microwaves Med Biol 4(3):216–224

Madary M, Metzinger TK (2016) Real virtuality: a code of ethical conduct. Recommendations for good scientific practice and the consumers of VR-technology. Front Robot AI 3:3

Marín-Morales J, Higuera-Trujillo JL, Greco A, Guixeres J, Llinares C, Scilingo EP, Alcañiz M, Valenza G (2018) Affective computing in virtual reality: emotion recognition from brain and heartbeat dynamics using wearable sensors. Sci Rep 8(1):1–15

Mauss IB, McCarter L, Levenson RW, Wilhelm FH, Gross JJ (2005) The tie that binds? Coherence among emotion experience, behavior, and physiology. Emotion 5(2):175–190

McDuff D, Gontarek S, Picard R (2014) Remote measurement of cognitive stress via heart rate variability. In: 36th annual international conference of the IEEE engineering in medicine and biology society, pp 2957–2960

McDuff DJ, Hernandez J, Gontarek S, Picard RW (2016) Cogcam: contact-free measurement of cognitive stress during computer tasks with a digital camera. In: Proceedings of the 2016 CHI conference on human factors in computing systems. Association for Computing Machinery, New York, USA, pp 4000–4004

Meyer OA, Omdahl MK, Makransky G (Oct2019) Investigating the effect of pre-training when learning through immersive virtual reality and video: a media and methods experiment. Comput Educ 140:103603

Miehlbradt J, Cuturi LF, Zanchi S, Gori M, Micera S (2021) Immersive virtual reality interferes with default head-trunk coordination strategies in young children. Sci Rep 11(1):1–13

Nguyen TTh, Duval T (2014) A survey of communication and awareness in collaborative virtual environments. In: 2014 international workshop on collaborative virtual environments (3DCVE). IEEE, pp 1–8

Nourbakhsh N, Wang Y, Chen F (2013) GSR and blink features for cognitive load classification. In: Kotzé P, Marsden G, Lindgaard G, Wesson J, Winckler M (eds) Human-computer interaction-INTERACT 2013. Springer, Heidelberg, pp 159–166

Peper E, Wilson V, Martin M, Rosegard E, Harvey R (2021) Avoid zoom fatigue, be present and learn. NeuroRegulation 8(1):47–47

Pham D-M, Stuerzlinger W (2019) Hawkey: efficient and versatile text entry for virtual reality. In: 25th ACM symposium on virtual reality software and technology, pp 1–11

Radianti J, Majchrzak TA, Fromm J, Wohlgenannt I (2020) A systematic review of immersive virtual reality applications for higher education: design elements, lessons learned, and research agenda. Comput Educ 147:103778

Rahman Y, Asish SM, Fisher NP, Bruce EC, Kulshreshth AK, Borst CW (2020) Exploring eye gaze visualization techniques for identifying distracted students in educational VR. In: 2020 IEEE conference on Virtual Reality and 3D User Interfaces (VR). IEEE, pp 868–877

Ramlogan S, Raman V, Sweet J (2014) A comparison of two forms of teaching instruction: video vs. live lecture for education in clinical periodontology. Eur J Dental Educ 18(1):31–38

Renner P, Pfeiffer T (2017) Attention guiding techniques using peripheral vision and eye tracking for feedback in augmented-reality-based assistance systems. In: 2017 IEEE Symposium on 3D User Interfaces (3DUI). IEEE, pp 186–194

Ritter III K (2016) Virtual solar energy center: a case study of the use of advanced visualization techniques for the comprehension of complex engineering products and processes. PhD thesis, University of Louisiana at Lafayette

Rivu R, Jiang R, Mäkelä V, Hassib M, Alt F (2021) Emotion elicitation techniques in virtual reality. IFIP conference on human-computer interaction. Springer, Heidelberg, pp 93–114

Russell J (1980) A circumplex model of affect. J Personality Soc Psychol 39:1161–1178

Russell JA (1978) Evidence of convergent validity on the dimensions of affect. J Personality Soc Psychol 36(10):1152

Segovia KY, Bailenson JN (2009) Virtually true: children's acquisition of false memories in virtual reality. Media Psychol 12(4):371–393

Steinicke F, Meinecke A, Lehmann-Willenbrock N (2020) A first pilot study to compare virtual group meetings using video conferences and (immersive) virtual reality. In: ACM symposium on Spatial User Interaction (SUI) 2020

Villanueva I, Campbell BD, Raikes AC, Jones SH, Putney LG (2018) A multimodal exploration of engineering students' emotions and electrodermal activity in design activities. J Eng Educ 107(3):414–441

Wang H, Chignell M, Ishizuka M (2006) Empathic tutoring software agents using real-time eye tracking. In: Proceedings of the 2006 symposium on eye tracking research & applications, pp 73–78

Woodworth JW, Broussard D, Borst CW (2020) Designing tools to improve collaborative interaction in a VR environment for teaching geosciences interpretation. In: Mensch und Computer 2020-Workshopband

Woodworth JW, Borst CW (2017) Design of a practical tv interface for teacher-guided VR field trips. In: 2017 IEEE 3rd Workshop on Everyday Virtual Reality (WEVR). IEEE, pp 1–6

Woodworth JW, Borst CW (2021) Designing immersive affective tasks for emotion elicitation in virtual reality. In: 2nd momentary emotion elicitation and capture workshop

Woodworth JW, Broussard D, Borst CW (2022) Redirecting desktop interface input to animate cross-reality avatars. In: 2022 IEEE conference on Virtual Reality and 3D User Interfaces (VR), pp 843–851

Woodworth RS (1899) Accuracy of voluntary movement. Psychol Rev: Monograph Suppl 3(3):i

Yao P, Lympouridis V, Zyda M (2021) Virtual equipment system: face mask and voodoo doll for user privacy and self-expression options in virtual reality. In: 2021 IEEE conference on Virtual Reality and 3D User Interfaces Abstracts and Workshops (VRW). IEEE, pp 747–748

Yoshimura A, Borst CW (2020a) Evaluation and comparison of desktop viewing and headset viewing of remote lectures in VR with mozilla hubs. In: ICAT-EGVE 2020—international conference on artificial reality and telexistence and Eurographics symposium on virtual environments

Yoshimura A, Borst CW (2020b) Remote instruction in virtual reality: a study of students attending class remotely from home with VR headsets. In: Hansen C, Nürnberger A, Preim B (eds) Mensch und Computer 2020 - Workshopband. Bonn, Gesellschaft für Informatik e.V

Yoshimura A, Borst CW (2021) A study of class meetings in VR: student experiences of attending lectures and of giving a project presentation. Front Virtual Reality 2:34

Yoshimura A, Khokhar A, Borst CW (2019a) Eye-gaze-triggered visual cues to restore attention in educational VR. In: 2019 IEEE conference on Virtual Reality and 3D User Interfaces (VR), IEEE

Yoshimura A, Khokhar A, Borst CW (2019b) Visual cues to restore student attention based on eye gaze drift, and application to an offshore training system. In: Symposium on spatial user interaction, pp 1–2

Youngblut C (1998) Educational uses of virtual reality technology. Technical report, Institute for defense analysis, Alexendria VA

Yu K, Gorbachev G, Eck U, Pankratz F, Navab N, Roth D (2021) Avatars for teleconsultation: effects of avatar embodiment techniques on user perception in 3d asymmetric telepresence. IEEE Trans Visualization Comput Graph 27(11):4129–4139

Zhang Y, Pfeuffer K, Chong MK, Alexander J, Bulling A, Gellersen H (2017) Look together: using gaze for assisting co-located collaborative search. Personal Ubiquitous Comput 21(1):173–186

Enhancing Multisensory Experience and Brand Value: Key Determinants for Extended, Augmented, and Virtual Reality Marketing Applications

Svetlana Bialkova

Abstract The rapid growth of extended reality (XR) technologies, such as augmented reality (AR), virtual reality (VR), and mixed reality (MR), provides avenues to turn market place into a highly innovative way of commerce. However, understanding customer's demands, combined with scarce examples on successful marketing in virtual reality, opens a knowledge gap. To close this gap, the current chapter enrols auditing of literature from the perspective of consumer needs and market demands. Combining theoretical insights with different AR/VR technologies and their real market applications, we suggest a framework on how to augment experience, encompassing processing from attention to action. The conceptual framework could be implemented in development of appropriate high-tech AR/VR environments, providing appealing multisensory experience, and thus, enriching the brand portfolio with innovation going beyond traditional marketing practices.

1 Introduction

Technological development fostered increase in the interest towards extended reality (XR) technologies, such as virtual reality (VR), augmented reality (AR), and mixed reality (MR). Although virtual worlds (simulated 3D environments for social and economic interaction) might open new avenues, the potential to do marketing in/between virtual worlds calls further investigation (Bialkova 2018, 2019a). Despite the efforts of different brands to launch digital commerce channels and stores in virtual world, commerce encompassing virtual reality platforms has a limited success, and some brands have even closed their virtual stores.

Previous studies have addressed possible reasons, as quality of virtual world and life (Animesh et al. 2011; Guo and Barnes 2009), individuals experience (Hoffman and Novak 2009; Takatalo et al. 2008), communal interactions and bounds (Piyathasanan et al. 2015; Spaulding 2010).

S. Bialkova (✉)
Liverpool Business School, Liverpool John Moores University, Liverpool, UK
e-mail: S.Bialkova@ljmu.ac.uk

© The Author(s), under exclusive license to Springer Nature Switzerland AG 2023
A. Simeone et al. (eds.), *Everyday Virtual and Augmented Reality*, Human–Computer Interaction Series, https://doi.org/10.1007/978-3-031-05804-2_7

While at the infancy of technology, the quality of virtual environments and life was reported to do not be at high level and precision (Nash et al. 2000), nowadays, the technology seems to be well developed. Although, the acknowledged potential of AR/VR/XR implementation in marketing and consumer practices, scientists (e.g. Alcañiz et al. 2019; Wedel et al. 2020) recognised a knowledge deficit on how to turn virtual worlds into innovative way of commerce, and thus, calling further investigation.

To explore the VR market potential, therefore, a shift has been going from virtual reality as a validating marketing research instrument for "real life" towards marketing within virtual reality itself. Several brands including leaders in respective market started to introduce different applications, e.g. IKEA place AR app (www.ikea.com), Coca-Cola augmented virtuality experience with the first Drinkable Ad (www.coca-colacompany.com), Walmart VR shop (www.walmart.com).

It is important to note hereby that various applications could be implemented along the reality-virtuality continuum (suggested by Milgram and Kishino 1994). See Fig. 1 for examples of enhanced consumer experience along the reality-virtuality continuum.

While in real environment the world is unmodelled, in VR the world is completely modelled. In augmented reality, virtual products are superposed on a real-life scene, and in augmented virtuality, virtual products and/or virtual contexts are augmented with real-life information.

Yet, the question is: which environment is most suitable and when to be implemented along the consumer journey. We have to point out hereby that marketing in real worlds and in virtual worlds may differ. From one side, the existing marketing strategies addressing real-life scenarios might be outdated and not appropriate for AR/VR/XR environments, which invites a remediation of previous tactics. From other side, on methodological level, there is a need to look closely at specific characteristics along the reality-virtuality continuum to advise implementation of most relevant approaches and technology. Moreover, on purely perceptual level, there might be a difference in the way information coming from different sensory modalities is integrated and interpreted. In this respect, it is important to understand how

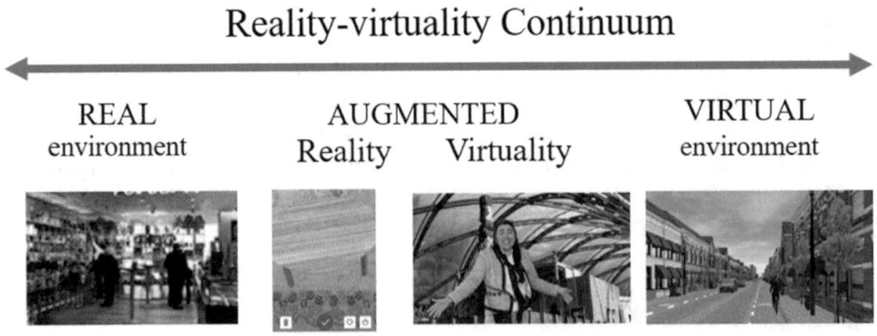

Reality-virtuality Continuum

Fig. 1 Reality-virtuality continuum

specific virtual reality features affect perception (in)between worlds, and what is the impact on the consequent consumer behaviour.

A lack of knowledge, however, on how brands may create brand value and generate real market profit via VR technology calls for creating new practices. Brands should explore innovative ways to enhance their image within the virtual worlds. For example, it would be useful to apply virtual reality as a persuasive communication tool. Academic research already suggested to compare virtual worlds to movie /TV soap opera (Muzellec et al. 2013, 2012), to employ virtual reality as a vehicle for advertising (Clemons 2008; Scaraboto et al. 2013; Tikkanen et al. 2009) and branding (Hemp 2006; Piyathasanan et al. 2015; Ramanathan and Purani 2014). It is puzzling, however, why consumers are still resistant towards these environments, despite the recognised benefit of AR/VR application for marketing practices.

We have to note, however, to implement working marketing strategies, it is crucial to understand first user needs and demands in virtual worlds, particularly concerning the human factor. Taken that buyer decision processes in virtual worlds are not that simple (Alcañiz et al. 2019; Flavián et al. 2019) and may not reflect the real-world buying behaviour (Bialkova 2019a; Papagiannidis et al. 2008), brands should look for new ways to reach, attract, and retain customers.

It may be useful to apply AR/VR/XR as a persuasive communication tool, to employ it as a vehicle for branding (Bialkova 2019a), advertising (Bialkova 2018), and commerce (Bialkova 2016). Especially taken the potential of virtual worlds for segmenting and targeting real-world users (Belisle and Bodur 2010; Hemp 2006), important aspect that calls further exploration is the delivery of (virtual) product/service to real-world customers. Moreover, avatars created in virtual worlds (an animated representation of the user, e.g. Holzwarth et al. 2006) do not always correspond to the real identity of the creator/user (Belisle and Bodur 2010; Belk 2013). Thus, it is still debatable what the avatar' purchase behaviour is; does it follow the same pattern as purchasing real-world goods for its creator (real customers). Therefore, understanding customers' demands, combined with failing industry initiatives and little available information concerning successful virtual reality marketing examples opens a knowledge gap, inviting further investigation.

We argue that augmenting specific virtual reality features and effects (e.g. visuals, sound, fostering interactivity) might possibly enhance experience. Enhanced experience was reported to lift the brand value (Bialkova 2019a), leading to brand advocacy (Bialkova 2019b; Bilakova and Ros 2021), and increased purchase intent (Bialkova and Barr 2022). To create value for business and generate real market profit, therefore, we assume, there is a need to provide meaningful connections to the brand in virtual worlds and beyond.

The current chapter addresses this challenging task. In particular, we explore potential avenues for successful marketing incorporating AR/VR/XR technology in order to:

(a) enrich the marketing space
(b) best communicate value
(c) bring consumer into the brand world

(d) optimise the user experience

(e) inspire memorable customer journey.

Present work covers the following aspects: First, auditing of existing literature and marketing practices concerning AR/VR/XR is provided. A special focus on consumer journey addresses user needs and demands when it comes to virtual environments and experience with/in. A holistic framework is suggested, summing up the key parameters emerging from attention to action as crucial in creating AR/VR/XR experiences shaping unforgettable consumer journey.

2 Marketing and Virtual Worlds

While few years ago, people were "visiting" virtual worlds, being mostly passive consumers of the content provided there, today, virtual reality platforms may "transfer" customers to alternative worlds, offering new opportunities for social and economic interactions. Due to the advance of technology, users are provided a high-tech environment where VR is not perceived as fictional, but rather extension of the reality (e.g. Takatalo et al. 2008) and the self (Belk 2013). Considering the virtual worlds as platforms for digital self-expression (e.g. Gabisch 2011; Piyathasanan et al. 2015), consumers may enter a world (VR platform) where they could create, produce, offer, and advocate the brand. This is a great opportunity not just for co-creation, but actually immersing the consumer in the middle of the experience, and the control of what happens. In traditional marketing, usually the brands are responsible for creation, production, and advocacy. Gratefully to the technology, we observe a change in the communication landscape, allowing consumers to be in the centre. Such customer centred approach provides a better understanding of their needs and demands, for delivering appropriate products and services.

The "virtual cave" in Heineken experience (www.heinekenexperience.com) is a classic example of enhanced experience (see Fig. 2, author personal visit and photo). More recent examples are coming from Samsung Gear and HTC Vive offering consumers experience anytime, anywhere they are (for detailed overview on further marketing cases, including relevant sources /links see Wedel et al. 2020).

Furthermore, virtual worlds may empower marketing for real-world products and services (Hemp 2006). Suggesting novel ways of assortment organisation and shopping (Speicher et al. 2018), opportunity for new products development, marketing within the virtual environment could be created (Ramanathan and Purani 2014), online and offline worlds could be connected (Piyathasanan et al. 2015). Note, however, it was argued whether consumers' behaviour in the virtual world has any influence on the actual purchase decisions in the real world (Clemons 2008), especially taken that VR had a negative effect on satisfaction (Pizzi et al. 2019).

Following the above notions, the question we address hereby is whether real-world products are actually bought when being marketed in virtual worlds. We further

Fig. 2 Example of branded experience in VR

questioned the purchase of virtual world products, and how to enhance the real brand value.

2.1 Brand Value Enhancement

Interaction with brands and products in the virtual worlds was recognised to increase consumers' product knowledge (Gabisch 2011), attitudes (Castillo and Bigne 2021), and purchase intentions (Bialkova and Barr 2022), to create and enhance brand awareness (Arakji and Lang 2008; Wedel et al. 2020). Furthermore, it was reported that virtual experience mediates customer loyalty in both virtual and real worlds (Piyathasanan et al. 2015), facilitates brand equity (Nah et al. 2011) and brand advocacy (Bialkova 2019b; Bialkova and Ros 2021).

One might ask how brand value is normally increased. In real marketing practices, various communication vehicles, advertising, and brand management strategies are incorporated. The crucial is that brand elements should be memorable, meaningful, likeable, to facilitate the leverage and perception of brand equity.

We might want to transfer this knowledge when developing appropriate AR/VR/XR applications. Note, however, virtual world might follow different patterns from those in the real world (Bialkova 2019a) concerning the value creation (Piyathasanan et al. 2015), and thus brand loyalty and marketing (Bialkova 2018). Moreover, behaviour could vary between real/virtual worlds as consumer needs/demands might be different than those expressed in the real-world counterparts. Whether this is the case, there is a need for further investigation, to better understand consumer demands and behaviour when it comes to AR/VR/XR. Such understanding will provide the necessary knowledge to design innovative high-tech solutions to enhance (user) experience and augment the consumer journey.

2.2 Augmenting the Experiential Journey

Experiential journey transferring consumers between worlds could be a key to successful branding. As already reported, implementing appropriate AR/VR/XR applications might enhance enjoyment, attractiveness, satisfaction (Bialkova 2018, 2019a). Pleasurable experiences combined with enhanced product/brand knowledge, increased purchase intention (Bilakova and Barr 2022), brand loyalty and recommendation (Bialkova and Ros 2019, 2021). Note, however, the effectiveness of AR/VR/XR environments is likely to vary along the customer journey, i.e. pre-purchase, purchase, post-purchase (Wedel et al. 2020). Although, a personalised experiential journey could be easily traced and analysed, its evaluation might further depend on the specific context.

Moreover, by activating various perceptual modalities, interacting with multiple touchpoints at different stages of the journey, consumers could be offered engaging and memorable experience. Taken that the customer demand and desire may reconfigure (Denegri-Knott and Molesworth 2013) over time and AR/VR experience, the question we address hereby is: *how to augment experience?*

In particular, it is important to know how consumers engage in virtual worlds, how they interact with the brand and each other, and how they achieve possible outcomes. Recent work in the context of advertising and branding reported that the background information modulates the way the VR environment is perceived, and thus, the attractiveness and enjoyment of the VR experience (Bialkova 2018, 2019b). The manipulated environmental factors modulated engagement, naturalness, presence, and liking of the VR environment. Experience was further enhanced, when parallel to visual, other modalities are stimulated. For example, integrating music within the VR environment was associated with higher engagement and liking (Bialkova and van Gisbergen 2017), and thus augmentation of experience (Bialkova 2019a). Although technology is still under development and studies are scarce on how to stimulate gustatory and olfactory modalities, there are some marketing practices integrating AR/VR in dining. For example, enhancing taste and olfaction (e.g. www.Sublimotionibiza.com) shown to reflect augmentation of experience.

Above cases show that the overall experience evaluation depends on the way stimuli from various modalities are perceived. Such evidences are important in building fundaments for developing the conceptual framework presented hereby.

3   The Conceptual Framework

Understanding the mechanisms underlying behaviour from attention to action is the core of current framework. The key concepts emerging from classical literature, namely, attention, sensation, perception, and action are elaborated, summed up in a model (see Fig. 3) and discussed in detail below.

3.1   Attention

Attention, defined as the process mediating perceptual selectivity for further action (Allport 1987; Yantis 2000), is incorporated in various models in marketing and consumer behaviour. The extent to which information is attended to and perceived plays a crucial role in a wide variety of consumer processing. In the AR/VR context, it was argued that the attention users pay to the environment (Witmer and Singer 1998) determines their sense of presence (Steuer 1992).

Attention of consumers, in both, real and virtual worlds, depends on various environmental characteristics like visual stimuli (colour, shape, form, objects, graphics), sound, smell, material (texture), and taste.

We further argue the selective nature of attention. From one side, the mindset with which the individual enters the virtual world could guide attention towards particular stimuli. Thus, selectivity of attention could be top-down, determined by the goal of consumer (Wedel et al. 2020) or the task (Yantis 2000). From other side, attention could be stimulus driven, bottom-up processing, i.e. on the basis of the salience of information within the visual field. Information is most likely to be noticed when it stands out in the crowd, either structurally (e.g. salience) or

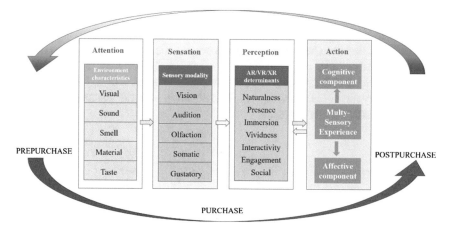

Fig. 3   Model from attention to action in AR/VR/XR experience

temporally (e.g. unexpectedness), as reported from psychology (Itti and Koch 2000). Attention grabbing mechanisms, in terms of gaze guiding was also applied as an adaptive computer-based tool, for complex technical systems (Weyers et al. 2020).

In real-life marketing practices, however, one may argue that tactics employing, e.g. subliminal advertising does not require attention. Evidences from psychophysics and neuroscience literature are opposing such statements. Although information could be processed non-consciously, i.e. subliminal and preconscious, such processing is modulated by spatial and temporal attention (for details, see Kouider and Dehaene 2007). Based on the above-mentioned, we could argue that attention is the bottleneck. The attended information is further processed in formation of senses.

3.2 Sensation

Sensation is defined in psychology as the process allowing brains to synthesise and organise the multisensory flow, coming via the five senses. Stimulations arriving through various sensory pathways are constantly updating the human brains (Thesen et al. 2004). A multifaceted, multisensory integration between various modalities was already reported from psychology and psychophysics (Talsma et al. 2010). Further support for the variety of multisensory phenomena comes from neuroscience. Sensory-specific brain responses and perceptual judgments concerning one sense can be affected in relations with other senses (Driver and Noesselt 2008; Thesen et al. 2004).

Creating sensory representations of the external world is fundamental to effective perception and cognitive functioning. Mostly sound and vision were modulated in AR/VR earlier. Gratefully to the advancement of technology, today, virtual worlds could be experienced through various sensory modalities, e.g. visual (Bialkova 2018), auditory (Bialkova 2019a; Bialkova and van Gisbergen 2017), olfactory (Flavián et al. 2021), and somatosensory including touch (Zielasko et al. 2019). Gustatory (Jaller et al. 2021) and body motion (Bialkova and Ettama 2019; Bialkova et al. 2018, 2022) stimulation was also reported to be possible. Involving all senses during experience, we assume, may transfer consumers easily between real and virtual worlds. Therefore, it is crucial to understand how different senses, i.e. input from various sensory modalities (vision, audition, olfaction, somatic, gustatory) shape the perception of AR/VR environments.

3.3 Perception

Perception reflects the process by which attended information is decoded and provided meaning to, in order to have an impact on further action, as acknowledged in psychology literature. Classical AR/VR studies pointed out that the way naturalness, presence, and immersion are perceived, is fundamental for the way the environment will be experienced. Naturalness is associated with the believability of the depiction of the environment itself and events within the environment (Freeman and Lessiter 2001). Naturalness was reported to influence the subjective experience of being in one place or environment, reflecting the presence (Witmer and Singer 1998). Vividness (Steuer 1992) and interactivity (Slater and Steed 2000; Steuer 1992) were recognised as crucial parameters loading on presence. Presence could be achieved even when someone is physically situated in a different environment (McMahan 2003), if this person is well engaged (Slater and Steed 2000). In the context of virtual environments, engagement (Steuer 1992) is associated with the degree of involvement and immersion (Freeman and Lessiter 2001). Studies were able to show that the better the naturalness and presence were perceived to be, the higher was the engagement (Bialkova and van Gisbergen 2017; Lessiter et al. 2001). Furthermore, the level of engagement would provide a better feeling of being inside the environment which is experienced by consumer. As a result, perception and liking of experience have been enhanced (Bialkova and van Gisbergen 2017; Bialkova 2019a).

Note that liking, along with enjoyment and attractiveness contribute to the affective (emotional) component of experience evaluation. Moreover, the level of emotions is influenced by the level of presence, while the feeling of presence is modulated by the "emotional" environments, a circular effect reported for VR environments (Riva et al. 2007). Do not forget, however, that presence and engagement might be also evaluated through cognitive component (Steuer 1992).

Such two-fold perspective, i.e. cognitive and affective, challenges marketers and tech experts to carefully consider what system is most appropriate, and in which context. Another challenge concerns what level of naturalness, presence, and immersion should be designed, to assure an optimal consumer experience. When consumer have to evaluate the functionality of the product, brand, etc. (i.e. enhancing cognitive component), it might be very appropriate to keep a high level of naturalness of the AR/VR environments. By contrast, when the aim is to stimulate feelings (i.e. affective component), it might be more appropriate to transfer consumers to imaginary worlds, providing opportunities to dream and experience fantasy.

3.4 Action

The action stage reflects the actual user behaviour. The perception of interactivity of the virtual environment will determine the sense of being able to take action (Sanchez-Vives and Slater 2005). We might even argue a circularity effect between the perception and action stage. Put differently, the more natural, interactive, and immersive the environment is perceived to be, the higher will be the possibility actions to be taken. As a result, the better the AR/VR/XR environments should be experienced. Note also, the better the virtual environment is experienced, the higher will be the perceived naturalness, presence, and immersion.

In this respect, we assume the more senses are involved, the higher will be the multisensory integration (Driver and Noesselt 2008; Talsma et al. 2010; Thesenet al.

2004). Furthermore, cognitive (e.g. reasoning) and affective (e.g. enjoyment, attractiveness) components should be taken into account. Cognition and affection should be addressed as complementary, fostering multisensory experience that might reflect, respectively, utilitarian (reason driven) and hedonic (emotion driven) purchase journey, as recently reported (Bilakova and Barr 2022).

Another aspect of the current model reflects the social interaction. Although innovative virtual platforms provide opportunity for social collaboration, some challenges might be encountered. These are related to technical, as well as legal issues. In terms of legal checks, notary or other body might be needed to guaranty the legitimacy of avatar creations, contracts, virtual identity/ fidelity of avatar-run businesses. This challenge calls for further advice and consideration by (legislative) authorities. Taken the digitalisation, AR and VR, such policy should be considered worldwide, i.e. transnational. In terms of technicality, the human factor should be taken into account in the system integration. Knowing the mechanisms underlying consumer/avatar behaviour will allow the creation of marketing tools that might successfully transform virtual (reality) to viral market.

4   Model Support and Future Avenues

Current framework was developed based on marketing practices, auditing the literature in psychology, psychophysics, usability and consumer behaviour, as well as classical AR/VR papers. To weight various aspects of the framework suggested, we bring to the attention of the reader some pilot studies from our lab.

In particular, multisensory integration was explored in one of the research lines. How visual and audio modalities interplay and how such interplay enhances experience was investigated via VR environments mimicking real-world scenarios when audio stimuli are manipulated. Naturalness, presence, engagement, and liking of the VR experience were addressed, to test the effect of the manipulated factors. Results are clear in showing that music could evoke complex cognitive and affective responses, and therefore, to alter consumer behaviour when exposed to VR (Bialkova and van Gisbergen 2017). We could further claim, combination of interactive audio and visual displays could stimulate the attention and sensation stage (in the model suggested hereby). As a consequence, the perception of the VR experiences is improved, which could lead to better evaluation and liking. These outcomes are clearly demonstrating that integrating music within the VR environment might increase engagement and liking, could augment the experience, and thus the consumer journey (Bialkova 2019a).

In another research line, movement was stimulated in a VR environment mimicking a real cities' streetscape. While participants were moving through the VR environment, some shops were advertised. The interplay between various background factors (i.e. reflecting attention and sensation stage in the model hereby) was reported to modulate the way consumers experience the naturalness of the environment (i.e. at perception stage). Naturalness further enhanced engagement, and thus, cognitive and affective responses. It was demonstrated that the background information (environmental factors) modulates the way the VR environment is perceived, which reflects the attractiveness and enjoyment of the VR experience (Bialkova 2018).

Naturalness, presence and engagement are crucial parameters determining how the VR experience is liked, as recent study from our lab also confirmed (Bialkova and Ros 2021). The study outcomes further show that the above-mentioned parameters are shaping the brand evaluation and consequent behaviour towards the brand and the company.

In another research line, we have explored how both, cognitive and affective aspects in terms of utilitarian and hedonic values navigate the experience and the purchase journey (Bialkova and Barr 2022). It was shown that utilitarian (i.e. needs and reasons driven) and hedonic (i.e. emotion driven) values are crucial in experience evaluation and consumer journey optimisation. The study further supports the notion that through high-tech applications, different stages, i.e. pre-purchase, purchase and post-purchase could be enhanced, as outlined in the conceptual framework hereby (see Fig. 3).

We have to point out that the current model provides fundaments to better understand mechanisms underlying experiential journey when employing AR/VR/ XR. The holistic framework also opens avenues for future exploration. One possibility for extension could be to look at integration of more sensory modalities, i.e. tactile, gustatory. Another exploration could compare the model effectiveness across various products, brands, retailers, and industries. Research could also focus on how unique selling point propositions could be best brought to the consumer via innovative high-tech environments.

Further innovation could be the implementation of eye-tracking techniques in VR mimicking real-life scenarios. Capturing where precisely the consumers eyes go, attention grabbing properties (attention stage) could be employed to predict buying behaviour (action stage).

Simulating VR environments mirroring the real-life shopping situations could possibly address the shortages of in-store observation being time and effort consuming, obtrusive and costly.

Based on the above-mentioned, we could argue that the implementation of AR/VR/XR could revolutionise the consumer research. Moreover, creating unique, personalised journeys will not just facilitate marketing practices, but it is expected to turn consumers into loyal customers.

5   Implications for Practice

The objective of the present work was to provide a better understanding on how to augment AR/VR/XR experience for everyday consumer applications. A holistic framework was suggested encompassing processing from attention to action in rendering virtual experience that is much more immersive and engaging for the user. Such augmented experience is a prerequisite for enhanced consumer journey.

Based on the framework, we nominated several propositions that could be immediately implemented in practice. The core pillars are:

- **From single to multisensory experience**
- **From static to dynamic user experience**
- **From individual to collaboration**
- **From local platform to global cloud.**

These propositions have been discussed in detail during WEVR 2022 (Bialkova 2022) and are summarised in Fig. 4 hereby.

In line with the presented framework, we have to mention that AR/VR/XR applications might be context specific, and that experience could either reflect real-life scenarios or create a fantasy world. Put differently, the current model could be used by brands to not just replicate their real-world trade dress, but to look for innovative ways to engage consumers, going beyond the local platform and traditional marketing environments.

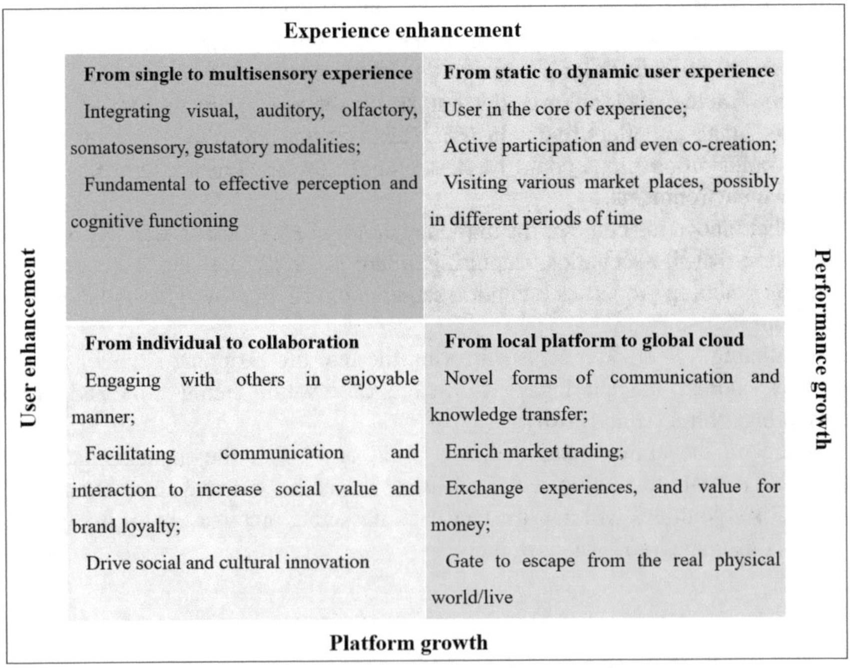

Experience enhancement	
From single to multisensory experience Integrating visual, auditory, olfactory, somatosensory, gustatory modalities; Fundamental to effective perception and cognitive functioning	**From static to dynamic user experience** User in the core of experience; Active participation and even co-creation; Visiting various market places, possibly in different periods of time
From individual to collaboration Engaging with others in enjoyable manner; Facilitating communication and interaction to increase social value and brand loyalty; Drive social and cultural innovation	**From local platform to global cloud** Novel forms of communication and knowledge transfer; Enrich market trading; Exchange experiences, and value for money; Gate to escape from the real physical world/live

User enhancement (left axis) · *Performance growth* (right axis) · **Platform growth** (bottom)

Fig. 4 AR/VR/XR penetration—propositions for practices

In sum

Present work suggests a holistic framework encompassing processing from attention to action, in an attempt to provide the much needed understanding on key parameters shaping experience at different stages along the consumer journey, i.e. pre-purchase, purchase, and post-purchase. The outcomes from lab and field studies strongly support the model introduced hereby. The framework could be directly implemented in practices, in development of appropriate AR/VR/XR applications to optimise brand portfolio and foster extraordinary experiential journey.

References

Animesh A, Pinsonneault A, Yang SB, Oh W (2011) An odyssey into virtual worlds: exploring the impacts of technological and spatial environments on intention to purchase virtual products. MIS Quarterly, pp 789–810

Alcañiz M, Bigne E, Guixeres J (2019) Virtual reality in marketing: a framework, review and research agenda. Front Psychol 10:1530

Allport A (1987) Selection for action: Some behavioral and neuro-physiological considerations of attention and action. In: Heuer H, Sanders AF (eds) Perspectives on perception and action. Erlbaum, Hills-dale, NJ, pp 395–419

Arakji RY, Lang KR (2008) Avatar business value analysis: a method for the evaluation of business value creation in virtual commerce. J Electron Commer Res 9(3):207–218

Belisle J, Bodur HO (2010) Avatars as information: perception of consumers based on their avatars in virtual worlds. Psychol Mark 27(8):741–765

Belk R (2013) Extended self in a digital world. J Consum Res 40(3):477–500

Bialkova S, Barr C (2022) Virtual try-on: how to enhance consumer experience? In: Proceedings of 29th IEEE, conference on virtual reality and 3D user interfaces (VR), 8th workshop on everyday virtual reality, Christchurch, New Zealand, 12–16 March 2022

Bialkova S, Ettema D, Dijst M (2022) How do design aspects influence the attractiveness of cycling streetscapes: results of virtual reality experiments in the Netherlands. Transport. Res. Part a: Policy and Practice 162:315–331

Bialkova S, Ros E (2021) Enhancing employer branding via high tech platforms: VR and digital, what works better and how? Managem. Rev.: Socio-Econ. Stud. 32:85–102

Bialkova S, Ros E (2019) Talent management: the potential of VR and digital innovations. In: Proceedings of EURAM2019: exploring the future of management. Lisbon, Portugal, 25–28 June 2019

Bialkova S, Ettema D (2019) Cycling renaissance: the VR potential in exploring static and moving environment elements. In: Proceedings of IEEEVR2019, 5th workshop on everyday virtual reality, Osaka, Japan, 23–27 March 2019

Bialkova S, Ettema D, Dijst M (2018) Urban future: unlocking cycling with VR applications. In: Proceedings of IEEE VR2018, VAR4Good: virtual and augmented reality for good, Reutlingen, Germany, 18–22 March 2018

Bialkova S, van Gisbergen MS (2017) When sound modulates vision: VR applications for art and entertainment. In: Proceedings of IEEE VR2017, 3rd workshop on everyday virtual reality, Los Angeles, US, 18–22 March 2019

Bialkova S (2022) From attention to action: key drivers to augment VR experience for everyday consumer applications. In: Proceedings of 29th IEEE, conference on virtual reality and 3D user interfaces (VR), 8th workshop on everyday virtual reality, Christchurch, New Zealand, 12–16 March 2022

Bialkova S (2019a) Consumers journey enhancement: the VR impact. In: Proceedings of EMAC2019, Hamburg, Germany, 28–31 May 2019

Bialkova S (2019b) Managing tomorrow: the VR impact, invited talk at EURAM2019, labs: augmented reality and virtual reality implications for management. In: Proceedings of EURAM2019b: exploring the future of management, Lisbon, Portugal, 25–28 June 2019

Bialkova S (2018) From indoor to outdoor: how virtual reality reshapes advertising? In: Proceedings of ICORIA2018, Valencia, Spain, 21–23 June 2018

Bialkova S (2016) Virtual worlds and real market perspectives. In: Virtual revolution 2016, Velthoven, The Netherlands. 1–3 March 2016

Castillo MJS, Bigne E (2021) A model of adoption of AR-based self-service technologies: a two country comparison. Int J Retail Distrib Managem 49(7):875–898

Clemons E (2008) The complex problem of monetizing virtual electronic social networks. Decis Support Syst 48(1):46–56

Denegri-Knott J, Molesworth M (2013) Redistributed consumer desire in digital virtual worlds of consumption. J Mark Manag 29(13–14):1561–1579

Driver J, Noesselt T (2008) Multisensory interplay reveals crossmodal influences on 'sensory-specific' brain regions. neural responses, and judgments. Neuron 57:11–23

Flavián C, Ibáñez-Sánchez S, Orús C (2019) The impact of virtual, augmented and mixed reality technologies on the customer experience. J Bus Res 100:547–560

Flavián C, Ibáñez-Sánchez S, Orús C (2021) The influence of scent on virtual reality experiences: the role of aroma-content congruence. J Bus Res 123:289–301

Freeman J, Lessiter J (2001) Here, there and everywhere: the effect of multichannel audio on presence. In: Proceedings of ICAD 2001, (Espoo, Finland, July 29–August 1, 2001)

Gabisch JA (2011) Virtual world brand experience and its impact on real world purchasing behavior. J Brand Manag 19(1):8–32

Guo Y, Barnes S (2009) Virtual item purchase behavior in virtual worlds: an exploratory investigation. Electron Commer Res 9:77–96

Hemp P (2006) Avatar-based marketing. Harv Bus Rev 84(6):48–57

Hoffman DL, Novak TP (2009) Flow online: lessons learned and future prospects. J Interact Mark 23(1):23–34

Holzwarth M, Janiszewski C, Neumann MN (2006) The influence of avatars on online consumer shopping behavior. J Mark 70(4):19–36

Itti L, Koch C (2000) A saliency-based search mechanism for overt and covert shifts of visual attention. Vision Res 40:1489–1506

Jaller C, Andersen NBS, Nilsson NC, Paisa R, Damsbo M, Serafin S (2021) MARTYR: exploring ingredients of virtual dining experiences. In: Proceedings of IEEE VR2021, 7th workshop on everyday virtual reality, Lisbon, Portugal, 27 March–3 April 2021

Kouider S, Dehaene S (2007) Levels of processing during non-conscious perception: a critical review of visual masking. Philosophical Trans Royal Soc b: Biol Sci 362(1481):857–875

Lessiter J, Freeman J, Keogh E, Davidoff J (2001) A cross-media presence questionnaire: the ITC-sense of presence inventory. Presence 10(3):282–329

McMahan A (2003) Immersion, engagement and presence. A method for analyzing 3D video game theory reader. In: Mark JP, Wolf, Perron B (eds) The video game, theory reader. NY, US, Routledge, Taylor & Francis Group, pp 67–86

Milgram P, Kishino F (1994) A taxonomy of mixed reality visual displays. IEICE Trans Inform Syst 77(12):1321–1329

Muzellec L, Kanitz C, Lynn T (2013) Fancy a coffee with friends in 'Central Perk'? reverse product placement, fictional brands and purchase intention. Int J Advert 32(3):399–417

Muzellec L, Lynn T, Lambkin M (2012) Branding in fictional and virtual environments: introducing a new conceptual domain and research agenda. Eur J Mark 46(6):811–826

Nah FF, Eschenbrenner E, DeWester D (2011) Enhancing brand equity through flow and telepresence: a comparison of 2D and 3D virtual worlds. MIS Q 35(3):731–747

Nash EB, Edwards GW, Thompson JA, Barfield W (2000) A review of presence and performance in virtual environments. Int J Human-Comput Interac 12(1):1–4

Papagiannidis S, Bourlakis M, Li F (2008) Making real money in virtual worlds: MMORPGs and emerging business opportunities, challenges and ethical implications in metaverses. Technol Forecast Soc Chang 75(5):610–622

Piyathasanan B, Mathies C, Wetzels M, Patterson PG, de Ruyter K (2015) A hierarchical model of virtual experience and its influences on the perceived value and loyalty of customers. Int J Electron Commer 19(2):126–158

Pizzi G, Scarpi D, Pichierri M, Vannucci V (2019) Virtual reality, real reactions? comparing consumer's perceptions and shopping orientation across physical and virtual-reality retail stores. Comput Hum Behav 96:1–12

Ramanathan J, Purani K (2014) Brand extension evaluation: real world and virtual world. J Product Brand Managem 23(7):504–515

Riva G, Alcañiz M al. (2007) Affective interactions using virtual reality: the link between presence and emotions. Cyberpsychol Behav 10(1):45–56

Sanchez-Vives MV, Slater M (2005) From presence to consciousness through virtual reality. Nature Neurosci Rev 6(4):332–339

Scaraboto D, Carter-Schneider L, Kedzior R (2013) At world's end: exploring consumer-marketer tensions in the closure of adverworlds. J Mark Manag 29(13–14):1518–1541

Slater M, Steed A (2000) A virtual presence counter. Presence 9(5):413–434

Spaulding TJ (2010) How can virtual communities create value for business? Electron Commer Res Appl 9(1):38–49

Speicher M, Hell P, Daiber F, Simeone A, Krüger A (2018) A virtual reality shopping experience using the apartment metaphor. In: AVI '18: Proceedings of the 2018 international conference on advanced visual interfaces

Steuer J (1992) Defining virtual reality: dimensions determining telepresence. J Commun 42(4):73–93

Takatalo J, Nyman G, Laaksonen L (2008) Components of human experience in virtual environments. Comput Hum Behav 24(1):1–15

Tikkanen H, Hietanen J, Henttonen T, Rokka J (2009) Exploring virtual worlds: success factors in virtual world marketing. Manag Decis 47(8):1357–1381

Talsma D, Senkowski D, Soto-Faraco S, Woldorff MG (2010) The multifaceted interplay between attention and multisensory integration. Trends in Cognitive Sci 14(9):400–410

Thesen T, Vibell JF, Calvert GA, Osterbauer RA (2004) Neuroimaging of multisensory processing in vision, audition, touch, and olfaction. Cogn Process 5:84–93

Yantis S (2000) Goal-directed and stimulus-driven determinants of attentional control. In: Monsell S, Driver J (eds) Control of cognitive processes: attention and performance XVIII. MIT (2000)

Wedel M, Bigne E, Zhang J (2020) Virtual and augmented reality: advancing research in consumer marketing. Int J Res Mark 37(3):443–465

Weyers B, Frank B, Kluge A (2020) A formal modeling framework for the implementation of gaze guiding as an adaptive computer-based job aid for the control of complex technical systems. Int J Human-Comput Interact 36(8):748–776

Witmer G, Singer MJ (1998) Measuring presence in virtual environments: a presence questionnaire. Presence: Teleoperators Virtual Environ 7(3):225–240

Zielasko D, Krüger M, Weyers B, Kuhlen TW (2019) Passive haptic menus for desk-based and HMD-projected virtual reality. In: Proceedings of IEEEVR2019, 5th workshop on everyday virtual reality, Osaka, Japan, 23-27 March 2019

Using Think-Aloud Protocol in Immersive VR Evaluations

Xuesong Zhang and Adalberto L. Simeone

Abstract There is a growing research interest concerning the use of VR as a medium in which to stage experimental evaluations. However, it is still unclear whether conventional usability evaluation methods can be directly applied to virtual reality evaluations and whether they will lead to similar insights when compared to the results of conventional usability real-world laboratory studies. Furthermore, the impact of graphic and interaction fidelity of the virtual prototype on the evaluation result is largely unexplored. Hence, we conducted two user studies with 44 participants. Results in the first study show that 61% of the reported usability problems were shared by both versions, highlighting the potential of Immersive Virtual Reality Evaluations (IVREs) as a method to evaluate early design concepts before committing to a physical prototype. In the second study, we found that usability issues related to the manual operation of the interactive device might not be identified if the interaction is implemented via supernatural techniques. In terms of graphical implications, designers should focus on those visual elements that communicate information to users. We discuss these implications and provide guidelines for deploying IVREs.

1 Introduction

The user-centered design (UCD) process starts with a concept based on the context of use, which is then followed by creating one or more prototypes at different fidelity levels (Lim et al. 2006). Prototypes are then iteratively refined through successive evaluations (Benyon 2019). However, building high-fidelity physical prototypes of a proposed concept or early idea is not always possible because of costs, time and practicality, or because the technology required could be immature or even unfeasible given current technological constraints.

X. Zhang (✉) · A. L. Simeone
Department of Computer Science, KU Leuven, Leuven, Belgium
e-mail: xuesong.zhang@kuleuven.be

A. L. Simeone
e-mail: adalberto.simeone@kuleuven.be

© The Author(s), under exclusive license to Springer Nature Switzerland AG 2023   197
A. Simeone et al. (eds.), *Everyday Virtual and Augmented Reality*, Human–Computer
Interaction Series, https://doi.org/10.1007/978-3-031-05804-2_8

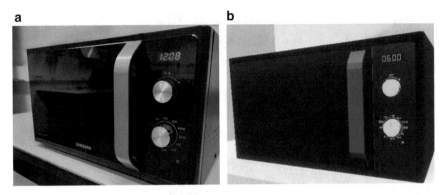

Fig. 1 Microwave (**a**) and its virtual twin (**b**) used in our user study

Virtual Reality (VR) can provide a way to address this challenge, since it allows us to simulate virtual counterparts of any device and technology, even non-existing ones. Voit et al. (2019) demonstrated the feasibility of inspecting the usability of an artifact in VR, as well as through online, laboratory, AR, and in situ studies. Further, Mäkelä et al. (2020) used VR as a medium to stage field studies in virtual environments (VEs) simulating the proposed context of use. We refer to this type of studies as "*Immersive Virtual Reality Evaluations*" (IVREs).

As a concept, IVREs propose the use of controllable VEs in which to stage the evaluation of a (virtual) prototype. Our hypothesis is that a significant share of the usability problems that will be uncovered in this manner would also present themselves if the virtual prototype were to be physically built. In this context, IVREs provide various advantages: (1) there is positive evidence that results obtained with VR evaluations can be transferred to the real world (Mathis et al. 2021); (2) we can stage field studies in VR that could be difficult to replicate in the real life (Mäkelä et al. 2020); (3) IVREs can be performed before a physical prototype is actually built, thus serving as a way to identify potential problems at an early stage; (4) since the evaluation happens fully in VR, IVRE can be performed from everyday environments instead of dedicated laboratories.

However, it is still unclear whether conventional usability evaluation methods can be as effective in VR as they are in reality in uncovering real usability issues from virtual prototypes. To answer this research question, we designed and conducted the first study, a comparative between-subjects user study: we evaluated the usability of a microwave oven model on both the real-world appliance and on an interactive "virtual twin". We define *virtual twins* as the explicitly virtual interactive counterpart to the more popular "digital twin" term (Tao et al. 2019), which focus more in the direct data-based connection and do not always require the existence of a three-dimensional model that replicates its interactive functionalities in VR. We chose to focus our study on a microwave, as they represent household appliances that many people are familiar with.

Both prototypes were evaluated via the *Think-Aloud Protocol (TAP)* (Ericsson and Simon 1984) and questionnaires such as the *System Usability Scale (SUS)* (Brooke 1996), *Post-Study System Usability Questionnaire (PSSUQ)* (Lewis 1995, 2002) to rate the user perceived usability and the *NASA Task Load Index (NASA-TLX)* (Hart 2006) to assess the task workload. For more information on these methods, please see Sect. 3.1.

Results from the first user study indicate that 61% of the usability issues present on the virtual prototype were also identified on the physical appliance. Participants reported similar numbers of identified usability problems in terms of type, when evaluating both prototypes with the *TAP* method. The SUS, PSSUQ, NASA-TLX questionnaires also offered similar scores when performing inspection in both settings. However, some usability issues were only detected with the physical prototype, since the haptic feedback is missing in VR. Although most of the usability problems that were solely found in VR were attributable to limitations of the interactive modality, VR participants behaved more actively and felt more free to interact with the virtual prototype because of the perceived lack of consequences from any wrongdoings.

Given the positive results in terms of overlapping problems, in the second study, we sought to understand whether the graphical appearance or the interactive fidelity of the virtual twin would affect the type and severity of the usability issues. Indeed, there is evidence in literature that the prototype representation itself or its interactive affordances can have an impact on the evaluator's behavior and perceived usability (Hoggenmüller et al. 2021; Simeone et al. 2017). Further, due to technical limitations of VR, it might be necessary to interact in a way that is different from its real-world analog. Interactions that we take for granted in the real world, such as pressing a button or turning a knob, are not so trivial in VR, especially when no haptic feedback is present (Nilsson et al. 2021) or the accuracy of the hand-tracking system is insufficient (Schneider et al. 2020).

In the second study, we created four different versions of the microwave oven that were modelled according to two levels of fidelity in both graphics (between *Simple* and *Physically Based Rendering* materials) and interaction (between *Natural* and *Supernatural* interaction modalities (McMahan et al. 2016; Lubos 2018; Yu and Bowman 2018), where simple 3D interaction metaphors replace complex real-world manipulations).

Similar to the first study, participants used the TAP method to evaluate the version of the microwave oven they were assigned to (see Sect. 6). We focused on the qualitative feedback of participants. Results indicate that supernatural interaction could make it difficult to identify problems which are related to manual manipulations, despite the fact that participants identified a comparable number of usability problems. In addition, more efforts should be made to achieve a less ambiguous graphical appearance during the implementation of virtual twin.

This chapter is an extended version of the paper entitled "Using the Think Aloud Protocol in an Immersive Virtual Reality Evaluation of a Virtual Twin," which was published in ACM SUI 2022. The contribution of this chapter is threefold: (1) We report the identified usability problems and analyze them depending on whether they affected both prototypes or solely one of the two. (2) We analyze the impact of graphic and interaction fidelity during the usability evaluation for the virtual prototypes. (3) We discuss which factors may affect the identification of usability problems in IVREs and provide a set of guidelines for performing them in the future studies.

2 Related Work

In this section, we present user studies employing VR to stage user studies and research related to the effects of graphics and interaction in VR.

2.1 Evaluations Performed in Virtual Reality

In 2007, Ye et al. (2007) investigated the possibility of applying VR technologies to computer-aided product design. Users viewed the generated 3D graphics through lightweight stereoscopic LCD glasses and perceived haptic feedback with a SensAble PHANToM Desktop device. Results showed that the proposed system offered a natural and intuitive interaction, which contributes to reducing the development time and design costs. The 2010 study by Bruno et al. (2010) is the closest to our first study. The authors compared the results of the usability evaluation of a real microwave, to those resulting from the evaluation of its three-dimensional twin experienced via a semi-immersive, stereoscopic, projected screen without head-tracking. Differently from our study, participants did not use the TAP: the experimenters observed them while they interacted with the two microwave ovens. Participants then filled in a usability satisfaction questionnaire. Results indicate that the number and type of reported problems were comparable across conditions.

In 2013, Falcão and Soares (2013) proposed the application of VR to the usability evaluation of consumer products. The authors stated that traditional evaluation with physical prototypes is expensive and difficult to rapidly iterate on. They suggested that employing VR technology could solve those limitations, but did not carry out any study.

More recently, with the increased affordability of VR HMD-based solutions (Bellalouna 2019), researchers began to explore the use of VR as a research method. In 2019, Voit et al. (2019) compared the evaluation of technological artifacts under different settings: online, VR, AR, laboratory setup, and in situ. Three standard questionnaires (AttrakDiff (Hassenzahl et al. 2003), ARI (Georgiou and Eleni 2017), and SUS were employed for the evaluation. They found that the medium used to assess artifacts affected the results, with VR providing comparable results to the real world.

In 2020, Mäkelä et al. (2020) analyzed the feasibility of applying VR as a testbed for the evaluation of different implementations of public displays. A largely similar user behavior was observed in both the VE and the real-world setting. Paneva et al. developed a "Levitation simulator" (2020), where a virtual twin allows users to prototype applications based on ultrasound hardware. They used the simulator to develop two levitation games, which were then implemented on the physical platform. Performance and engagement levels with the developed games were found to be comparable to those reported with the real apparatus.

In 2021, Mathis et al. (2021) replicated an authentication schema from a real-world laboratory setting into a VE. Results indicated that the virtual version has similar usability as the physical prototype in terms of entry accuracy, entry time, and perceived workload, as measured by task completion times and NASA-TLX scores (Hart 2006). Saffo et al. (2021) also leveraged a social VR platform (VRChat) and replicated two published user studies: a quantitative study on Fitt's law and a qualitative study on tabletop collaboration. Those two social VR studies yielded analogous results as in the original study, which contributes positive evidence to the validity of using social VR to perform HCI evaluations.

With this work, we further contribute to the growing field of work on studies ran in VR, with a study comparing applying the TAP method to a conventional inspection and to one performed in immersive VR.

2.2 Effect of Prototype Representation in Terms of Graphic Appearance

There is evidence that using realistic lighting and graphics affects immersive users perceive the sense of presence in the VE. Previous work shows that when visual realism is improved, participants can perceive greater presence and respond with more realistic behavior (Slater et al. 2009; Yu et al. 2012). Furthermore, Simeone et al. found that the graphical appearance of a material affect user behavior in the VE (Simeone et al. 2017). In 2021, Hoggenmuller et al. presented a comparative user study of real-world VR (i.e., 360° video in VR), computer-generated VR, and real-world video (Hoggenmüller et al. 2021). By comparing the results gathered from these three prototype representations, authors found that in the real-world VR representation, despite users perceiving high presence, the user experience was similar to the other two representations. However, qualitative data showed participants focused on different experiential and perceptual aspects with different representations, highlighting that the choice of a proper graphic appearance is important in collecting user feedback.

2.3 Effect of the Interactivity Fidelity of Prototype

In this chapter, we define the virtual prototypes explicitly as the virtual interactive counterpart to the more popular term "digital twin" (Tao et al. 2019), which does not always require the existence of a three-dimensional object that replicates its interactive functionalities in VR. The ability to interact is an important feature of the virtual twin. McMahan et al. pointed out the interaction fidelity along with display fidelity affects user performance, presence, engagement, and system usability (McMahan et al. 2012). Furthermore, the interaction fidelity is an "uncanny valley" in terms of user performance: the low fidelity interaction contributes to comparable results as the high fidelity (McMahan et al. 2016). User performance is better than with the mid-fidelity approach. Rogers et al. further suggested the impact of interaction fidelity varies between interaction tasks; however, users prefer the high interaction fidelity since it is more immersive and enjoyable (Rogers et al. 2019). To our knowledge, there is no other empirical work investigating the impact of interaction fidelity on IVREs.

3   User Study 1: Physical Versus Virtual Prototypes

We designed a between-subjects user study with the aim of comparing the results of a usability evaluation of a microwave oven in a real-world laboratory setting, with those resulting from the inspection of its virtual twin while the evaluator is immersed in a VE. Both evaluations were performed using the *Think-Aloud Protocol (TAP)* and standard questionnaires including *SUS, PSSUQ, NASA-TLX*. The independent variable in this study was the STUDY MODALITY: {Real Environment (RE), Virtual Environment (VE)}.

We recorded the entire evaluation process and transcribed the participants' dialogs. We further analyzed the data resulting from the TAP to identify the problems, the scope each related to, and their severity. Participants were asked to inspect a microwave oven. As a common kitchen appliance, microwaves share functions whose implementation varies between manufacturers. In the study, participants acted as the evaluators. We assigned them a set of tasks that used the microwave's advanced functions to achieve a desired effect (such as defrosting food based on the time or the weight, the combination of grill and microwave function).

While participants all shared to some extents a basic understanding of how a microwave works, we expected that the specific way in which the oven interfaces are implemented across manufacturers would have led to the surfacing of various usability problems. Further, we hypothesized that a share of these problems would have manifested themselves in the virtual twin as well. The study thus aims to investigate the extent of this overlap, and the nature and severity of the identified problems, through qualitative analysis. The results provide further insights on whether performing the IVRE alone on a concept of a product that does not yet exist physically could become a valid complementary tool to help refine and iterate faster on design activities, before committing to a physical prototype.

3.1 Usability Evaluation Methods

Think-Aloud Protocol. The Think-Aloud Protocol (TAP) asks participants to verbalize their thoughts while performing specific tasks (Ericsson and Simon 1984). The information collected provides an account of which usability problems were experienced and indications as to the source of these issues.

Alhadreti and Mayhew compared three TAP types to the evaluation of the user interface of a university library website (Alhadreti and Mayhew 2018). They were: the *concurrent* TAP method, where users verbalize their thoughts while interacting (Ericsson and Simon 1984); the *retrospective* TAP method, where users provide a report after finishing interacting with the object of the evaluation (Ericsson and Simon 1984); the *hybrid* method, which represents the combination of the first two types (Følstad and Hornbæk 2010). Results show that the concurrent TAP method detected more usability problems than the retrospective TAP. No significant differences were found between concurrent and hybrid method in terms of number of problems. The concurrent TAP needed the shortest amount of time in terms of conduction and analysis among those methods. For these reasons, we chose the concurrent TAP as the usability evaluation method to use in our user studies.

Questionnaires. Using questionnaires in usability evaluations is a common practice that allows experimenters to collect data in a quick and cost-effective way (Zaharias and Poylymenakou 2009). The *System Usability Scale (SUS)* (Brooke 1996) is a widely used validated questionnaire, since SUS is a valid and reliable tool to quickly measure the perceived usability of products or services (Brooke 2013). SUS is a cheap, effective, and robust tool and works even with a small sample (8–12 users) to get a valid assessment (Tullis and Stetson 2004; Bangor et al. 2009). The SUS questionnaire consists of ten different questions with a five-point scale ranging from *1: strongly disagree* to *5: strongly agree*. Researchers usually use a scoring system (from *0: negative* to *100: positive*) that enables the comparison of two versions of an application (Brooke 2013).

We also used the *Post-Study System Usability Questionnaire (PSSUQ)* (the shorter version) in our user study, which consists of 16 items and measures the system usability from *System Usefulness*, *Information Quality* to *Interface Quality* (Lewis 2002). In PSSUQ, unlike SUS, a seven-point scale was used, ranging from *1: strongly agree* to *7: strongly disagree*. Thus, a lower score means a better evaluation. This questionnaire is suitable for evaluating different types of products at different development stages based on its generalizability (Lewis 2002).

To measure the perceived workload while accomplishing tasks, we use the *NASA Task Load Index (NASA-TLX)*, which consists of six subscales, namely *Mental Demand*, *Physical Demand*, *Temporal Demands*, *Frustration*, *Effort*, and *Performance* (Hart 2006). A twenty-point scale (*1: Low, 20: High*) was used here. The summary of unweighted scores represents the overall workload experienced from 6 to 120.

Those questionnaires have been used in previous IVRE studies, e.g., (Voit et al. 2019; Mathis et al. 2021), thus we applied them in our study as well.

3.2 Apparatus

We created a virtual twin of a real microwave appliance (Fig. 1a) by Samsung (MG23F301E). This microwave was released in 2014 (according to its manual[1]) and has been superseded by an improved model released in 2021. It is fully functional and owned by one of the authors. Based on this model, we created a three-dimensional replica using Blender (Fig. 1b). One of the features of this microwave oven is that if there is no further change after setting the function or timer, the microwave will automatically start cooking within two seconds. While participants could overall be assumed to be familiar with the basic functionality of a microwave, we expected to find various usability problems depending on how well its physical interface had been designed.

The virtual twin has the same dimensions as the physical microwave. Its interactive features were implemented in Unity 2020.3.3,[2] and it was rendered with the High Definition Rendering Pipeline.[3] Participants interacted with the virtual twin through a HTC Vive Pro HMD.[4] Interaction with the microwave dials and buttons was implemented via collision-based selection with a Vive controller, due to the insufficient accuracy of the embedded hand-based detection. In the VE, the controller appears as a virtual hand with a small cube aligned to the index finger as a reference. The addition of this reference cube was necessary because during pilot testing, users without VR experience noted that it was difficult to determine whether the hand actually touched the button.

When the reference cube collides with a button, participants can press the trigger to confirm the selection, which triggers the action associated with the collided button on the microwave. If the cube collides with a dial, participants need to press the trigger and hold while turning their wrist to rotate the dial. During the experiment, participants also needed to open the microwave door to put in or take out (virtual) food, if necessary. The door was likewise opened by holding the trigger on the controller in the proximity of the handle and pulling (respectively, pushing) it until it was fully opened (closed). The virtual twin simulated all the functionalities of the physical microwave. It also plays sounds and updates the information on the screen in the same way the real oven does when certain button combinations are pressed. An animation was created to simulate the defrost/heat/microwave/grill process inside the microwave.

The group that interacted with the physical appliance did so in our laboratory, where the oven had been temporarily placed. A separate cup containing water is secured inside the microwave oven to prevent it from running empty. No food or other drinks were actually heated in this condition. The user study was approved by the Ethical Review Board of our institution.

---

[1] https://www.manua.ls/samsung/mg23f301eas/manual?p=1.

[2] https://unity3d.com/unity/whats-new/2020.3.3.

[3] https://docs.unity3d.com/Packages/com.unity.render-pipelines.high-definition@11.0/manual/index.html.

[4] https://www.vive.com/eu/support/vive-pro-hmd/category_howto/about-the-headset.html.

3.3 Demographics

We recruited 24 participants (13 male, 11 female) between the ages of 23 and 32 (MEAN = 26.96, SD = 2.63) for this user study. Twelve participants were randomly assigned to each group. They were recruited through internal mailing lists, word-of-mouth and social media. There was no compensation for participation in this user study.

3.4 Procedure

After filling a consent and a demographics form, we introduced participants to the TAP evaluation method and the procedure to perform it. Then, participants were asked to sit in front of the (virtual) microwave to perform the evaluation. Participants had to complete eight tasks with the (virtual) microwave, in randomized order (see Table 1). The tasks required participants to press certain buttons and rotate the dials to defrost/heat/microwave/grill food with a specified power for a certain duration. These tasks were designed to prompt participants to pay attention to the icons, operate all the buttons or knobs, and experience all the functions of the microwave oven. A cup is prepared and treated as the food described in the task. The brief instructions detailing how to perform them came from the manual and were relayed to the participants by the experimenter. Before the formal evaluation, participants went through a training session to get familiar with the interaction in the VE. The experimenter introduced the interaction with the HMD and its controller, where participants could practice the interaction action.

After participants confirmed they understood the purpose of the evaluation, the experimenter gave them a signal to start. While performing it, participants described their actions and thoughts. They finished the task by either completing or abandoning it. Participants were allowed to abandon the task after three unsuccessful attempts to complete it. Three tasks were abandoned by two participants. In total, 192 trials were performed (8 tasks × 24 participants). We recorded the RE sessions with a smartphone camera, and VE sessions with OBS[5] to record the first-person view.

After evaluating the microwave, we asked participants to fill in four web-based questionnaires: the SUS, the PSSUQ, the NASA-TLX, and a custom questionnaire with ten required five-point scale questions (where 1 is strongly disagree and 5 is strongly agree). In the custom questionnaire, two questions aimed to understand participants' opinion on whether performing the TAP affected their task performance; five questions aimed at eliciting their view on the TAP method. The remaining questions aimed to understand the impact of the experimenter's presence on the study. Then, the participants proceeded to freely explore the microwave in either the real or virtual environment without completing tasks. After this exploration phase, participants needed to fill in another custom questionnaire with three questions with

---

[5] OBS- https://obsproject.com/.

Table 1 Task list for each microwave

Task 1	Defrost food for 3 min
Task 2	Set clock to 15:34
Task 3	Microwave 30 s on 600 W
Task 4	Keep the food warm for 1 min 30 s
Task 5	Grill for 2 min
Task 6	Heat 4 min 30 s with the high microwave and grill function
Task 7	Heat 10 min with the low microwave and grill function
Task 8	Defrost 500 g food

a five-point scale. Those questions asked participants to compare the physical and virtual models in terms of the similarity of their appearance and their operational similarity (1: completely inconsistent; 5: completely consistent). We also asked them to predict whether performing the task with the virtual prototype would require more time than with the physical prototype (1: strongly disagree; 5: strongly agree). At the end of the study, we conducted semi-structured interviews to let participants walk us through their feedback on the use of the TAP in the RE and in the VE. Each evaluation lasted about 60 min.

4   Results of User Study 1

In this section, we report the quantitative data collected during the study. The identified usability problems were differentiated according to whether they affected one or both prototypes. We then categorized them into four common areas. Finally, we report the results of the questionnaires filled by the participants after the evaluation and the task completion times.

4.1   Detected Usability Problems from Think-Aloud Protocol

Distribution of the detected problems. We followed a two-stage extraction process to identify the usability problems, leading from individual problems to final problems, as proposed by Alhadreti and Mayhew (2018). After this process, a total of 46 distinct usability problems were identified; of these, 28 overlapping problems were detected for both the virtual and real microwave. Five problems were only found by the participants in the RE, and 13 problems are unique to the VE (see Fig. 2).

| 28 | 5 | 13 |

■ Overlap ▪ RE ▪ VE

Fig. 2 Distribution of detected usability problems

We compared the number of detected problems by performing a Kruskal-Wallis H-test on the data, as in Alhadreti and Mayhew's work (2018). There was no significant difference in terms of STUDY MODALITY ($p = 0.975$): the number of reported usability problems was comparable across both conditions (VE: MEAN = 8.91, SD = 4.30; RE: MEAN = 8.92, SD = 4.21).

Categorization of the detected usability problems. We grouped them into four categories according to the motivations behind their occurrences (from the users' perspective). Their distribution is shown in Table 2.

C1: *Misoperation of the appliance due to misunderstanding the process.*
The setting-start processes of the functions are not always same within the same microwave. However, if the user does not fully understand or remember the process correctly, they might then not know what the next step to perform is. Hence, the user might press the wrong button or get stuck in the process. For example, if there is no other operation by the user after two seconds of the set time or function, the microwave oven will automatically activate. During the user study, five participants pressed the clock button after setting the function and timer, and the microwave started running at the same time by accident. They assumed the clock button represents the *"start"* function and pressed this button again for the next task. However, the button did not work as expected, because pressing it enters the time setting mode.

C2: *Misoperation due to not being able to find the desired button/dial/functions.*
Participants know what the next step is. However, they cannot find the desired function or button. For example, participants need to set the clock to 15:34 in *Task 2*. They need to change the minute digit after setting the hour digit. However, seven participants did not know which button they should have pressed to change the mode from hours to minutes.

C3: *Confusion caused by similar functions.*
The appliance provides two or more similar functions under a different menu, and the participant could not distinguish them. Hence, the participant chose the wrong function and cannot then reach their goal. For example, there are two defrosting functions based on either the time or the weight, respectively.

C4: *Confusion caused by the text, icon, position, shape of button/knob.*
The icon and text on the device surface is ambiguous, and user might misunderstand the function intended by the designers. The description of the text or the button shape misleads users to operate them incorrectly. For example, participants pressed the knob, which can only be rotated.

Table 2 Allocation of the number of reported usability problems between VE and RE in terms of problem type and severity

	Overlap					RE					VR				
	SUM	H	M	L	E	SUM	H	M	L	E	SUM	H	M	L	E
C1	9	4	3	2	0	1	0	1	0	0	2	0	0	1	1
C2	5	1	2	1	1	2	1	0	0	1	0	0	0	0	0
C3	5	2	2	1	0	0	0	0	0	0	0	0	0	0	0
C4	9	1	2	6	0	2	0	0	1	1	11	0	1	9	1

Distribution of the detected problem in terms of the severity. According to the problem's impact on the performance (task completion time), each problem is assigned with one of four severities: *H: Critical*; *M: Major*; *L: Low*; and *E: Enhancement* (Dumas et al. 1999; Alhadreti and Mayhew 2017; Zhao et al. 2014; Alhadreti and Mayhew 2018). Their distribution is shown in Table 2.

The list of detected usability problems. The following are the usability problems we identified through a two-stage extraction process (Alhadreti and Mayhew 2018), which were identified in both settings, or only identified in the RE or the VE. We will discuss these usability issues in more detail in the *Discussion* (Sect. 5).

Unique usability problems in the VE

UP1 *Participants perceived the image as blurred. (C4, L, 9 times)*
UP2 *Participants tried to start the microwave by pressing the knob. (C4, E, 4 times)*
UP3 *The knob rotation is not intuitive and slow. (C4, L, 3 times)*
UP4 *The knob rotation is tiresome. (C4, L, 3 times)*
UP5 *Participants cannot open the door. (C4, L, 2 times)*

Unique usability problems in the RE

UP6 *Confusion on how to set the timer. (C2, M, 10 times)*
UP7 *Attempting to start the microwave by pressing the clock button. (C4, E, 8 times)*
UP8 *Using an incorrect knob to adjust the minute setting. (C4, L, 1 time)*
UP9 *The microwave door is hard to open and close. (C4, L, 2 times)*

Overlapping problems in both the RE and VE

UP10 *Participants are confused by similar icons (two defrost icons, three grill-microwave combination icons).(C4, L, RE: 4 times; VE: 7 times)*

UP11 *Participants are confused by similar defrost functions. (C3, H, RE: 2 times; VE: 2 times)*

UP12 *The user misselected another function adjacent to the position of the target function. (C4, M, RE: 2 times; VE: 3 times)*

UP13 *Lack of a START button. (C2, L, RE: 6 times; VE: 8 times)*

UP14 *Lack of a STOP button. (C2, H, RE: 3 times; VE: 3 times)*

UP15 *Activating an empty microwave. (C1, H, RE: 1 time; VE: 2 times)*

UP16 *The knob is not sensitive to small angle rotation. (C4, L, RE: 4 times; VE: 5 times)*

4.2 Custom Questionnaire—TAP Experience

We ran Kruskal-Wallis H tests on the questionnaire results to detect if there were differences when conducting TAP in the RE and in the VE as in Alhadreti and Mayhew (2018). No significant differences were detected. Table 3 shows the results.

4.3 SUS

The SUS scores were first calculated (Brooke 2013), then Shapiro-Wilk tests were run to inspect the normality of the distribution. There is no evidence that the SUS scores of the physical microwave ($W(12) = 0.96$, $p = 0.785$) and its virtual twin ($W(12) = 0.92$, $p = 0.285$) deviate significantly from a normal distribution.

Table 3 Result of the TAP experience questionnaire, where 1 stands for "strongly disagree" and 5 is for "strongly agree"

	VE		RE		
	MEAN	SD	MEAN	SD	p
It felt tiring to perform the TAP	2.75	1.29	2.83	1.34	0.881
It felt unnatural to perform the TAP	2.50	1.24	3.50	1.51	0.098
It felt unpleasant to perform the TAP	2.00	0.95	2.50	1.31	0.384
It felt difficult to perform the TAP	1.92	0.79	2.83	1.47	0.114
It felt time consuming to perform the TAP	2.83	1.27	3.83	1.19	0.067
The presence of the evaluator was unnatural	1.83	0.72	2.58	1.38	0.167
The presence of the evaluator felt unpleasant	1.58	0.67	2.00	1.21	0.531
The presence of the evaluator felt disturbing	1.33	0.65	1.83	1.03	0.181

One-way ANOVA tests were run to determine if there were significant differences in terms of the SUS scores attribute to the microwave across the virtual and real conditions, as also used by Alhadreti and Mayhew (2018). Participants rated the virtual twin (MEAN = 61.25, SD = 11.75) as having a marginally higher usability than the physical microwave (MEAN = 55.63, SD = 16.00), where values between 50.9 between 71.4 correspond to a good level of usability (Bangor et al. 2009). However, the difference was not significant ($p = 0.339$).

4.4 PSSUQ

One-way ANOVA tests were run to determine if there were differences in terms of the PSSUQ scores of the physical microwave and its virtual counterpart. Overall, participants rated the physical microwave (MEAN = 2.12, SD = 1.38) as having lower performance and were less satisfied with it, compared to its virtual counterpart (MEAN = 1.90, SD = 1.01); the virtual microwave was also rated as having higher system usefulness, higher information quality, and higher interface quality; however, no significance was detected among the results ($p = 0.669$). Table 4 shows the partial results.

4.5 NASA-TLX

One-way ANOVA tests were run to determine if there were differences in terms of workload between interaction with the virtual twin or with the real appliance. Overall, participants perceived comparable levels of workload in both the RE (MEAN = 41.92, SD = 15.27) and in the VE (MEAN = 45.92, SD = 17.80) without statistical significance ($p = 0.561$) (Fig. 3).

Table 4 Partial result of PSSUQ questionnaire, where 1 stands for "strongly agree" and 7 is for "strongly disagree"

	VE		RE		
	MEAN	SD	MEAN	SD	p
Overall	1.90	1.01	2.12	1.38	0.669
System usefulness	1.74	1.01	1.76	1.50	0.958
Information quality	2.32	1.38	2.58	1.69	0.687
Interface quality	1.75	1.31	1.89	1.37	0.802

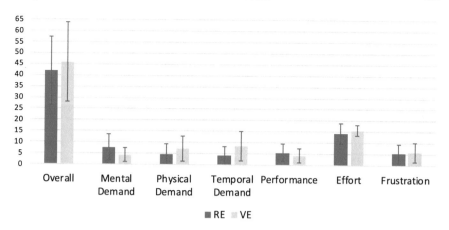

Fig. 3 NASA-TLX scores of the microwave and its virtual twin. The error bars indicate the standard deviation

4.6 Similarity of the Virtual Microwave

After the formal evaluation with TAP, participants were asked to freely interact with the other microwave. During this exploration session, they were not required to complete any task. To understand the perceived experience difference when using the two prototypes, we invited them to answer the following three questions afterward:

- *I think the virtual model is identical to the real microwave oven in terms of appearance. (1: strongly disagree; 5: strongly agree)*
- *I think the virtual model is identical to the real microwave oven in terms of working mechanism. (1: strongly disagree; 5: strongly agree)*
- *I feel that it would take more time when interacting with virtual microwaves than when interacting with physical microwaves. (1: interacting with virtual microwave takes less time; 3: there is no time difference; 5: interacting with virtual microwave takes more time).*

Participants were generally in agreement on the similarity of the implementation of the virtual twin based on the results from the custom questionnaire. They thought that the virtual twin represented a close approximation of the physical appliance in terms of both visual appearance (VE: MEAN = 4.08, SD = 1.08; RE: MEAN = 3.25, SD = 1.36) and operation (VE: MEAN = 3.58, SD = 1.56; RE: MEAN = 3.17, SD = 1.47). However, participants believed interacting with the virtual microwave takes more time than with the physical one (VE: MEAN = 4.50, SD = 0.67; RE: MEAN = 4.50, SD = 0.80). Scores here refer to which microwave type they interacted first.

Table 5 Table reports the full results of the analysis of the task completion times

	VE		RE			
	MEAN	SD	MEAN	SD	$H(2)$	p
Task 1	45.88	15.43	29.67	18.53	4.204	0.040
Task 2	59.83	29.80	73.40	53.30	0.004	0.951
Task 3	34.87	17.23	40.45	20.83	0.641	0.423
Task 4	57.25	41.44	27.71	14.19	5.079	0.024
Task 5	57.02	32.01	32.50	22.10	4.449	0.035
Task 6	54.13	18.00	41.36	37.59	3.649	0.056
Task 7	56.99	19.60	45.83	34.22	2.903	0.088
Task 8	45.01	19.37	52.00	41.02	0.041	0.840
Total time	405.98	88.88	336.12	184.16	3.205	0.073

4.7 Task Completion Times

Task completion times (TCTs) were recorded from the moment when the experimenter gave the signal to start and until the participant communicated they were finished with the task. Participants were free to abandon the task as specified in Sect. 3.4. In total, there was one participant who abandoned two tasks in the RE, while one task was abandoned by one participant in the VE.

Since a Shapiro-Wilk test determined that the TCTs of the microwave significantly deviated from a normal distribution, we used non-parametric methods. Kruskal-Wallis H tests were run on the data to determine if there were differences in terms of TCTs between the data measured in the VE condition and those measured in the RE.

Overall, participants took more time in the VE condition (MEAN = 405.98, SD = 88.88) to complete all eight tasks than in the RE (MEAN = 336.12, SD = 184.16). Participants performed tasks 1, 4, 5 significantly quicker in the RE than in the VE (T1: $p = 0.04$; T4: $p = 0.024$; T5: $p = 0.035$). The full results of all TCTs are shown in Table 5.

5 Discussion of User Study 1

In this section, we discuss the usability issues that were found as a result of both the IVRE and the conventional laboratory-based evaluation.

Table 6 Resolution used in contemporary retail HMDs (Kreylos 2016), we used a HTC Vive Pro in our user study

HMD	Resolution per eye (px)
Oculus Rift S	1440×1280
Oculus Quest 2	1982×1920
HTC Vive	1080×1200
HTC Vive Pro	1440×1600

5.1 Unique Problems in the VE

Through the IVRE, participants reported 13 unique problems that were not found in the inspection of the physical appliance. We classified these into four categories according to the underlying causes (see Sect. 4.1). The most commonly reported usability problems (UPn) in the IVRE were of type C4: eleven such problems were issues related to the "physical" interface of the virtual twin (see Table 2).

The resolution of the HMDs affects the user's perception of the information in the VE. Usability problems related to blur image, such as UP1, was caused by the low resolution of the used HMD (see Table 6). After the evaluation process, we asked participants in the RE whether they perceived icons to be blurry. They confirmed those were false positives, as it was not the case in the RE. The resolution of the headset led to difficulties in interpreting the information as intended by the designers, which affected the user experience. We anticipate that as VR headset technology matures, this will become less of a problem for IVREs in the near future.

The different interaction modality compared to the real world also resulted in other unique VE usability problems (i.e., UP3, UP4).

P7, P8 reported that the knob turning action in VE did not match with their experience. People typically use their fingers to turn knobs; however, wrist rotation is necessary when using a controller in the VE. The interaction with the virtual twin did not reproduce the natural interaction style that is possible in the RE and was reported as slower than expected. Introducing a haptic proxy for the most common interactable controls could mitigate the occurrence of this problem (Simeone et al. 2015).

Similarly, seven participants in the VE reported that they felt tired when rotating the knob, since the interaction is performed mid-air without arm support in a non-ergonomic position. This is similar to the gorilla arm syndrome (Boring et al. 2009). We expect that in the near future, with improved hand-tracking accuracy, natural hand-based interaction will alleviate this problem and reduce the effect of fatigue resulting from holding a controller with a non-negligible weight. Alternatively, using smaller form-factor controllers could provide an interim alternative, as the Vive wands weigh 307 g compared to the 137 g weight of the Oculus Quest 2 controllers.

We also noticed that the insufficient prior VR experience would lead to VE unique usability problems (e.g., UP5). Two participants had no prior experience with manipulating objects in VR and encountered problems while opening the microwave door. They forgot to press the controller trigger when they tried to open the door. Thus, the system did not detect the collision, and the door did not turn to follow the user's hand movements. Our training session lasted for two minutes. A longer session with activities to complete in order to progress could reduce these problems.

5.2 Unique Problems in the RE

When evaluating the microwave with the TAP, five problems were only detected in the RE. These problems are largely dependent on the participant's individual experience and understanding of the system (e.g., UP6, UP7, UP8). These usability issues reveal that the system state is not clear enough to the user. Users' previous experience with similar products can also influence them. *P16* reported that timer button is placed on the bottom right, which was the *"same position as the start button of my own microwave"*. This led to the misoperation.

The lack of haptic feedback of the virtual model is also partly responsible for the unique usability issues in the VE. UP9 was only found affecting the real microwave, due to the haptic feedback of the physical model, which was absent in the VE. *P1* mentioned that the door was difficult to open and to close properly, as it required more strength than expected. In the VE, participants only needed to press the controller trigger to manipulate the door. This usability problem related to the amount of force necessary to operate the door could only be identified in the RE.

5.3 Overlapping Problems in both the RE and VE

When evaluating the microwave with TAP, 61% of the usability problems of the microwave were identified in both the RE and VE conditions.

In both conditions, participants exhibited similar behavior. We followed up the study with a semi-structured interview where we inquired about their experience with this microwave model, and there were only three participants who had prior experience with operating this microwave. The high number of overlapping problems is in line with findings by Bruno and Muzzupappa (2010), where participants experienced similar difficulties in understanding the microwave features in both the real-life laboratory and its virtual replica settings.

We also noticed participants exhibited different behavior when they encountered the same usability problem. In the RE, participants received different haptic sensations when they touch the buttons on the microwave or grab the cup. This feedback varies depending on the material. However, there is no haptic feedback after the controller collides with different virtual objects in the VE. This leads to differences in the way users perceive system state and perform operations, as implied in UP16.

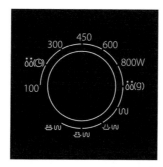

Fig. 4 Icons around the bottom right knob, as seen on the virtual twin

Despite the HMD resolution further complicating participants' perception, each icon on the physical microwave is smaller than 0.5 cm × 0.5 cm, which limits the space available for the icon design. In both conditions, participants pointed out that they encountered problems in understanding the meaning of the icons. Such as *P14* assuming that the "(g)" label is a special icon; eleven participants had problems distinguishing between the three grill-microwave icons because their differences are minimal. Those icons would need to be redesigned in order to become more easily recognizable.

Usability problems related to the product design were identified in both VE and RE settings, such as UP11, UP13, UP14, UP15. Users can correctly interpret the working mechanism of the prototype in the VE, because they can interact with the same virtual buttons of RE in shape, size, and position, and the virtual microwaves have similar sound and animation responses to mimic the working process. These design faults were present in the virtual prototype too, and participants could identify them. Likewise, the usability problems related to inappropriate placement can be identified in both setting, such as UP12. The icons for weight-based defrost and grill functions are located at the 3 and 4 o'clock positions around the bottom right knob (see Fig. 4). Since participants were asked to sit in front of the (virtual) microwave, both icons may have been (partially) obscured by the knobs in view. Indeed, we observed *P20 (RE)* and *P22 (VE)* both misselect one of the functions, since both are adjacent to each other.

However, we noticed participants acted differently in the RE and VE when they encountered the same problem. For example, U16, in the time/weight setting, when users turn the upper knob less than 30 °C, the time/weight information on the screen will not change. We believe this represents a feature *working as intended* to prevent misoperation. *P17 (RE)* was confused and commented "*I think it is not the right knob*", since they were certain that the rotation action did occur, while *P3, P9* (VE) continued to try to rotate the knob with the controller and commented "*It's hard to rotate in VR*".

5.4   Task Completion Time

Three out of the eight tasks took significantly longer in the VE than in the real-world setting. These three tasks required participants to select a function and then set a certain time interval from 90 s to 180 s. Participants were asked to continuously rotate the knob, and within this time range, the timer increased by 10 s for every 30 °C rotation movement, which required participants to precisely control the knob. When the time interval was not within this range, there was no significant difference in TCTs. Thus, this difference was solely attributable to the interaction technique used to rotate the knob in the VE.

5.5   Experience with Think-Aloud Protocol

Results show that that participants experienced the TAP in the VE and in the RE in a similar fashion. During the user study, the experimenter guides the TAP process by giving the participant essential instructions (e.g., "*could you describe your current action?*") to carry on the study. These interruptions on behalf of the experimenter have often been associated with "Breaks-in-Presence" (Slater and Steed 2000) experienced by the participant. However, in the case of the TAP, the user is explicitly asked to describe their thinking and actions from the start. Thus, the connection between the VE and real world was always there.

However, participants reacted differently to the knowledge of the presence of the evaluator when conducting the TAP. Some, like *P6* were surprised by this "Cross-Reality" (Cools et al. 2021) co-presence: "*It's strange, I know there is another person in the room, but I can't see them*". Conversely, *P10* had the opposite reaction: "*I felt extra comfortable with the presence of the evaluator, this because I felt that they knew the next steps very well*". Some participants did not notice the evaluator: "*I did not even notice the evaluator during the VR session. The headset blocks out the physical environment*". (*P4*). Indeed, the evaluator did not have an avatar in the VE, because they did not interact with the user directly neither in the RE nor in the VE conditions.

6   User Study 2: Graphics × Interactivity Fidelity

In our previous study, we found that both the interaction modalities and the rendering quality of a virtual twin had an impact on the results of an usability evaluation. The focus of this study was these two aspects.

We compared the perceived usability, the task workload, the presence experience, as well as the task completion time when users use the TAP in an immersive VE to inspect a virtual twin of a microwave oven. The TAP was applied here again, so that verbal expressions can be used to understand users' intentions and behaviors. By replicating the functionalities of the microwave in VR in the exact same way as the real appliance operates in the real world, we exclude confounding factors that might be introduced by the design of an ex novo interactive device.

This user study followed a 2 × 2 factorial design with two between-subjects variables, i.e., GRAPHICS FIDELITY, INTERACTIVE FIDELITY. The levels in each independent variables were:

- GRAPHICS FIDELITY: {Color Based Rendering (CBR), Physically Based Rendering (PBR) }
- INTERACTIVE FIDELITY: {Natural Interaction(NI), Supernatural Interaction (SI)}.

This user study also followed a split-plot design. We assigned five participants to each condition to find out the usability issues, since four or five users could identified 80% of usability problems when performing the TAP (Virzi 1992; Hwang and Salvendy 2010).

6.1 Interactivity Fidelity

The *interactivity fidelity* indicates the extents of the similarity between an action performed in VR and its analogous action in the real world (McMahan et al. 2016). In this study, only the interaction with the knob and door was implemented with different interaction fidelities.

In the SI condition, a user needs to touch the knob with their virtual hand and press either the left or the right area on the trackpad to turn the knob counter-clockwise or clockwise (Fig. 5a). Each click is equivalent to 30° rotation, which is the minimum increment with the real microwave. In the NI condition, a user needs to physically rotate their wrist in correspondence of the knob while pressing the trigger button. The knob rotates along with the user's wrist movement (Fig. 7b).

Likewise, the door of the microwave oven can be controlled with two approaches. In the SI, pressing the trigger of the controller while touching the virtual door starts an animation that rotates the door to the fully open or closed position, depending on its initial state. In contrast, the user needs to keep holding the trigger and simultaneously move the door along with the controller in the case of NI.

6.2 Graphics Fidelity

The *Graphics Fidelity* represents an indication of the similarity between materials used to render the microwave oven and those of the physical appliance. Basic Unity *HDRP/Lit* shaders were created in the CBR style (6a), to match the diffuse (Albedo in the Unity terminology) colors from various parts of the virtual microwave oven (enclosure, glass door, handle, buttons, etc.) to those from the physical appliance,

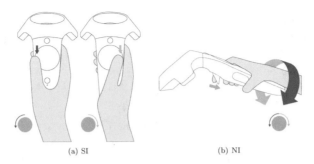

(a) SI   (b) NI

Fig. 5 Rotating the knob using the controller with different interactivity fidelities

(a) CBR style   (b) PBR style

Fig. 6 Graphics fidelity

whereas PBR simulates the physical properties of light (Pharr et al. 2016), for example, absorption and reflection. We used several PBR materials from the *Measured Material Library for High Definition Render Pipeline*[6] to render the plastic, glass, and metal parts of the virtual twin (see Fig. 6b).

6.3   Apparatus and Implementation

We used the same process to implement the virtual twins and apparatus as in USER STUDY 1 (Sect. 3.2).

6.4   Demographics

Twenty participants (four females) were recruited for the laboratory-based user study aged from 25 to 38 (MEAN = 30.10, SD = 4.32). Eight participants had no experience with VR before. We assigned five participants to each of the four groups. Each

---

[6] Library: https://github.com/Unity-Technologies/MeasuredMaterialLibraryHDRP.

participant was compensated with a ten € shopping voucher. The user study was approved by the Ethical Review Board of our institution.

6.5   Procedure

The procedure was similar to USER STUDY 1 (Sect. 3.4). Participants filled in three different questionnaires after completing all tasks with the assigned virtual microwave oven: SUS, NASA-TLX, Igroup Presence Questionnaire (IPQ) (Schubert et al. 2001; Regenbrecht and Schubert 2002). We used IPQ to rate the participants' perceived presence experience in VR. Then, a semi-structured interview was conducted. At the end, we asked them to experience the virtual twin in another combination of interactivity and graphics fidelity and express their preference.

7   Result of User Study 2

In this section, we report the qualitative data collected during the study, the identified usability issues and the user preferences for interactive fidelity.

7.1   SUS, NASA-TLX, IPQ

No significant difference was found between the SUS, NASA-TLX, and IPQ scores when performing evaluation neither with different levels of graphics or interactivity fidelity, nor with the different combinations of these fidelities.

7.2   Preference for Graphics and Interaction Fidelity

Participants showed different preferences for SI and NI in the door and knob manipulation. About 62.5% participants reported they preferred the button click instead of rotating the knob. Half of the participants stated they liked the pulling action for opening the door of the microwave oven.

Only *P10* noticed the graphics difference of the virtual replicas and commented "*this one (with PBR) looks like it has a better quality and is more expensive*". The other participants reported they were "*focusing on the task*", and the graphics difference is "*too slight to notice*".

7.3 Detected Usability Problems

Only new unique usability problems, which were identified in each condition, are listed below.

UP17 *The microwave oven's door was not fully closed (SI only)*
UP18 *Mismatch between the actions in VR and real life (NI only)*
UP19 *Click left button to turn right (SI only)*
UP20 *Cumbersome rotation (NI only)*
UP21 *Inconsistency spatial presence experience (CBR only)*
UP22 *The indicator bar is hard to observe (PBR only).*

8 Discussion of User Study 2

8.1 Interactive Fidelity

According to the semi-structured interview, the continuous drag action in NI was rated by participants as "natural" while the click action in SI as "quick" by the participants. Our participants were split evenly on which of the two approaches they preferred.

The absence of haptic feedback induces certain misoperations in the NI, despite a sound being played by the virtual twin as feedback to indicate that the door has been closed. However, as on the real model, there is no other indication if the door is left open. Participants did not push the door in the closed position properly and incorrectly believed the door was closed from their visual perspective, because of the missing haptic feedback compared to the real-life equivalent, and resulted in the device fail to work. While in the SI, the whole open/close process is unambiguously completed through one click. So participants do not need to check the door status carefully. This, however, suggests that SI could cause UPs related to the manual operation to not be detected, as these actions are performed by the system instead of the user.

Participants reported that they preferred clicking the button in the SI over rotating the controller in the NI for turning the knob. Users need to operate the knob more frequently than opening the door in each task. This caused a user preference to appear. *P18* stated *"when clicking the button, it sounds like the clicking sound of gears biting together when rotating the knob in the real life"*. This insight suggests potential benefits in introducing multi-sensory (Obrist et al. 2017), pseudo-haptic (Pusch and Lécuyer 2011) in the future IVRE designs. *P9* also prefers the click action, which is *"easy and quick"*, while *P17* described the wrist-based rotation action as more *"natural"*.

In SI, we observed that when participants reached the knob rotation limit, they then wanted to rotate the knob counter-clockwise to reach the desired function on the right side of the indicator bar (see Fig. 4). Participants clicked the right button that is actually used for clockwise turning. They were then stuck and complained that the system did not work as expected. After several tries, they figured out they needed to press the left button to reach the desired position on the right side. They rated this interaction as *"needing high mental demand"*.

Surprisingly, the SI has caused users to misunderstand the knob mechanism. Since the rotation was completed by clicking the trackpad, *P17* stated *"these should have been buttons, not rotary knobs"*. Furthermore, participants misunderstood how to operate the knob. Two participants attempted to press the rotary button to achieve their goal. *P15* explained that this action was based primarily on his/her everyday experience that rotary knobs of this shape are sometimes pressable. While the rotation action in NI is still different from itself in the real world, the NI does not affect how users understand the interacting object. The interaction fidelity has different impact on user experience, and preference varies from the tasks, in line with the work by Rogers et al. (2019).

8.2 Graphics Fidelity

In our study, the graphics fidelity did not affect participants' opinion on the microwave oven's usability. About 18 participants (8 PBR, 10 CBR) reported that the blurred icons on the microwave oven were difficult to observe, which forced them to bend down close to the microwave oven; this problem was caused by the low resolution of the VR headset and occurred in both graphics fidelities as in USER STUDY 1. In both graphics settings, participants also complained that icons were hard to recognize. This was caused by the design of the real microwave oven itself, as the icons did not express their meaning with sufficient clarity.

Despite the use of PBR to render the microwave oven, we used pictures of our laboratory as textures for the room used in the VE, instead of replicating a 3D version of all the furniture and equipment (see Fig. 7), since a VE that looked different from the physical room could have constituted a "Break-in-Presence" (Chertoff et al. 2008).

The initial purpose of setting up the VE was to replicate our real-world laboratory to give the glass material surroundings that could be reflected. During the study, *P6* was distracted by the reflection on the glass and started to focus on the VE. Then stated *"it's strange, the wall is flat"*. Being unlit textures, the walls were not impacted by the lighting. The contrast between the high graphical fidelity of the PBR version contrasted with the lower fidelity of the environment, which was not noticed by the participants in the CBR. Future works should explore how the fidelity of the surrounding environment affects the focus where the interaction lies.

(a)Reflectionsontheglass   (b)Virtualenvironment

Fig. 7 Setting of the VE and its reflections on the glass

8.3 IVRE for Human-Centered Usability Evaluation

After comparing the usability problems found in both versions of the evaluations, we found that 61% of these affected both real and virtual prototypes. Crucially, this study was performed with precisely the intention of assessing the extent of this overlap. However, we ideally envision the IVRE to be performed *before* a physical prototype is implemented. In that case, if a physical equivalent of the virtual microwave had not yet been built, the IVRE would have uncovered numerous problems that could also have affected the physical version. Thus, we think that performing an IVRE can represent an efficient method to uncover usability problems in VR and use the insights gained to further refine the design, before finalizing it into a physical prototype.

   We recommend product designers, researchers, and other stakeholders to consider the following guidelines when performing an IVRE.

- *Implement natural interaction techniques that approximate as closely as possible the way the product will be interacted with in the real world.*
  As our results suggest, differences in the interaction modality will be likely flagged as usability problems. However, in line with previous findings from Voit et al. (2019), these are attributable to the VR interaction techniques, rather than the product itself. Evaluators should thus identify and categorize these problems accordingly and reflect on the likelihood of these interactivity issues affecting a physical prototype. Moreover, although both interactive variants of the fidelity led to the identification of a comparable numbers of usability problems, it is worth noting that those related to the manual operation of a device might not have been identified if it had been implemented through supernatural interaction.
- *Providing enough training sessions before performing an IVRE.*
  If the interaction in IVRE does not match the real world's and involves additional devices, such as controllers, designers should introduce users to the VR interaction via a training session. Completing a quick "tutorial" before proceeding to the actual can help to rule out simple issues related to inexperience with the VR interface.
- *Use haptic proxies to uncover related problems.*
  A problem that was uniquely identified in the RE (UP9) was not identified via the

IVRE due to the lack of a physical proxy. Due to the positive effects of incorporating haptic feedback in VR experiences on the believability of the experience (Bruno and Muzzupappa 2010; Nilsson et al. 2021; Simeone et al. 2015) to further enhance the fidelity of the interaction and uncover related problems in VR, future work should explore the inclusion of how different types of haptic proxies in IVREs affect the results (e.g., from passive and completely static proxies to proxies with working but faked buttons or actuators).

- *Emphasize the visual accuracy of the virtual twin.*
  According to our results, we found that visual cues did affect users when evaluating the virtual twin. Making sure that text, icons, buttons, labels are replicated to the same degree of accuracy can provide beneficial cues on their affordances to users. In line with previous research suggesting that the graphical realism of the scene can affect user behavior (Simeone et al. 2017), we also think that by improving the physical accuracy of the materials properties, shadows and lighting used in the scene and on the virtual twin can minimize the occurrence of related problems (e.g., see UP1). Future work should also explore multi-sensory VR experiences, if relevant (Mahalil et al. 2020).

- *IVREs can be especially suited for performing tasks that could be difficult to replicate in the RE.*
  Participants (*P3, P6, P11, P12*) commented that they felt more free to explore the virtual twin's function since "*It won't break*". Analogously, hazardous scenarios (e.g., the microwave catching fire) could be tested in VR without repercussions. In the future, an IVRE coupled with a high-fidelity physics system could also be used to "stress test" devices and simulate conditions that might lead to structural integrity problems.

9 Conclusion

In this chapter, we compared the results obtained after performing an evaluation based on the Think-Aloud Protocol on a real kitchen appliance, to those resulting from inspecting a virtual twin of the same everyday appliance with 24 participants. Furthermore, we analyzed the impact of graphic and interaction fidelity on evaluating the usability of virtual replicas based on a user study with 20 participants.

Results showed that there is a 61% overlap in terms of identified usability problems observed in both the real and virtual evaluations. The results highlight the potential of using Immersive Virtual Reality Evaluations (IVREs) to assess the usability of early VR concepts of physical artifacts and still obtain insightful results that can inform and improve the design of the physical version, which can also reduce the need to build expensive physical prototype. No significant effect of the graphics and interaction fidelity was found. However, participants detected unique usability problems under different settings. The different levels of interactive fidelity did not affect their understanding of the prototype operation in real life. The class of usability problems related to manual operations of the interactive device could be missed if those actions are replaced by supernatural analogs.

However, IVREs are mediated by the VR interfaces used. Some usability issues uniquely found on the virtual twin are attributable to limitations of the VR technology itself, such as the low resolution which affected the interpretation of text and icons. The lack of haptic feedback in the VR condition did not allow to identify related problems that were only identified after inspecting the physical appliance. Thus, we suggest that future work should focus on studying the impact of the graphical and haptic fidelity on IVREs.

Acknowledgements This research is supported by Internal Funds KU Leuven (HFGD8312-C14/20/078).

References

Alhadreti O, Mayhew P (2017) To intervene or not to intervene: an investigation of three think-aloud protocols in usability testing. J Usability Stud 12(3):111–132

Alhadreti O, Mayhew P (2018) Rethinking thinking aloud: a comparison of three think-aloud protocols. In: Proceedings of the 2018 CHI conference on human factors in computing systems, pp 1–12

Bangor A, Kortum P, Miller J (2009) Determining what individual SUS scores mean: adding an adjective rating scale. J Usability Stud 4(3):114–123

Bellalouna F (2019) Vr-based design process of industrial products. In: Proceedings of international conference on competitive manufacturing (COMA–19), South Africa, Stellenbosch, pp 239–245

Benyon D (2019) Designing user experience, Pearson Educación. ISBN: 9781292155531

Boring S, Jurmu M, Butz A (2009) Scroll, tilt or move it: using mobile phones to continuously control pointers on large public displays. In: Proceedings of the 21st annual conference of the Australian computer-human interaction special interest group: design: open 24/7, pp 161–168

Brooke J (1996) Sus: a 'quick and dirty' usability scale, Usability evaluation in industry 189

Brooke J (2013) Sus: a retrospective. J Usability Stud 8(2):29–40

Bruno F, Muzzupappa M (2010) Product interface design: a participatory approach based on virtual reality. Int J Human-Comput Studi 68(5):254–269

Chertoff DB, Schatz SL, McDaniel R, Bowers CA (2008) Improving presence theory through experiential design, presence: teleoperators and virtual environments 17(4):405–413

Cools R, Han J, Adalberto SL (2021) Selectvisar: selective visualisation of virtual environments in augmented reality. In: Designing interactive systems conference (New York, NY, USA), DIS '21, Association for Computing. Machinery, pp 275–282

Dumas JS, Dumas JS, Redish J (1999) A practical guide to usability testing. Intellect Books

Ericsson KA, Simon HA (1984) Protocol analysis: verbal reports as data. The MIT Press

Falcão CS, Soares MM (2013) Application of virtual reality technologies in consumer product usability. In: In: Marcus A (ed.) Design, User Experience, and usability. Web, mobile, and product design (Berlin, Heidelberg). Springer Berlin Heidelberg, pp 342–351

Følstad A, Hornbæk K (2010) Work-domain knowledge in usability evaluation: experiences with cooperative usability testing. J Syst Softw 83(11):2019–2030. Interplay between Usability Evaluation and Software Development

Georgiou Y, Eleni KA (2017) The development and validation of the ARI questionnaire: an instrument for measuring immersion in location-based augmented reality settings. Int J Human-Comput Stud 98:24–37

Hart SG (2006) NASA-task load index (NASA-TLX); 20 years later. Proc Human Fact Ergonom Soc Ann Meet 50(9):904–908

Hassenzahl M, Burmester M, Koller F (2003) AttrakDiff: a questionnaire to measure perceived hedonic and pragmatic quality. Men Comput 57:187–196

Hoggenmüller M, Tomitsch M, Hespanhol L, Tran TTM, Worrall S, Nebot E (2021) Context-based interface prototyping: understanding the effect of prototype representation on user feedback. In: Proceedings of the 2021 CHI conference on human factors in computing systems (New York, NY, USA), CHI '21, Association for Computing Machinery

Hwang W, Salvendy G (2010) Number of people required for usability evaluation: the 102 rule. Commun. ACM 53(5):130–133

Kreylos O (2016) Optical properties of current vr hmds

Laugwitz B, Held T, Schrepp M (2008) Construction and evaluation of a user experience questionnaire. In: Holzinger A (ed) HCI and usability for education and work (Berlin, Heidelberg). Springer, Berlin Heidelberg, pp 63–76

Lewis JR (1995) IBM computer usability satisfaction questionnaires: psychometric evaluation and instructions for use. Int J Human-Comput Interact 7(1):57–78

Lewis JR (2002) Psychometric evaluation of the PSSUQ using data from five years of usability studies. Int J Human-Comput Interact 14(3–4):463–488

Lim Y, Pangam A, Periyasami S, Aneja S (2006) Comparative analysis of high- and low-fidelity prototypes for more valid usability evaluations of mobile devices. In: Proceedings of the 4th nordic conference on human-computer interaction: changing roles (New York, NY, USA), NordiCHI '06, Association for Computing Machinery, pp 291–300

Lubos PB (2018) Supernatural and comfortable user interfaces for basic 3d interaction tasks, Ph.D. thesis, State and University Library Hamburg Carl von Ossietzky

Mahalil I, Yusof AM, Ibrahim N (2020) A literature review on the effects of 6-dimensional virtual reality's sport applications toward higher presense. In: 2020 8th International conference on information technology and multimedia (ICIMU), pp 277–282

Mäkelä V, Radiah R, Alsherif S, Khamis M, Xiao C, Borchert L, Schmidt A, Alt F (2020) Virtual field studies: conducting studies on public displays in virtual reality. In: Proceedings of the 2020 CHI conference on human factors in computing systems (New York, NY, USA), CHI '20, Association for Computing Machinery, pp 1–15

Mathis F, Vaniea K, Khamis M (2021) Replicueauth: validating the use of a lab-based virtual reality setup for evaluating authentication systems. In: Proceedings of the 39th annual ACM conference on human factors in computing systems (New York, NY, USA), CHI '21, ACM

McMahan Ryan P, Bowman Doug A, Zielinski David J, Brady Rachael B (2012) Evaluating display fidelity and interaction fidelity in a virtual reality game. IEEE Trans Visual Comput Graph 18(4):626–633

McMahan RP, Lai C, Pal SK (2016) Interaction fidelity: the uncanny valley of virtual reality interactions, virtual, augmented and mixed reality (Cham) (Stephanie Lackey and Randall Shumaker, eds.), Springer International Publishing, pp 59–70

Nilsson NC, Zenner A, Simeone AL (2021) Propping up virtual reality with haptic proxies. IEEE Comput Graph Appl (in press), to appear

Obrist M, Gatti E, Maggioni E, Thanh Vi C, Velasco C (2017) Multisensory experiences in HCI. IEEE MultiMedia 24(2):9–13

Paneva V, Bachynskyi M, Müller J (2020) Levitation simulator: prototyping ultrasonic levitation interfaces in virtual reality. In: Proceedings of the 2020 CHI conference on human factors in computing systems (New York, NY, USA), CHI '20, Association for Computing Machinery, pp 1–12

Pharr M, Jakob W, Humphreys G (2016) From theory to implementation, Morgan Kaufmann, Phys Based Rendering

Pusch A, Lécuyer A (2011) Pseudo-haptics: from the theoretical foundations to practical system design guidelines. In: Proceedings of the 13th international conference on multimodal interfaces (New York, NY, USA), ICMI '11, Association for Computing Machinery, pp 57–64

Regenbrecht H, Schubert T (2002) Real and illusory interactions enhance presence in virtual environments. Presence 11(4):425–434

Rogers K, Funke J, Frommel J, Stamm S, Weber M (2019) Exploring interaction fidelity in virtual reality: object manipulation and whole-body movements. In: Proceedings of the 2019 CHI conference on human factors in computing systems (New York, NY, USA), CHI '19, Association for Computing Machinery, pp 1–14

Saffo D, Di Bartolomeo S, Yildirim C, Dunne C (2021) Remote and collaborative virtual reality experiments via social vr platforms. In: Proceedings of the 2021 CHI conference on human factors in computing systems (New York, NY, USA), CHI '21, Association for Computing Machinery

Schneider D, Otte A, Kublin AS, Martschenko A, Kristensson PO, Ofek E, Pahud M, Grubert J (2020) Accuracy of commodity finger tracking systems for virtual reality head-mounted displays. In: 2020 IEEE conference on virtual reality and 3D user interfaces abstracts and workshops (VRW), pp 804–805

Schubert T, Friedmann F, Regenbrecht H (2001) I group presence questionnaire. Teleoperators Virtual Environ 41:115–124

Simeone AL, Mavridou I, Powell W (2017) Altering user movement behaviour in virtual environments. IEEE Trans Vis Comput Graph 23(4):1312–1321

Simeone AL, Velloso E, Gellersen H (2015) Substitutional reality: using the physical environment to design virtual reality experiences. In: Proceedings of the 33rd annual ACM conference on human factors in computing systems (New York, NY, USA), CHI '15, Association for Computing Machinery, pp 3307–3316

Slater M, Khanna P, Mortensen J, Yu I (2009) Visual realism enhances realistic response in an immersive virtual environment. IEEE Comput Graph Appl 29(3):76–84

Slater M, Steed A (2000) A virtual presence counter. Presence: Teleoperators Virt Environ 9(5):413–434

Tao F, Zhang H, Liu A, Nee AYC (2019) Digital twin in industry: state-of-the-art. IEEE Trans Ind Inf 15(4):2405–2415

Tullis TS, Stetson JN (2004) A comparison of questionnaires for assessing website usability. Usability professional association conference, vol. 1, Minneapolis, USA, pp 1–12

Virzi RA (1992) Refining the test phase of usability evaluation: how many subjects is enough? Human Factors 34(4):457–468

Voit A, Mayer S, Schwind V, Henze N (2019) Online, vr, ar, lab, and in-situ: Comparison of research methods to evaluate smart artifacts. In: Proceedings of the 2019 CHI conference on human factors in computing systems (New York, NY, USA), CHI '19, Association for Computing Machinery, pp 1–12

Ye J, Badiyani S, Raja V, Schlegel T (2007) Applications of virtual reality in product design evaluation. In: Jacko JA (ed) Human-computer interaction. HCI applications and services (Berlin, Heidelberg), Springer, Berlin Heidelberg, pp 1190–1199

Yu I, Mortensen J, Khanna P, Spanlang B, Slater M (2012) Visual realism enhances realistic response in an immersive virtual environment–part 2. IEEE Comput Graph Appl 32(6):36–45

Yu R, Bowman DA (2018) Force push: exploring expressive gesture-to-force mappings for remote object manipulation in virtual reality. Frontiers in ICT 25

Zaharias P, Poylymenakou A (2009) Developing a usability evaluation method for e-learning applications: beyond functional usability. Int. J Human-Comput Int 25(1):75–98

Zhao T, McDonald S, Edwards HM (2014) The impact of two different think-aloud instructions in a usability test: a case of just following orders? Behav Inf Tech 33(2):163–183

Adaptive Virtual Neuroarchitecture

Abhinandan Jain, Pattie Maes, and Misha Sra

Abstract Our surrounding environment impacts our cognitive-emotional processes on a daily basis and shapes our physical, psychological and social wellbeing. Although the effects of the built environment on our psycho-physiological processes are well studied, virtual environment design with a potentially similar impact on the user has received limited attention. Based on the influence of space design on a user and combining that with the dynamic affordances of virtual spaces, we present the idea of *adaptive virtual neuroarchitecture (AVN)*, where virtual environments respond to the user and the user's real-world context while simultaneously influencing them both in real time. To show how AVN has been explored in current research, we present a sampling of recent work that demonstrates reciprocal relationships using physical affordances (space, objects), the user's state (physiological, cognitive, emotional), and the virtual world used in the design of novel virtual reality experiences. We believe AVN has the potential to help us learn how to design spaces and environments that can enhance the wellbeing of their inhabitants.

1 Introduction

Twentieth-century philosopher Maurice Merleau-Ponty wrote, space is existential and existence is spatial (Merleau-Ponty 1996). That is to say, we are always somewhere. Everyday we awake in space, move in space, eat, sleep, and work in space. As Winnicott and Merleau-Ponty state, our bodies are fundamentally related to the space that we inhabit and this embodiment enables us to experience our lived real-

A. Jain (✉) · P. Maes
MIT Media Lab, Cambridge, USA
e-mail: abyjain@mit.edu

P. Maes
e-mail: pattie@media.mit.edu

M. Sra
UCSB, Santa Barbara, USA
e-mail: sra@cs.ucsb.edu

ity, allowing us to not only perceive our own existence but also the world around us (Goldberg 2021). Though (Murray, 1999) describes the body, as both a "holistic sense organ" and an "assemblage of sense apparatus", we do not actively reflect on bodily perception in our daily lives. Despite non-conscious reflection on bodily perception by individuals, architects take the aggregate perceptual processes into account for designing the built environment. Knowing that people spend most of their daily time indoors, buildings can be an important focal point for promoting wellbeing by optimizing the occupant's experience of the indoors space. We believe bodily perceptual processes can similarly form the basis of built environment design in virtual reality (VR).

Though our interpretation of the real world is a continually evolving process through our interactions with the environment, the built environment itself is largely static. Most physical space adaptations are usually achieved through landscape or interior design. For example, urban planners create and maintain green spaces (e.g., parks, yards, terraces), personalizing them with thought given to things like visual impact, shade, or other benefits (e.g., fruit, smell) and changes in color (e.g., fall foliage, annuals vs perennials) over time. Similarly, people expend considerable effort and time in designing their homes, choosing furniture, flooring, lighting, paint, and colors to adapt their living spaces to themselves.

In recent years, there has been "convergent agreement from architects, designers, psychologists, and neuroscientists about the multifactorial nature of the reciprocal interaction between humans and built space" and the desire to understand how it can impact human wellbeing (Chiamulera et al. 2017a). Neuroarchitecture is an emerging term defined as the application of neuroscience specifically pertaining to the use of knowledge on human perception, cognition, and behavior for the design of physical spaces (Metzger 0000). It is a new interdisciplinary area that studies the interaction between the brain and built spaces (Chiamulera et al. 2017a). We believe virtual neuroarchitecture is a natural extension of neuroarchitecture especially since VR experiences evoke a sense of presence or "being there", much like physical spaces do and lead to a different immersive experience than that of 3D video game worlds on a computer screen. In contrast with physical spaces where material, objects, effort, cost, and time are required to modify and adapt the space to specific needs or purposes, virtual spaces can respond to the user and adapt to their cognitive and emotional states dynamically with an immediacy and convenience that is only possible with digital content.

We call this **adaptive** (dynamic and reciprocal) connection between a physical space, a virtual space, and the user *adaptive virtual neuroarchitecture (AVN)*. By dynamic, we refer to the automatic transformation of the virtual space in response to changes in the user's physical space and changes in the user themselves (e.g., physiological data, emotional data). By reciprocal, we mean the establishment of a continuous feedback loop between the virtual space, the physical space, and the user. Both types of connections eventually establish computer-to-human interaction, where a digitally generated world interacts with user's perception with the goal of influencing their cognitive and emotional states. In the design space of virtual neuroarchitecture, the example projects we present in Sects. 3.1 and 3.2 specifically focus on adaptive virtual environments. A virtual environment is composed of both inanimate and animate elements such as buildings, trees, furniture, animals, and virtual humans. Each of these elements can respond to a user, either through direct interaction or automatically based on user data. For this work, we constrain our examples to changes in the inanimate elements that happen either via user interaction or automatically. Our hope is that this design space and the questions raised by the example projects highlight new opportunities for the design of computer-to-human interactions and for probing the potential impact of AVN on human wellbeing at physical, cognitive, emotional, and social levels.

We begin below by discussing embodied cognition, specifically how the mind and the body interacting together in an environment shape our actions and behaviors. To support this discussion, we provide examples of the built environment's impact on an individual's affective and cognitive processes. In Sect. 3, we present AVN in more detail with a few example projects that utilize characteristics of the real world and the human body to create dynamic spatial experiences that have the potential to influence a user's affective and behavioral processes. More specifically, we explore the dynamics in two broad categories of *Adaptive Spaces* and *Adaptive Experiences*. Lastly, we highlight potential applications of AVN in education, training, wellbeing, and architectural design.

2 The Mind, the Body, and the Environment

2.1 *Embodied Cognition*

In the last few decades, research has shifted from an understanding of the mind as an independent information processor toward understanding cognitive processes in relation to the environment (Friedenberg and Silverman 2006). This shift from Descartes' mind-body dualism toward embodied cognition has placed emphasis on the body and the environment in providing a foundation for facilitating and supporting cognition. Proponents argue that cognition takes place in the context of a physical environment and continuously evolves through interaction with this environment which involves the processes of perception and action (Wilson Dec 2002). That is to say, the mind works collectively with the body toward making sense of the world. The process involves "sensation—gathering of information; perception—analysis of gathered information; cognition—synthesis of the information; and generalization—representation of the information" (Lindsay and Norman 2013; Jain et al. 2020).

Research suggests that not all incoming sensations and corresponding processing becomes part of conscious awareness. These sensations can factor into our unconscious (not aware), conscious (aware), or metacognitive (aware of being aware) processing (Schooler et al. 2015). Which pathway is used depends upon the signal's characteristics such as its attentional or cognitive demands or its correlation to prior mental representations (Jain et al. 2020). Human cognition, affect, or behavior can, thus, be influenced through multiple sensory processing pathways.

The non-conscious processing of information leads the mind and body into structuring actions even before awareness of intention to act forms. Such non-conscious prenoetic processes create the schema for potential actions within the environment the individual is situated in (Bower and Gallagher, 2013). For example, the decision to grasp an object is determined by the presence of an object within reach and by our having hands. Similarly, seeing always happens from somewhere, and it depends on the body and head pose of the viewer as well as any constraints in the surrounding environment (Bower and Gallagher 2013; Soto-Faraco et al. Oct 2004). As Leder summarizes it, "To see something as reachable and thereby open to my use is to implicitly experience my body's capacity of reach" (Leder 1990). This implies that incoming sensory stimuli to the body are organized within the body schema and continuously updated with sensory input and body movement. This embodied model of processing and cognition applies to VR and the design of adaptive VR spaces, regardless of an avatar embodiment. A change in the user's situational space, i.e., the physical space the user is located in at the time of the VR experience, generates a new schema for potential actions and outcomes in the virtual space. We discuss a VR project that exemplifies this idea in 3.1.1.

2.2 Environmental Interactions with Psycho-physiological Processes

The view of cognition being embodied is consolidated with established knowledge of the effects of built space on perception, affect, and behavioral responses (Ulrich et al. 1991).

"We shape our buildings; thereafter they shape us" said Sir Winston Churchill in his speech on the rebuilding of the House of Commons, emphasizing the impact of shape (oblong instead of semi-circular) and size (not big enough to contain all Members) on governance. Churchill understood the influence of the built environment on its inhabitants. Research has since shown how a building's characteristics such as shape, lighting, acoustics, texture, colors or scale, influence the thoughts, emotional states, cognitive load, health, and behavior of its occupants (Ellard 2015; Li 2019; Roessler 2012; Choi et al. 2014). Our surrounding environment is an essential part of our daily lived experience with many people spending over 90% of their day inside a building. Therefore, indoors spaces have continuous cognitive-emotional influence on shaping our behavior (Chiamulera et al. 2017a).

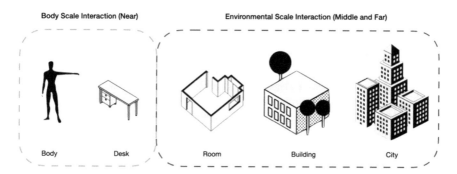

Fig. 1 Near spaces are within reach of the body, and we categorize them as body scale spaces. Middle and far spaces are where the surrounding environment and architecture start impacting us

2.2.1 Perceiving Space Through the Body

Perceiving space involves sensory input into the eyes with head and body movements determining what the eyes look at. Different types of body movements allow us to apprehend proximal and distal spaces through head turning or object grasping and translation, respectively. Humans experience space at three main scales of near, middle, and far (Franz 2005). Near allows us to understand small object geometries by grasping and manipulating them with our hands. Middle space is experienced at a room-scale where lighting, contrast, and texture become important in helping understand the objects, the space, and its relationship to the body. In middle space, only portions of objects are visible at any moment when viewed from a specific location. However, the user can easily move around the space to interact with objects, e.g., a user can walk up to a table or sit down on a couch. At the far scale, touch-based interaction is not possible and our ability to perceive objects is limited to understanding forms and shapes as viewed from a distance (e.g., the outlines of buildings or shapes of trees). Complexity and details that are perceivable at near and middle scales are often not perceivable at this scale. Perception of space, similar to the middle space, is influenced by lighting and texture but also by shadows, vistas, skylines, and the ability to move across longer distances, whether by foot or in a vehicle. We situate the study of virtual neuroarchitecture in the middle and far spaces where the environment's features, both spatial and object-based, can start to interact and shape cognitive processes (Fig. 1). VR allows us to design experiences in near, middle, and far spaces, in contrast to AR which, in practice, is largely limited to near and middle space experiences. While object-based interactions in any physical environment are limited to near and middle spaces, in a virtual environment even far spaces can enable object interaction through digital enhancements of a user's abilities such as Gravity Gloves as seen in the Half-Life:Alyx VR game which allows a user to pull objects to their hands or virtual arm lengthening to reach far objects (Poupyrev et al. 1996) or teleportation to allow rapid movement across space (Bozgeyikli et al. 2016).

2.2.2   Space and Wellbeing

Architects and urban designers have employed all levels of scale and the body's relationship to space in the design of cities, buildings, public (indoors and outdoors), and private spaces for centuries. Prior work has demonstrated the impact of such architectural and environmental characteristics on cognitive processes. For example, static properties such as materials, colors, and dynamic elements of space such as background noise have been shown to facilitate individual creative performance (McCoy and Evans 2002; Mehta et al. 2012). Decreasing distance between walls, lowering the ceiling height or altering window heights has been shown to significantly impact user emotional states (Presti et al. 2022). Correspondingly, exposure to poor architectural and indoor environmental conditions has been found to negatively impact occupants' cognitive functions such as decision-making (Allen et al. 2016; MacNaughton et al. 2017) and shown to have adverse effects on performance and productivity (Fisk 2000; Wyon 2004). Environmental psychology research has helped design hospitals, schools, and residential units that can lead to optimal cognitive performance conditions or increase productivity. For example, studies have found that in classrooms with increased natural light, students achieved higher test scores in contrast to those with lower natural light (Mott et al. 2012) or cold vs. warm hues in classrooms improve attention and memory performance (Llinares et al. 2021). For spaces where access to views of the outdoors is not possible, studies have shown simulated green settings to have positive effects on mood, self-esteem, and self-reported feelings of stress and depression (Bowler et al. 2010; Barton and Pretty 2010; Mcsweeney et al. 2014). Prior work has also shown how the addition of "hospital green" walls and nature landscape views from windows helped speed up the healing process of patients by 8.5% (Ulrich 1984) and reduce need for pain relief (Ulrich 1981). Given that humans in urban areas tend to spend inordinately large amounts of their time indoors, even more so given the recent COVID-19 pandemic, the design of space, and understanding its impact on our wellbeing have never been more critical.

2.2.3   Multi-sensory Experiences in Space

Multi-sensory stimulation and synesthetic experiences have been found to be a causal factor for generating esthetic emotions and creating metanoic (spiritually moving) or transformative experiences for the observer in an architectural space (Spence 2020). For example, the scale, lighting, and synchronous reverberation in a cathedral create an immersive and almost hypnotic multi-sensory experience with audio, visual, and emotional input (Blesser and Salter 2007). However, incongruency of such stimuli can create psychological tension and cognitive conflict. As shown in prior work, disproportionate spatial features can lead to strange sound reverberations causing discomfort or the poor use of colors and lighting can impact an occupant's mood negatively (Blesser and Salter 2007).

Just as we respond cognitively and emotionally to the built environment, as shown in the examples presented above, virtual environment properties, such as color, lightning, and texture, also impact us akin to the impact felt in the real world (Naz et al. 2017). Additionally, dynamic elements of the physical environment which adapt to the user have been shown to enhance a user's cognitive processes (Zhao et al. 2017; Cho et al. 2002), mood (Plante et al. 2003), and wellbeing (Depledge et al. 2011). For example, mediated atmosphere uses a digital display to change the perceived environment based on the user's physiology and shows positive impact on the user's focus and stress levels (Zhao et al. 2017). Such demonstrated effects, of static and adaptive elements in the physical environment, on a user's psycho-physiological processes are our primary inspiration to explore the design of adaptive (dynamically responsive and reciprocal) virtual environments.

3 Adaptive Virtual Neuroarchitecture

Architecture has provided us with the built environment, surrounding us in structures which integrate elements that can influence our physiological, psychological, and social-cognitive processes (Ulrich 1991; Li 2019). Neuroarchitecture is an emerging interdisciplinary area that applies the understanding of perception, cognition, and behavior from neuroscience to architectural design with the goal of optimizing the positive impact of the built environment on the occupants at cognitive-emotional and behavioral levels (Chiamulera et al. 2017a; Higuera-Trujillo et al. 2021). However, the physical world is largely static and renovating the physical environment frequently to study, evaluate, or optimize the interaction between the brain and built spaces and subsequent influence on a user's cognitive processes can be expensive, cumbersome, and logistically less feasible. Recent work in the design of flexible architectural spaces explores using robotic elements to reconfigure the user's space at the press of a button. While this makes the physical space dynamic, it may be limited in functionality due to the modifications being constrained by the physical space extents (Larrea-Tamayo 2015).

VR presents opportunities for designing architectural spaces with a layer of dynamism which can allow us to achieve, in a sense, "programmable matter". The term "programmable matter" was introduced in 1991 by Toffoli and Margolus[1] to refer to matter that has the ability to change its physical properties.

With AVN, we propose the design of VR spaces and experiences that are dynamic, responsive, and integrate reciprocity between the physical and virtual environments and a user's physiological and cognitive states. We can map a physical environment's properties such as texture, color, lighting, acoustics, size, layout, or style to the design of a virtual environment and modify them often and as quickly as desired. Furthermore, we can map a user's physiological or psychological responses to virtual space modifications and create feedback loops between the virtual dynamism and the

---

[1] https://en.wikipedia.org/wiki/Programmable_matter.

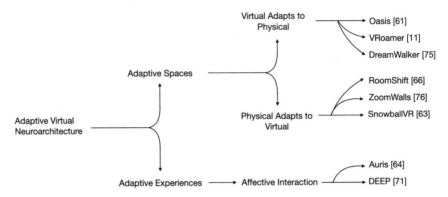

Fig. 2 We categorize adaptive virtual neuroarchitecture (AVN) into Adaptive Spaces and Adaptive Experiences and showcase example projects in each category

physiological signals to create a sense of harmony between the two. The dynamic remodeling of the virtual environment can be frequent, continuous, or occasional depending on what the user needs. The remodeled virtual environment can translate across different scales (near, middle, or far) depending upon the user's situation and desire. The degree of virtual responsiveness can be manipulated by the degree of input signal (user's sensor data and/or changes in their physical space), while the direction of change can be determined by the user. For example, if the user's heart rate increases slowly, the environment can respond to it slowly with modifications to features such as lighting, color, or space. These modifications can either be in a direction that results in an increase in the user's heart rate or calms them down, which could be decided by the user or the interaction designer. However, allowing developers to make the decision on how to modify a user's physiological and psychological responses raises ethical concerns related to limiting user agency and manipulating the user to a degree potentially greater than achievable by changes in visual imagery alone. We can also create multi-sensory feedback loops that include stimuli other than the visual and auditory signals such as olfaction (Amores and Maes 2017), proprioception (Sra et al. 2019; Lopes et al. 0000), and temperature (Brooks et al. 2020). These multi-sensory feedback loops can each uniquely impact cognitive processes (e.g., healing, mindfulness, wellbeing) by augmenting changes to the virtual environment and reciprocal changes to the user's perception of the updated virtual environment. We can imagine the virtual environment to be a fluid or liquid space that continuously morphs due to the user's presence and movement through it. Multi-sensory haptic feedback such as electrical muscle stimulation (Lopes et al. 2015), weight perception (Choi et al. 2017), and terrain texture (Je et al. 2021) can further increase the user's sense of presence in the VR space and reinforce desired environmental effects on the user through simultaneous changes in elements such as lighting, weather, and atmosphere.

To better understand AVN, we have designed and built a few working prototypes, some of which we present here along with work by other researchers. We present

Fig. 3 Oasis system creates a 3D map of the physical environment, automatically detecting open walkable areas which allow the system to generate virtual environments with corresponding walkable areas. While the physical affordance of walking is the same in both environments, the visual experience and spatial feel can be quite different. For example, as seen in the figure above, a hallway is transformed into an open countryside which still allows the user to walk freely while wearing a wireless headset device in the mapped physical/virtual space without breaking immersion. Figure from the paper (Sra et al. 2016)

these example projects in two broad categories of *Adaptive Spaces* and *Adaptive Experiences* (Fig. 2). In *Adaptive Spaces*, the virtual and the physical world interact with each other, with the virtual environment often adapting to the physical space and in some cases, the physical space changing in response to the virtual space. In *Adaptive Experiences*, we present VR projects which build upon physiological or psychological constructs that influence our cognitive processes (Fig. 2). This not a comprehensive survey of prior work. Our primary goal is to highlight AVN in research and use the selected examples to present new and interesting design opportunities for future work in this area.

3.1   Adaptive Spaces

One of the major challenges in the design of adaptive VR environments is the mapping of a physical space to a virtual space such that the user is able to take advantage of the real world spatial and tactile affordances which can augment their virtual experience. Most VR systems render a pre-defined tracking space boundary to separate the physical world from the virtual, breaking the user's experience at the boundary by a visual or haptic reminder of the divide between the two seemingly separate worlds anytime the user approaches the boundary. While this is understandably done to prevent the user from colliding with physical objects, there is opportunity for more advanced integration between the user, their physical environment, and the virtual world.

One option that has been explored in generating virtual spaces that adapt to the user's physical environment is using a depth camera to scan the user's surroundings, reconstruct geometry, infer walkable areas, and detect physical objects. This data is used to generate a VR environment which replaces the reconstructed walls and furniture with similarly sized and positioned virtual elements such that the user can freely walk in the physical space without running into any obstacles. The objects in the physical space provide haptic feedback to the user through their emulated virtual counterparts (Sra et al. 2016; Shapira and Freedman 2016; Simeone et al. 2015). A related exploration used robotic or human manipulated furniture and walls that conformed to changes in the virtual environment to provide the user a corresponding adaptable physical space and related haptic feedback (Suzuki et al. 2020; Yixian et al. 2020). Using the real world as a template, a single physical space can be used to create multiple unique and visually different virtual environments with tactile feedback in ways that maintain user safety by preserving the geometry and semantics of the real world (Sra et al. 2016; Shapira and Freedman 2016). The idea can be expanded into creating blended spaces for remotely located multi-user experiences that allow each user to freely walk around and interact as if they are in the same physical space (Sra et al. 2017). Exploring the degrees to which the physical world is blended with a virtual world (Hartmann et al. 2019) can help understand how we perceive these hybrid spaces, paving the way for a future where the virtual and the physical will allow for seamless transition between them, without risk of injury.

3.1.1   Virtual Adapts to Physical

Oasis

Oasis automatically generates immersive and interactive VR worlds that adapt to the user's physical space (Sra et al. 2017, 2016). The system uses a 3D capture of an indoor scene to isolate walkable areas, interactions, and obstacles. Individual objects from the physical world (e.g., chairs) are mapped to objects in the virtual environment and tracked in real time for providing haptic feedback (Fig. 3). The mapping of physical objects to their virtual counterparts creates a dynamic experience

Fig. 4 Dreamwalker creates a real-time VR experience in an outdoor physical environment. Figure from the original paper included with author permission (Yang et al. 2019)

where users receive full haptic feedback from their interactions with virtual proxies. The user's actions in the virtual environment are also reflected in the real world (e.g., sitting down in a virtual/physical chair), and chair movements in the physical world are reflected in the corresponding movements of the virtual chair. This dynamic (real time response) and reciprocal (bidirectional) relationship creates a connected situated experience between the physical and the virtual worlds. This subsequently increases presence for the user in the virtual world and creates a more engaging user experience. Oasis presents a step toward creating fully dynamic relationships between the physical and virtual worlds. Oasis also highlights transformation of space scale from middle space in the physical world to a far scale in the virtual world while mapping characteristics of the physical world dynamically to the virtual world. However, Oasis has limited object tracking and is bounded by finite walkable areas of the real-world environment. It therefore does not exemplify a strong reciprocal spatial relationship where all changes in the virtual world are reflected in the physical world.

VRoamer and Dreamwalker

VRoamer (Cheng et al. 2019) is a proof of concept system which detects collisions with obstacles in real time and places virtual obstacles in the user's path to prevent them from a potential collision (Fig. 5). VRoamer builds upon Oasis but differs in that the collisions with physical objects are dynamically detected and represented in the virtual world when walking on a pre-planned indoor path. Dreamwalker (Yang et al. 2019) builds upon VRoamer where it improves tracking while walking outdoors wearing a VR headset and includes walkable areas such as slopes, curbs, and non-planar surfaces. It uses GPS data and SLAM for tracking and places a pre-created virtual environment along a known physical path for an outdoor walking experience in VR. Dreamwalker allows for longer walkable paths with real-time collision detection of moving obstacles (Fig. 4). Whereas in Oasis a movable object like a chair is

Fig. 5 VRoamer's dungeon environment with virtual obstacles shown in response to physical obstacles in the user's environment. Figure from the paper (Cheng et al. 2019)

pre-scanned and only tracked in real time, Dreamwalker allows for detecting previously unseen obstacles and representing them in the VR environment at runtime. In both VRoamer and Dreamwalker, representations of detected obstacles (static and moving) create a dynamic connection between the physical and virtual worlds as interactions in the physical space are reflected in the virtual space. However, neither VRoamer nor Dreamwalker establishes a reciprocal relationship between the real and virtual spaces since changes in the virtual world are not reflected in the physical environment.

Oasis, VRoamer and Dreamwalker are examples of virtual neuroarchitecture systems that enable multiple visual reconfigurations of the user's static physical space virtually, while maintaining a connection between the two spaces based on the affordance of walkability. Adaptive virtual spaces open up the opportunity to study the impact of size (closed room vs open yard), shape (smooth curves vs sharp edges and corners), textures, colors, lightning, or weather on the user while maintaining the walkability of the user's actual environment. The automated generation in Oasis and real-time mapping in VRoamer combined with the outdoors path planning in Dreamwalker may one day allow for building VR environments on a city-wide scale which adapt to create personalized experiences for all individuals (Fig. 5).

3.1.2 Physical Adapts to Virtual

RoomShift and ZoomWalls

RoomShift (Suzuki et al. 2020) is a room size dynamic environment where physical objects move in response to a user's virtual movements and position themselves in appropriate locations around the user to provide haptic feedback (Fig. 6). It utilizes a swarm of shape changing robotic assistants, similar to shelf-moving robots. The goal is to enable physical interactions such as touching, sitting, placing things, and leaning while the user is immersed in VR. The system continuously tracks virtual touchable surfaces in close proximity to the user in VR and directs the robot swarm to transport physical objects to the positions without clashing with other robots or the user.

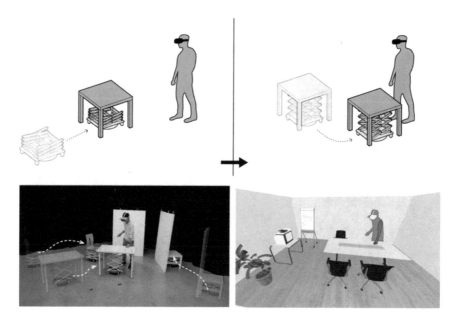

Fig. 6 In RoomShift, robotic assistants move furniture around the user who is immersed in VR, demonstrating a way to represent changes in the virtual environment on the user's physical space. Figure from the original paper included with author permission (Suzuki et al. 2020)

ZoomWalls (Yixian et al. 2020), similar to RoomShift, creates a dynamic physical environment by reconfiguring robotic props that match interaction with virtual structures like walls/doors. The robots re-position themselves so as to create a simulated wall segment of the room/area. This simulation allows to create size-based illusions of the surroundings for the user. Having walls follow closely makes the user feel they are enclosed in a much tighter space, while distributing them makes the space size seem bigger. The user study demonstrates increase in presence and immersion for the users.

SnowballVR

A dynamic match between a fort made of actuated cardboard boxes with a corresponding virtual snow fort enables manipulating physical objects based on virtual events in SnowballVR (Sra et al. 2016). The snow fort takes advantage of the connection between the virtual and physical to provide haptic (boxes), aural (sound of boxes collapsing), and spatial (matching snow fort in position, scale, and orientation) feedback to the user. Additionally, a visual mechanism that controls the collapsible boxes can engage the non-VR users (Fig. 7) in this spectator focused VR experience. Without the need for a screen, non-VR users can determine how the virtual snowball fight is progressing based on how many snow fort boxes they see and hear collapse. The connection between the virtual and the physical is unidirectional, from VR to the physical world.

Fig. 7 SnowballVR showing two users, one shooting virtual snowballs using a modified Nerf gun and the other dodging the snowballs by hiding behind a physical/virtual snow fort. Figure from the paper (Sra et al. 2016)

RoomShift, ZoomWalls, and SnowballVR showcase the dynamic modulation of physical space in response to the user's behavior in a virtual environment, and do so without pre-configuration, as has been necessary in prior work exploring passive haptics for room-scale feedback (Insko 2001).These projects show both a uni- and bidirectional relationship between the virtual and physical spaces as objects are updated in both worlds when their properties change in either. This opens up new questions related to boundaries and evolution of a user's sense of presence and being in a space when space itself becomes fluid.

3.2   *Adaptive Experiences*

From the modest barn to the majestic monuments, the elements of architectural design like proportion and scale, light, color, and shape have been shown to impact humans in tangible ways. Whether it is entering the Cathédrale Notre-Dame de Paris for the first time and feeling simultaneously awed and humbled or entering a cavernous office daily and feeling time slow down, space has an undeniable emotional impact on both its short- and long-term inhabitants. For example, (Marín-Morales et al., 2018) proposed a new methodology to recognize a user's emotional state in VR when presented architectural stimuli such as illumination, color, and geometry to evoke different emotional states. Their findings demonstrate the ability of VR to elicit desired emotions and highlight potential for novel applications in areas such as diverse as architecture, health, education, and gaming. In another work, 360° panoramas were compared with immersive virtual environments in terms of psychological and physiological responses and a user's sense of presence. Analysis showed that 360° panoramas were considered close to reality in terms of a user's psychological response, whereas the VR worlds elicited a higher physiological response. A correlation between the two responses indicated the user's sense of presence (Higuera-Trujillo et al. 2017). Such psychological and physiological influence of the virtual environment presents opportunities for the design of experiences and space that are personalized to the user for palpable cognitive and emotional impact. In this section, we present two example projects where dynamic virtual experiences impact physiological and psychological states of the user.

3.2.1 Affective Interactions

Auris (Sra et al., 2017) is a VR world generation system that uses data from songs (audio and lyrics) to create virtual worlds that encapsulate and represent the mood of the song visually through space, texture, lighting, and design. Layers of textures created using Inception[2] with song data allow for the creation surreal environments for presenting a new type of dynamic and immersive 3D music experience (Fig. 8). The user study showed that after experiencing the virtual environment, the user's mood reflected the mood depicted by the generated world. We would like to note that the choice of direction of influence, i.e., if the user is in a sad mood, should they enter a happy environment or a sad environment, should reside with the user since there is possibility of making the user's mood worse by forcing a different mood on them. Based on this work, the multi-sensory feedback and interactive experience of the song-based space have the potential to impact a user's mood and can be used for the design of applications related to therapy, relaxation, or stress management. Auris represents an example of dynamic environment transformation based on a detected mood in a song which is a psychological construct that influences the user's experience of and response to the environment. While a song's mood data is labeled collectively by a large group of individuals, the impact of the song-based VR space is evaluated on the individual.

DEEP (van Rooij et al., 2016) is an immersive underwater fantasy VR world aimed at providing a calm and relaxing experience for the user. DEEP uses biofeedback to support breathing for a meditative experience. The system uses variable resistor stretch sensors to measure diaphragm expansions and modifies the virtual world using that data in real time. For example, based on the user's breathing cycles, the environment changes motion dynamics of objects resulting in a biofeedback loop. The goal is to use respiration physiology to help enable anxiety regulation and improve cognitive performance (van Rooij et al. 2016). The feedback loop demonstrates a reciprocal relationship where the environment transforms and influences the user's physiology implicitly and vice-versa.

---

[2] https://ai.googleblog.com/2015/06/inceptionism-going-deeper-into-neural.html.

Fig. 8 Auris generates mood-based VR worlds from music to create spatial and interactive experiences of listening to music. Happy (left) and sad (right) worlds generated from "The Bird and The Worm" and "Blue Prelude" by Nina Simone respectively. Figure from the paper (Sra et al. 2017)

Both Auris and DEEP showcase the use of psychological and physiological constructs, respectively, in the generation of a virtual world which in turn effects the user. Both projects present the design of virtual environments that are either based on or closely integrated with a user's physiological or psychological responses. While there is a lot of prior work that explores the integration of physiological signals with interaction in VR (Davies and Harrison 1996; Sra et al. 2018), there are limited projects that specifically alter the virtual environment based on the user's data.

4 Applications

AVN presents a new design space for developing experiences which are intertwined with a user's surroundings, physiology, or psychology. Such experiences allow for subtle or overt environmental (physical and virtual) manipulations which in turn have an effect on the user such as impacting cognitive functions and improving wellbeing. With newer devices like PhysioHMD (Galea[3]) (Bernal et al. 2018), there is opportunity to simplify the process of conducting neuroarchitecture experiments. Here, we present a few potential applications of AVN in education and training, wellbeing, and architectural design which are largely inspired by broad areas of interest in the VR research community. Many other areas of interest in virtual, augmented, and mixed reality (XR for short) such as entertainment, socialization, and teamwork could also benefit from the concept of AVN.

---

[3] https://galea.co/.

4.1 Education and Training

Our bodily and environmental experiences are closely linked in facilitating the learning process (Shapiro 2011; Sullivan 2018). Researchers have emphasized the significance of being in and experiencing an environment in order to learn effectively (Montessori 1959). Environmental characteristics such as illumination have shown positive effects on the learning process (Mott et al. 2012). With AVN, we imagine creating personalized and adaptive environments which optimize mood and emotions based on user's physiology, to facilitate learning. For example, changing environmental settings based on user's cognitive load and affective state to personalize the learning process, matching the pace, and difficulty of content to the user. Another way researchers have shown the effectiveness on learning and memorization is by using spatially distributed cues in a user's surroundings. For example, NeverMind (Rosello et al. 2016) uses the "method of loci" memorization technique in augmented reality to help users memorize more effectively, creating a connection between a familiar walking path and corresponding virtual objects placed along that path. This inspires the idea of using learning materials by spatially distributing and embedding them in a virtual environment to influence learning motivation, engagement, and recall.

VR has been used for training since the mid-90s with consumer VR devices now increasingly being used for medical (Ruthenbeck and Reynolds 2015), safety (Sacks et al. 2013), customer experience.[4], and other forms of training. Virtual training requires a close match between the physical space and the virtual worlds as well as a match in the actions performed in order for the experience to meaningfully transfer to real situations. By creating virtual environments, interactions and objects that are similar to their real-world counterparts, with or without haptics, training scenarios have already proven to be better than video learning of similar tasks (Ahir et al. 2020; Checa and Bustillo 2020). With AVN, we believe, creating a continuum of experiences across multiple characteristics of virtual and physical worlds enables utilization of the virtual world reconfigurability with the physical world tangibility for the design of new types of dynamic learning and training experiences.

4.2 Therapy and Wellbeing

Research has shown various effects of the surroundings on an individual's psychological state such as mood, anxiety, stress (Roessler 2012; Bowler et al. 2010; Barton and Pretty 2010; Blesser and Salter 2007) as well as on healing processes of the body (Ulrich 1981, 1984). A now famous study by (Langer, 2009) demonstrated positive impact of surroundings on the physical health and wellbeing of elderly subjects, when they retreated to a setting that was reminiscent of their 20 years younger selves. Virtual neuroarchitecture provides this potential of recreating time-shifted environments based on surrounding physical environments as the examples in Sect. 3.1.1

---

[4] https://www.strivr.com/blog/customer-experience-training-virtual-reality/

show. Researchers have also used VR as an affective intervention to induce calmness and reduce anxiety by creating real-time adaptive environments based on the user's physiological signals (Amores et al. 2019; Fernandez et al. 2019). These projects are presented in Sect. 3.2.1. Adaptive Experiences for therapy can be enhanced with wearable devices which may track data over time as well as provide vibrotactile feedback. Using false feedback techniques has also been demonstrated to increase focus and calmness (Costa et al. 2016, 2019; Choi and Ishii 2020) through the integration of the user's physiological data into their experience.

4.3   Architectural Design

VR environments are being utilized in Computer-Aided Architectural Design (CAAD) for simulating indoor spaces before finalizing architectural designs (Milovanovic et al. 2017). Spatial and acoustics modeling of an environment is simulated before construction begins to get a better understanding of the characteristics of the space (Vorländer et al. 2015; Portman et al. 2015), especially crucial for the design of music and other sound related venues but also valuable for the design of quiet spaces like churches or apartment buildings for maintaining privacy. Research has identified the need for more immersive, scalable, multi-sensory, and interactive experiences as a future challenge for creating better CAAD tools (Milovanovic et al. 2017; Portman et al. 2015).

AVN has the potential to emulate dynamic user-based spatial modifications from the virtual environment to the physical environment as presented in Sect. 3.1.1. The ease of reconfigurability from the virtual environment and concurrent reciprocity in the physical environment present an opportunity to understand the experience and impact of multiple designs in parallel, allowing for rapid modifications or granular adjustment of individual parameters, enabling evaluation of a space over time and and testing with as few or as many users as needed, before expending time and cost in construction.

5   Conclusion

Our surrounding environment impacts us continuously in our daily lives, affecting our physiological and psychological processes. Both indoor and outdoor spaces can impact our experiences and motivations and shape our behaviors. However, the built environment is often static, impersonal (especially shared indoor spaces and public outdoor spaces), and inflexible. VR as a tool addresses these shortcomings and presents new opportunities for transforming spaces into dynamic experiences with the potential to positively impact users.

In this chapter, we presented the idea of *adaptive virtual neuroarchitecture (AVN)* and defined it as a dynamic and reciprocal connection between the physical space, the virtual space, and the user. AVN designs can not only adapt to and transform the user's surroundings but also their mental state, often through a feedback loop that integrates a user's physiological data into the virtual experience. Our idea of AVN builds on current knowledge of embodied cognition to inform the design of adaptive virtual environments as well as the emerging field of neuroarchitecture. Through a few example projects from our own work and others, we presented how adaptive virtual worlds and experiences that interact with both the user's surroundings and their cognitive states can open up new research questions and opportunities for future work in the design of virtual environments and experiences.

References

Ahir K, Govani K, Gajera R, Shah M (2020) Application on virtual reality for enhanced education learning, military training and sports. Augmented Human Res 5(1):1–9

Allen JG, MacNaughton P, Satish U, Santanam S, Vallarino J, Spengler JD (2016) Associations of cognitive function scores with carbon dioxide, ventilation, and volatile organic compound exposures in office workers: a controlled exposure study of green and conventional office environments. Environ Health Perspect 124(6):805–812

Amores J, Fuste A, Richer R (2019) Deep reality: towards increasing relaxation in VR by subtly changing light, sound and movement based on HR, EDA, and EEG. In: Extended abstracts of the 2019 CHI conference on human factors in computing systems, pp 1–2

Amores J, Maes P (2017) Essence: Olfactory interfaces for unconscious influence of mood and cognitive performance. In: Proceedings of the 2017 CHI conference on human factors in computing systems, pp 28–34

Barton J, Pretty J (2010) What is the best dose of nature and green exercise for improving mental health? A multi-study analysis. Environ Sci Technol 44(10):3947–3955

Bernal G, Yang T, Jain A, Maes P (2018) Physiohmd: a conformable, modular toolkit for collecting physiological data from head-mounted displays. In: Proceedings of the 2018 ACM international symposium on wearable computers, pp 160–167

Blesser B, Salter L-R (2007) Spaces speak, are you listening. The Cambridge, MA

Bower M, Gallagher S (2013) Bodily affects as prenoetic elements in enactive perception. Phenomenol Mind 4(1):78–93

Bowler DE, Buyung-Ali LM, Knight TM, Pullin AS (2010) A systematic review of evidence for the added benefits to health of exposure to natural environments. BMC Public Health 10(1):1–10

Bozgeyikli E, Raij A, Katkoori S, Dubey R (2016) Point & teleport locomotion technique for virtual reality. In: Proceedings of the 2016 annual symposium on computer-human interaction in play, pp 205–216

Brooks J, Nagels S, Lopes P (2020) Trigeminal-based temperature illusions. In: Proceedings of the 2020 CHI conference on human factors in computing systems, pp 1–12

Checa D, Bustillo A (2020) A review of immersive virtual reality serious games to enhance learning and training. Multimedia Tools Appl 79(9):5501–5527

Cheng L-P, Ofek E, Holz C, Wilson AD (2019) Vroamer: generating on-the-fly VR experiences while walking inside large, unknown real-world building environments. In: 2019 IEEE conference on Virtual Reality and 3D user interfaces (VR). IEEE, pp 359–366

Cristiano C, Elisa F, Giulia B, Stefano F, Francesco T, Bogdan M, Thomas Z, Sandra B (2017) Virtual reality for neuroarchitecture: cue reactivity in built spaces. Front Psychol 8:185

Cho B-H, Ku J, Jang DP, Kim S, Lee YH, Kim IY, Lee JH, Kim SI (2002) The effect of virtual reality cognitive training for attention enhancement. CyberPsychology Behav 5(2):129–137

Choi H-H, Van Merriënboer JJG, Paas F (2014) Effects of the physical environment on cognitive load and learning: towards a new model of cognitive load. Educ Psychol Rev 26(2):225–244

Choi I, Culbertson H, Miller MR, Olwal A, Follmer S (2017) Grabity: a wearable haptic interface for simulating weight and grasping in virtual reality. In: Proceedings of the 30th annual ACM symposium on user interface software and technology, pp 119–130

Choi KY, Ishii H (2020) ambienbeat: wrist-worn mobile tactile biofeedback for heart rate rhythmic regulation. In: Proceedings of the fourteenth international conference on tangible, embedded, and embodied interaction, pp 17–30

Costa J, Adams AT, Jung MF, Guimbretière F, Choudhury T (2016) Emotioncheck: leveraging bodily signals and false feedback to regulate our emotions. In: Proceedings of the 2016 ACM international joint conference on pervasive and ubiquitous computing, pp 758–769

Costa J, Guimbretière F, Jung MF, Choudhury T (2019) Boostmeup: improving cognitive performance in the moment by unobtrusively regulating emotions with a smartwatch. In: Proceedings of the ACM on interactive, mobile, wearable and ubiquitous technologies, vol 3, issue 2, pp 1–23

Davies C, Harrison J (1996) Osmose: towards broadening the aesthetics of virtual reality. ACM SIGGRAPH Comput Graph 30(4):25–28

Depledge MH, Stone RJ, Bird WJ (2011) Can natural and virtual environments be used to promote improved human health and wellbeing? Environ Sci Technol 45(11):4660–4665

Ellard C (2015) Places of the heart: the psychogeography of everyday life. Bellevue Literary Press

Fernandez JA, Fusté A, Richer R, Maes P (2019) Deep reality: an underwater VR experience to promote relaxation by unconscious HR, EDA, and brain activity biofeedback. In: ACM SIGGRAPH 2019 Virtual, Augmented, and Mixed Reality, pp 1–1 (2019)

Fisk WJ (2000) Health and productivity gains from better indoor environments and their relationship with building energy efficiency. Ann Rev Energy Environ 25(1):537–566

Franz G (2005) An empirical approach to the experience of architectural space. PhD thesis, Bauhaus-Universität Weimar, Germany

Friedenberg J, Silverman G (2006) Cognitive science?: an introduction to the study of mind. Sage, Thousand Oaks

Goldberg P (2021) 12 embodiment, dissociation, and the rhythm of life. In: Body as psychoanalytic object: clinical applications from Winnicott to Bion and beyond, p 12

Hartmann J, Holz C, Ofek E, Wilson AD (2019) Realitycheck: Blending virtual environments with situated physical reality. In: Proceedings of the 2019 CHI conference on human factors in computing systems, pp 1–12

Higuera-Trujillo JL, Llinares C, Macagno E (2021) The cognitive-emotional design and study of architectural space: a scoping review of neuroarchitecture and its precursor approaches. Sensors 21(6):2193

Higuera-Trujillo JL, Maldonado JL-T, Millán CL (2017) Psychological and physiological human responses to simulated and real environments: a comparison between photographs, 360 panoramas, and virtual reality. Appl Ergon 65:398–409

Insko BE (2001) Passive haptics significantly enhances virtual environments. The University of North Carolina at Chapel Hill

Jain A, Horowitz AH, Schoeller F, Leigh S, Maes P, Sra M (2020) Designing interactions beyond conscious control: a new model for wearable interfaces. In: Proceedings of the ACM on interactive, mobile, wearable and ubiquitous technologies, vol 4, issue 3, Sept 2020

Je S, Lim H, Moon K, Teng S-Y, Brooks J, Lopes P, Bianchi A (2021) Elevate: A walkable pin-array for large shape-changing terrains. In: Proceedings of the 2021 CHI conference on human factors in computing systems, pp 1–11

Langer EJ (2009) Counterclockwise: mindful health and the power of possibility. Ballantine Books

Larrea-Tamayo H (2015) ARkits: architectural robotics kits. PhD thesis, Massachusetts Institute of Technology

Leder D (1990) The absent body. University of Chicago Press

Li G (2019) The dynamics of architectural form: Space, emotion and memory. Art Des Rev 7(4):187–205

Lindsay PH, Norman DA (2013) Human information processing: an introduction to psychology. Academic Press

Llinares C, Higuera-Trujillo JL, Serra J (2021) Cold and warm coloured classrooms. Effects on students' attention and memory measured through psychological and neurophysiological responses. Buildi Environ 196:107726

Lopes P, Ion A, Baudisch P (2015) Impacto: simulating physical impact by combining tactile stimulation with electrical muscle stimulation. In: Proceedings of the 28th annual ACM symposium on user interface software & technology, pp 11–19

Lopes P, Young S, Cheng L, Marwecki P, Baudisch P. Providing haptics to walls and other heavy objects in virtual reality by means of electrical muscle stimulation. In: Proceedings of conference on human factors in computing systems

MacNaughton P, Satish U, Laurent JGC, Flanigan S, Vallarino J, Coull B, Spengler JD, Allen JG (2017) The impact of working in a green certified building on cognitive function and health. Build Environ 114:178–186

Marín-Morales J, Higuera-Trujillo JL, Greco A, Guixeres J, Llinares C, Scilingo EP, Alcañiz M, Valenza G (2018) Affective computing in virtual reality: emotion recognition from brain and heartbeat dynamics using wearable sensors. Sci Rep 8(1):1–15

McCoy JM, Evans GW (2002) The potential role of the physical environment in fostering creativity. Creativity Res J 14(3–4):409–426

Mcsweeney J, Rainham D, Johnson SA, Sherry SB, Singleton J (2014) Indoor nature exposure (ine): a health-promotion framework. Health Promotion Int 30(1):126–139

Mehta R, Zhu R, Cheema A (2012) Is noise always bad? Exploring the effects of ambient noise on creative cognition. J Consumer Res 39(4):784–799

Merleau-Ponty M (1996) Phenomenology of perception. Motilal Banarsidass Publishe

Metzger C. Neuroarchitecture. Jovis Verlag GmbH

Milovanovic J, Moreau G, Siret D, Miguet F (2017) Virtual and augmented reality in architectural design and education. In: 17th international conference, CAAD Futures 2017

Montessori M (1959) The absorbent mind. Lulu.com

Mott MS, Robinson DH, Walden A, Burnette J, Rutherford AS (2012) Illuminating the effects of dynamic lighting on student learning. Sage Open 2(2):2158244012445585

Murray C (1999) Towards a phenomenology of the body in virtual reality. Res Philos Technol 19:149–173

Naz A, Kopper R, McMahan RP, Nadin M (2017) Emotional qualities of VR space. In: 2017 IEEE Virtual Reality (VR). IEEE, pp 3–11

Plante TG, Aldridge A, Bogden R, Hanelin C (2003) Might virtual reality promote the mood benefits of exercise? Comput Human Behav 19(4):495–509

Portman ME, Natapov A, Fisher-Gewirtzman D (2015) To go where no man has gone before: virtual reality in architecture, landscape architecture and environmental planning. Comput Environ Urban Syst 54:376–384

Poupyrev I, Billinghurst M, Weghorst S, Ichikawa T (1996) The go-go interaction technique: non-linear mapping for direct manipulation in VR. In: Proceedings of the 9th annual ACM symposium on user interface software and technology, pp 79–80

Presti P, Ruzzon D, Avanzini P, Caruana F, Rizzolatti G, Vecchiato G (2022) Measuring arousal and valence generated by the dynamic experience of architectural forms in virtual environments. Sci Rep 12(1):1–12

Roessler KK (2012) Healthy architecture! Can environments evoke emotional responses? Global J Health Sci 4(4):83

Rosello O, Exposito M, Maes P (2016) Nevermind: using augmented reality for memorization. In: Proceedings of the 29th annual symposium on user interface software and technology, pp 215–216

Ruthenbeck GS, Reynolds KJ (2015) Virtual reality for medical training: the state-of-the-art. J Simul 9(1):16–26

Sacks R, Perlman A, Barak R (2013) Construction safety training using immersive virtual reality. Constr Manage Econ 31(9):1005–1017

Schooler JW, Mrazek MD, Baird B, Winkielman P (2015) Minding the mind: the value of distinguishing among unconscious, conscious, and metaconscious processes

Shapira L, Freedman D (2016) Reality skins: creating immersive and tactile virtual environments. In: 2016 IEEE International Symposium on Mixed and Augmented Reality (ISMAR). IEEE, pp 115–124

Shapiro L (2011) Embodied cognition. Routledge

Simeone AL, Velloso E, Gellersen H (2015) Substitutional reality: using the physical environment to design virtual reality experiences. In: Proceedings of the 33rd annual ACM conference on human factors in computing systems, pp 3307–3316

Salvador S-F, Angelica R, Charles S (2004) Tactile selective attention and body posture: assessing the multisensory contributions of vision and proprioception. Percept Psychophys 66(7):1077–1094

Spence C (2020) Senses of place: architectural design for the multisensory mind. Cogn Res: Principles Implications 5(1):1–26

Sra M, Garrido-Jurado S, Maes P (2017) Oasis: procedurally generated social virtual spaces from 3d scanned real spaces. IEEE Trans Visualization Comput Graph 24(12):3174–3187

Sra M, Garrido-Jurado S, Schmandt C, Maes P (2016) Procedurally generated virtual reality from 3d reconstructed physical space. In: Proceedings of the 22nd ACM conference on virtual reality software and technology, pp 191–200

Sra M, Jain A, Maes P (2019) Adding proprioceptive feedback to virtual reality experiences using galvanic vestibular stimulation. In: Proceedings of the 2019 CHI conference on human factors in computing systems, pp 1–14

Sra M, Jain D, Caetano AP, Calvo A, Hilton E, Schmandt C (2016) Resolving spatial variation and allowing spectator participation in multiplayer VR In: Proceedings of the 29th annual symposium on user interface software and technology, pp 221–222

Sra M, Maes P, Vijayaraghavan P, Roy D (2017) Auris: creating affective virtual spaces from music. In: Proceedings of the 23rd ACM symposium on virtual reality software and technology, pp 1–11

Sra M, Xu X, Maes P (2018) Breathvr: leveraging breathing as a directly controlled interface for virtual reality games. In: Proceedings of the 2018 CHI conference on human factors in computing systems, pp 1–12

Sullivan JV (2018) Learning and embodied cognition: a review and proposal. Psychol Learn Teach 17(2):128–143

Suzuki R, Hedayati H, Zheng C, Bohn JL, Szafir D, Yi-Luen Do E, Gross MD, Leithinger D (2020) Roomshift: room-scale dynamic haptics for VR with furniture-moving swarm robots. In: Proceedings of the 2020 CHI conference on human factors in computing systems, pp 1–11

Ulrich RS (1981) Natural versus urban scenes: some psychophysiological effects. Environ Behav 13(5):523–556

Ulrich RS (1991) Effects of interior design on wellness: theory and recent scientific research. In: Journal of health care interior design: proceedings from the... symposium on health care interior design, vol 3, pp 97–109

Ulrich RS, Simons RF, Losito BD, Evelyn F, Miles MA, Michael Z (1991) Stress recovery during exposure to natural and urban environments. J Environ Psychol 11(3):201–230

Ulrich RS (1984) View through a window may influence recovery from surgery. Science 224(4647):420–421

van Rooij M, Lobel A, Harris O, Smit N, Granic I (2016) Deep: a biofeedback virtual reality game for children at-risk for anxiety. In: Proceedings of the 2016 CHI conference extended abstracts on human factors in computing systems, CHI EA '16, New York, NY, USA. Association for Computing Machinery, pp 1989–1997

Vorländer M, Schröder D, Pelzer S, Wefers F (2015) Virtual reality for architectural acoustics. J Build Performance Simul 8(1):15–25

Wilson M (2002) Six views of embodied cognition. Psychonomic Bull Rev 9(4):625–636

Wyon DP (2004) The effects of indoor air quality on performance and productivity. Indoor Air 14:92–101

Yang (Junrui) J, Holz C, Ofek E, Wilson AD (2019) Dreamwalker: substituting real-world walking experiences with a virtual reality. In: Proceedings of the 32nd annual ACM symposium on user interface software and technology, pp 1093–1107

Yixian Y, Takashima K, Tang A, Tanno T, Fujita K, Kitamura Y (2020) Zoomwalls: dynamic walls that simulate haptic infrastructure for room-scale VR world. In: Proceedings of the 33rd annual ACM symposium on user interface software and technology, pp 223–235

Zhao N, Azaria A, Paradiso JA (2017) Mediated atmospheres: a multimodal mediated work environment. In: Proceedings of the ACM on interactive, mobile, wearable and ubiquitous technologies, vol 1, issue 2, pp 1–23

Printed in the United States
by Baker & Taylor Publisher Services